Using Corpora to Analyze Gender

Using Corpora to Analyze Gender

PAUL BAKER

BLOOMSBURY
LONDON • NEW DELHI • NEW YORK • SYDNEY

Bloomsbury Academic

An imprint of Bloomsbury Publishing Plc

50 Bedford Square
London
WC1B 3DP
UK

1385 Broadway
New York
NY 10018
USA

www.bloomsbury.com

First published 2014

British Library Cataloguing-in-Publication Data
A catalogue record for this book is available from the British Library.

ISBN: HB: 978-1-4411-1058-9
PB: 978-1-4411-0877-7
ePub: 978-1-4725-2707-3
ePDF: 978-1-4725-2483-6

Library of Congress Cataloging-in-Publication Data
A catalog record for this book is available from the Library of Congress.

Typeset by Newgen Knowledge Works (P) Ltd., Chennai, India
Printed and bound in India

CONTENTS

ACKNOWLEDGEMENTS

I would like to express thanks to the following:

The research presented in this paper was supported by the ESRC Centre for Corpus Approaches to Social Science, ESRC grant reference ES/K002155/1.

Members of the Research in Gender, Language and Sexuality group and the Corpus Research seminar group at Lancaster University, who provided useful feedback for earlier drafts of some of the analysis described in this book.

Andrew Hardie, for providing me with male and female spoken data from the British National Corpus, to a somewhat exacting format.

John Swales, Uta Romer and Matt O'Donnell for patiently answering my questions about the MICASE corpus.

Paul Rayson, Mike Scott, Laurence Anthony and Adam Kilgarriff for providing corpus analysis software, without whom this book could not have been written.

I would also like to thank Jane Sunderland and Judith Baxter, for their continuing support and good ideas over the years.

CHAPTER ONE

Introduction

How many times did you say 'I love you' today?

In 2012, four days before Valentine's Day, I was contacted by a journalist who worked for an international newspaper. He was writing an article 'on linguistic differences between men and women' and was primarily interested in 'outlining the main linguistic differences, along with sentences/paragraphs as spoken by men/women to illustrate such differences'. He wanted me to give him a list of some gendered differences and he cited a study by Harrison and Shortall (2011), which had surveyed 171 college students and found that males report falling in love earlier than women and saying 'I love you' earlier.

I replied to the journalist, saying that it is difficult to create such a list as the amount of data needed would be enormous. We would require millions of words of spoken language data, taken from large numbers of people from a wide range of backgrounds and locations. It would be a good idea to sample data at various points in time to ensure that any differences we found were stable rather than being due to something specific about a particular period of a particular society. With regard to the paper that the journalist had cited, I suggested that perhaps we cannot generalize too widely from a study which used a relatively small number of participants (99 women and 72 men) who were of similar age and current circumstances (students) and asked to remember and then report on their own linguistic behaviour (Harrison and Shortall also refer to some of these issues in the discussion section of their article[1]). To illustrate, I sent the journalist some information about the phrase 'I love you' in the British National Corpus (BNC), a large reference corpus consisting of 100 million words of British English of which 10 million words are transcriptions of recorded conversations. For about 71 per cent of this conversational data we know whether the speaker was male or female. Although the BNC can only directly tell us about language use in British society at the point in time that the data was collected (the early 1990s), as one of the biggest sources of naturally occurring spoken language data, at the time of writing, it is still one of the best resources that corpus linguists have access to.

I found that *I love you* only occurred 64 times in the spoken part of the BNC, and while the female speakers in the corpus said it about three times as much as the males, the majority picture was that most of the speakers did not say 'I love you' (at least when they were being recorded). I offered, humorously, that people should perhaps be encouraged to say the phrase more often.

Unsurprisingly, the journalist didn't reply. I had not produced a list of words and phrases which would either confirm stereotypes about gendered language use or refute them. Either way, such a finding could have constituted 'news'. Instead, my response could be summarized as 'there is not enough evidence to draw much of a conclusion'. February 14th was approaching and my response was unlikely to cohere with any narrative that the journalist wanted to create.

From gender difference to gendered discourses

The above anecdote is illustrative of a dissonance between academic research in the field of Gender and Language over the last 20 years or so, and public/media perceptions of gender and language. But this discrepancy was not always the case. The 'gender differences paradigm'[2] was actually an early academic approach, linked to Lakoff's (1975) 'male dominance' theory of language use (the view that males used language to dominate women). Fishman (1977) expanded on and contributed to this theory by proposing that women engaged in what she memorably called 'interactional shitwork', which among other things involved using questions and hedges to force responses from men in order to facilitate conversation.

While Lakoff and Fishman focused more on the notion of male dominance than gender difference per se, there was an underlying assumption that for men to be dominant and women to be dominated, then the sexes must also use language differently. Towards the end of the 1980s, another approach, popularized by Tannen (1990) emphasized gender *differences* rather than male dominance. This was a perspective influenced by interactional sociolinguistics and broadly based around the view that males and females had distinct and separate 'genderlects' which resulted in 'cross-cultural miscommunications'. Tannen argued that men viewed conversation as a contest, whereas women used conversation to exchange confirmation and support. On the surface, this 'difference' paradigm could be seen as a more politically neutral and thus uncontroversial[3] way of thinking about gender and language. In eschewing second-wave[4] feminist claims of patriarchal dominance, 'gender difference' does not characterize men as oppressors and women as victims, nor does it position anybody's language use as 'superior' to anybody else's. The difference paradigm instead views males and females as growing up in largely separate speech communities and learning different ways of socializing and using language. Linguistic gender differences are therefore used to 'explain' interpersonal conflict within (heterosexual) couples. Such conflicts are said to be due to misunderstandings as males and females attach different meanings to the same utterances as well as having different needs. Some proponents of the paradigm claim that the sexes need to be educated in order to understand each other's language. 'Difference' is thus a 'grand' theory, simple to grasp, blame-free and offering an explanation and solution to couples' conflict that is widely applicable. It is easy to see why it has become so popular, particularly in the media, spawning numerous relationship 'self-help' books and newspaper articles about amusing linguistic gender differences that seem to confirm what we already knew or suspected about men and women.

But while the gender differences paradigm is popular in the media, within academia, there has been a considerable amount of disagreement over whether men and women actually do use language differently to a significant degree, with some researchers arguing that differences do exist (e.g. Locke 2011), and others indicating that linguistic gender difference is a myth (e.g. Cameron 2008). Among those who argue for difference, there are a range of views about where such differences come from – perhaps they can be attributed to essential biological differences relating to chemicals in the brain, different reproductive systems or body musculature and size which can all impact on how people come to see themselves and are viewed by others. Possibly the differences are related to the ways that society socializes males and females differently, with different expectations regarding appropriate language behaviour for boys and girls. In the 1990s, taking a post-structuralist perspective, Judith Butler proposed that gender is performative – a form of *doing* rather than a form of *being*, so rather than people speaking a certain way because they are male or female, instead they use language (among other aspects of behaviour) in order to perform a male or female identity, according to current social conventions about how the sexes should behave. Butler pointed to female impersonators, showing that gender performances can be subverted and are therefore not intrinsically linked to a single sex. People learn what their correct gender performance for their sex should be by observing and copying other people around them. Therefore Butler (1990: 31) notes, 'The parodic repetition of "the original". . . reveals the original to be nothing other than a parody of the idea of the natural and the original.' Butler also links gender performance to sexuality, referring to a 'heterosexual matrix' (ibid.: 5). She argues that '. . . for bodies to cohere and make sense there must be a stable sex expressed through a stable gender (masculine expresses male, feminine expresses female) that is oppositionally and hierarchically defined through the compulsory practice of heterosexuality' (ibid.: 151).

Since the 1990s then, in the field of Gender and Language, there has been a move away from studies which shoehorn all males and all females into separate categories for comparison, and a shift instead towards research which has explored differences among women or differences among men, for example, by focusing on the ways that gender interacts with other identity categories (Eckert and McConnnell-Ginet 1992). Such an approach has also helped to formulate an alternative set of research questions, which focus around the ways that language use helps to create, reflect and challenge the societal conventions that Butler pointed to as influencing the ways that men and women talk. Terms like *social convention* and *expectations* can be related to the concept of *discourse* which Foucault (1972: 49) defines as 'practices which systematically form the objects of which they speak' while Burr (1995: 48) suggests that discourse is the production of 'meanings, metaphors, representations, images, stories, statements and so on that in some way together produce a particular version of events'. Gill (1993: 166) has noted that language has increasingly become important across the social sciences, due to the 'influence of post-structuralist ideas which stressed the thoroughly discursive, textual nature of social life' and Cameron (1998: 947) points out that in fact, this 'linguistic' turn was mainly a turn to discourse analysis. Livia and Hall (1997: 12) argue that '. . . it is discourse that produces the speaker, and not the other way round, because the performance will be intelligible, only if it "emerges in the context of binding conventions"'.

Within the field of Gender and Language then, a number of key approaches have utilized the turn to discourse, including work in discursive psychology which combines elements from conversation analysis, ethnomethodology and rhetorical social psychology. Some researchers have introduced elements of post-structuralist theory or critical discourse analysis into discursive psychology, such as Edley and Wetherell (1999) who examined young men's talk about fatherhood. Others have shown how techniques used in Conversation Analysis can be adopted for feminist research, for example Kitzinger (2008: 136) has shown how 'gender – or sexuality, or power, or oppression – is produced and reproduced in interaction'. A different approach combines critical discourse analysis and feminist linguistics to form FCDA (Feminist Critical Discourse Analysis). FCDA involves the critique of 'discourses which sustain a patriarchal social order: that is, relations of power that systematically privilege men as a social group and disadvantage, exclude and disempower women as a social group' (Lazar 2005: 5). FCDA is thus concerned with outlining how language use sustains unequal gender relations, with its main aims being emancipation and transformation. While FCDA also has the remit of showing how taken-for-granted assumptions around gender can be negotiated and contested as well as (re)produced, a third approach offered by Baxter, is more firmly focused on negotiation. Baxter's FPDA (Feminist Post-Structuralist Discourse Analysis) 'suggests that females always adopt multiple subject positions, and that it is far too reductive to constitute women in general, or indeed any individual woman, simply as victims of male oppression' (Baxter 2003: 10). Instead, FPDA involves close qualitative analyses of texts (often detailed transcripts of conversations) to show how participants (particularly those who may be conceived of as relatively powerless) can experience 'moments of power', whereas powerful people can be positioned as momentarily powerless.

A useful concept in the field of Gender and Language is the idea of *gendered discourses*, which Sunderland (2004) suggests can be identified through the analysis of traces in language use:

> People do not . . . recognise a discourse . . . in any straightforward way . . . Not only is it not identified or named, and is not self-evident or visible as a discrete chunk of a given text, it can never be 'there' in its entirety. What is there are certain linguistic features: 'marks on a page', words spoken or even people's memories of previous conversations . . . which – if sufficient and coherent – may suggest that they are 'traces' of a particular discourse. (ibid.: 28)

Sunderland acknowledges that the identification and naming of a gendered discourse is a highly subjective process, and her approach involves categorizing discourses in terms of their function (e.g. conservative, resistant, subversive or damaging) and relationship to each other (e.g. two discourses may be competing or mutually supportive or one may be dominant and the other subordinate). This relational aspect of discourse helps to explain why people can appear to be inconsistent in their positions as they may be drawing on conflicting discourses.

The above feminist approaches to discourse analysis also all place emphasis on intertextuality (relations between texts), interdiscursivity (relations between discourses) and self-reflexivity, advocating that researchers acknowledge their own theoretical positions and reflect on their research practices 'lest these inadvertently contribute towards the perpetuation, rather than the subversion, of hierarchically differential treatment of women' (Lazar 2005: 15).

Another aspect that many of the discourse-based types of Gender and Language research have in common, is that they often involve a 'close' or qualitative analysis of a small number of short texts (as well as taking into account the practices surrounding the creation, distribution and reception of those texts). There are good reasons for this, one being that the identification and critique of discourse is a complicated and often slow process, requiring attention to detail and consideration of many types of context (see Flowerdew forthcoming). As Mills (1998: 247–8) points out, the successes of feminism have helped to curb some of the more obviously harmful forms of sexist language use, although it could be argued that rather than being fully eradicated, sexist discourse has become increasingly more complex, sophisticated and ambiguous and thus more difficult to identify. Mills (ibid.) argues 'What is necessary now is a form of feminist analysis which can analyse the complexity of sexism . . . now that feminism has made sexism more problematic.'

So while discourse analysis has become popular within Gender and Language, this has tended to be based on detailed qualitative studies using smaller excerpts of texts rather than approaches that involve techniques from Corpus Linguistics (described in more detail in the following section), which work well on large amounts of data, sometimes comprising millions or even billions of words. As an illustration of the extent of the impact of Corpus Linguistics on the field of Gender and Language, I examined frequencies of the word *corpus* and its plural *corpora* in 63 articles published in issues 1–6 (between 2007–12) of the journal *Gender and Language*. Twenty five articles contained at least one mention of the word *corpus* or *corpora*, although this does not necessarily indicate that these were articles which used Corpus Linguistics methods. Indeed, authors mainly used the term to refer to their data set as a corpus but they carried out their analysis using purely qualitative methods. I would classify only four papers (6.3% of the total) as taking a Corpus Linguistics approach (Johnson and Ensslin (2007), Charteris-Black and Seale (2009), Baker (2010) and King (2011)). Additionally, Holmgreen (2009) used a corpus to verify some of her findings but her main method was qualitative. There is evidence that some researchers in Gender and Language are using corpus approaches, although they seem to be in the minority.

A chief motivation for writing this book then, is to consider and demonstrate some of the ways that Corpus Linguistics can be of value to people working in the field of Gender and Language. I would not encourage researchers to abandon their existing methods but rather offer Corpus Linguistics as a supplementary approach. This book is therefore mainly written for two types of people. First, those who are interested in Gender and Language and would like to know more about how Corpus Linguistics can help them in their research, and second, people already working in Corpus Linguistics who do not consider themselves to be familiar with the field of Gender and Language, but would like to examine gender in their corpus research. I assume that readers have a basic level of computer literacy (e.g. they know how to create, alter and find files and folders on a computer, can send emails and access information on the World Wide Web through a browser like Internet Explorer) but are not computer programmers or statisticians and do not necessarily want to be. Indeed, an aim of this book is to demonstrate how much can be achieved within a Corpus Linguistics paradigm without needing to be a computer or maths wizard, although with that said, such people have been and continue to be central to the development of the field. I hope that this book will empower 'non-techy' Gender and Language researchers to feel confident in building and exploiting corpora, while encouraging corpus linguists to incorporate some of the more recent thinking about Gender and Language into their own studies. Therefore, each of the analysis chapters in this book (Chapters Two to Seven) combine the analysis of different types of corpora, with a variety of aims in mind, using a range of techniques, as well as addressing issues and problems as they arise. I have tried to provide as much coverage as possible and an overview of the book is presented at the end of this chapter.

However, in the following section, as a way of becoming better acquainted with the method, I will first discuss some of the key terms and concepts surrounding Corpus Linguistics, in order to try to better explain why it is worth considering as a method within Gender and Language.

Building a corpus . . .

Because a large part of Corpus Linguistics is based in its methodology – ways of conducting analysis, it is versatile enough to be applied to many topics, although as I have argued elsewhere (Baker 2005: 7–14), people working in the field of Gender and Language have sometimes been slow to exploit its potential, perhaps due to a variety of different reasons: unfamiliarity, lack of access to data and tools of analysis, a misperception that it is a purely quantitative approach or dislike of computers. In this section I begin by providing the rationale behind Corpus Linguistics, then move on to discuss some of the main ways that analysis can be carried out.

The word *corpus* is Latin for *body*, so Corpus Linguistics refers to a body of language. This body usually consists of collections of texts, either in full, or comprising smaller excerpts from them. The key point is that these texts involve authentic cases of language use as it occurs in the 'real world', as opposed to say a made-up sentence by a linguist in order to demonstrate a particular point. Invented sentences like 'The cat sat on the mat' do not always accurately reflect the ways that people actually use language. Corpus Linguistics is therefore an approach that is grounded in empiricism and has much in common with other approaches in the social sciences where samples are taken in order to make generalizations about a wider population. The connected concepts of sampling and representativeness underpin all Corpus Linguistics research – a corpus needs to be sampled in such a way that we can be confident that it actually is representative of the language variety that we are studying. For example, if we were interested in sampling the speech of teenage girls in England, we would need to ensure that we collected transcriptions of speech from girls from a range of locations (e.g. North, South, Midlands), social and ethnic groups and circumstances (at home, at school, shopping, out with friends, visiting relatives, going to doctor's appointments, etc.). We would also need to ensure that the sampling was relatively balanced, with no type of girl or speech event being overly represented in comparison with the others. Ideally, each girl should contribute about the same amount of speech so no single person's speech idiosyncrasies skew our data set (although sometimes practical realities mean that this is not always possible and other measures which take distribution of features into account need to be taken in order to avoid jumping to the wrong conclusions).

A corpus is usually comprised of text files that can be stored on a computer. In the case of texts that were initially in written form (such as newspaper articles, books, emails, etc.) such storage is relatively easy to achieve, especially if the texts are already in electronic form. Texts that are only available in paper form (such as hand-written letters) need to be converted to electronic form, either by keying them in or using optical character recognition software (if the text has been typed). For spoken texts such as recordings of conversations, the speech needs to be transcribed, and corpus builders must consider how or whether they will use a scheme for representing features like laughter, people speaking quietly and external noises. Some corpora are multimodal in that they contain combinations of images (moving or still) and language (written or spoken), and again, coding schemes need to be applied so that all the relevant information is incorporated into the corpus.

Even with a written text like a newspaper article, within Corpus Linguistics it is common to assign annotations (or tags) to it in order to make the task of analysis easier. Many corpus texts contain headers which either occur at their start or are linked to a separate file. Headers contain tags which give meta-information about the text, such as who created it, where and when, what genre it is from, whether any spelling irregularities have been corrected and so on. A transcript of a conversation might include information about each speaker's age, sex or social class – such information is useful if we want to focus on certain types of speakers. As well as appearing in headers, tags can also be found within the main body of texts. For example, we might want to mark punctuation in a certain way so that it is not misinterpreted, particularly if the text will be used across a range of different operating systems. A mark like 'could be an opening quotation mark, a closing quotation mark or an apostrophe, so incorporating information about the actual function of each 'in a corpus, via tags would be useful if say, we wanted to bring up all the quotes in a corpus. In order to retain the original formatting of a text, elements like bullet points, paragraph breaks and italics can also be marked – as much of this information is stripped from texts when they are converted into plain text for analysis with corpus software.

It is also often helpful to be able to disambiguate certain uses or meanings of words – for example, *love* can be a verb, common noun or proper noun as well as referring to an emotion or a tennis score. Tags can be attached to words which reflect the grammatical or semantic group that they belong to. Figure 1.1 shows a small part of a file from the BNC, with tags to mark each utterance <u>, the grammatical class of each word <w>, sentences <s> and vocalizations like laughter <vocal>. Tags can also contain attributes and values. For example, the tag <u has the attribute *who* (referring to speaker identity) which is assigned a value, in the case below, this is a code number like PS04U which refers to an individual speaker.

Figure 1.1 also shows the same text without tagging. As tagged data can be difficult to read, especially to people not used to working with tags, most corpus analysis software will allow the tags to be hidden or ignored. For example, unless specified, the tool WordSmith will ignore anything between the symbols <and> which are commonly used to denote tags in XML, one of the most commonly used annotation schemes.

Some corpora can claim total representativeness of a genre while others cannot. For example, if we build a corpus containing all of the published novels written by one author in the twentieth century then we have full representation of that author's published fictional output over that century. On the other hand, a corpus of teenage girls' speech can never capture every utterance ever made and only acts as a representative sample. Hunston (2002: 14–15) makes an important distinction between reference and specialized corpora (the former are also known as general corpora). A reference corpus is intended to act as a representative of a particular language variety such as American English. Reference corpora will contain a wide range of text types, and will usually have to be very large – consisting of many millions or billions of words. A specialized corpus, on the other hand, is usually less ambitious, consisting of a set of texts which are intended to represent (either partially or fully) a specific genre or text type. An example of a

---

<u who=PS04U>

<s n="00012(03900)"><w PPIS1>I <w VV0>mean <w PPY>you <w VV0>know <w RGQ>how <w DA1>much <w NN2>boxes <w VBR>are<c YSTP>. </s>
</u>
<u who=PS04Y>
<s n="00013(03901)"><w RR>Quite<c YSTP>. <vocal desc=laugh></s>
</u>

I mean you know how much boxes are.

Quite.

FIGURE 1.1 *Excerpt of file KBF from the British National Corpus, with and without tags.*

specialized corpus would be a corpus of American newspaper articles about a particular topic between the years 2000 and 2010, or a collection of tweets made within the United Kingdom in February 2013, or the collected novels of a single author. The distinction between *reference* and *specialized* is more linear than binary, however, as it could be argued that all corpora are intended to act as a reference for something, while all corpora are specialized to an extent. So the BNC, which is often given as an example of a reference corpus still specializes in British English taken from a discrete, and relatively short time period rather than being representative of all English or even all British English.

Depending on the type of text being collected and the aims of the corpus builder, issues surrounding ethics and copyright need to be addressed. If the corpus is intended for personal use only and the texts are already widely available in the public domain, then researchers may not feel that they need to request anyone's permission in order to use them, although if you intend to publish your findings in a book or journal article and want to reproduce a large stretch of text from within a corpus, then usually permission from copyright holders must be sought.

With corpora that are built with the intention of being sold to other researchers, then it is more important to ask permission to use those texts. Additionally, the collection of texts which involve personal information, such as emails or transcripts containing personal details also require the researcher to ask the people who contributed towards those texts for permission to work with them. Even if speakers or email writers are happy to allow their personal information to appear in a corpus, it is still wise to redact or alter texts so that identities cannot be traced. Anonymity needs to be carefully considered, as McEnery and Hardie (2012: 57–70) in a discussion of a number of ethical issues concerning corpus building and distribution, note that even when names are anonymized this may still not be enough to protect the identity of a speaker.

Why do we need so much text though? Why not just stick to the analysis of a few well-chosen texts? In many cases, such analyses are valid and interesting. However, if we want to make wider generalizations about language in use, the more text we have, the better. A corpus can help us to avoid accusations that we have cherry-picked examples in order to prove a preconceived point. If we want to argue, say, that a certain radio program is sexist, we could choose to analyse a five-minute stretch of conversation from it, which we already know to be sexist. However, our argument is more convincing if we can show that the sexism is pervasive across many episodes, day after day, and that we have not conveniently ignored many cases where the radio program actually challenges sexism. A corpus analysis can tell us what is typical then.

Even when just working with a single text, a corpus can allow us to investigate hunches about uses of certain words or phrases within it. Consider a short text where the author describes a woman as *clucking*. We might argue that this is a negative representation, equating the woman's speech as like that of a hen and thus annoying and/or irrelevant. However, in order to show that the author is drawing on a reasonably well-understood sexist discourse, it would be useful to find more examples in a large reference corpus. Does *clucking* (or related verbs like *quacking* and *twittering*), often occur with reference to women (but not so much with men) in such a corpus? As another example, imagine that we want to analyse a short newspaper article that contains the phrase 'gay activists are always calling for tolerance and understanding'. We might want to argue that the author is implicitly biased against gay activists, although the context around the sentence is somewhat ambiguous. However, if we go to a reference corpus like the BNC and examine similar constructions like: [humans] *are always* [-ing form of verb], we find that many of them involve cases of people who are being criticized for complaining about something and that this is often followed by an additional pattern where someone is represented as saying, claiming or doing something, which the writer then refutes as incorrect or unwise. We therefore have evidence that the author who is writing about gay activists is using a construction which implies a negative stance, and that readers who are reasonably familiar with English will be primed to pick up on this, without it needing to be made explicit. Corpora can therefore reveal something about hidden meanings associated with words and phrases, affording us a more robust way of pointing out biases.

To continue, the following section describes some of the more commonly used techniques of analysis in Corpus Linguistics.

. . . and analysing it

Once collected, it is possible to analyse a corpus by reading all of it (and this is one approach I take, to an extent, in Chapter Three), but most Corpus Linguistics research involves the use of specialized software which can perform complex calculations on the language data very quickly. The advantage of such tools is that they are fast and accurate, performing calculations in seconds that would take humans many hours or days to carry out and be likely to contain errors.

Some corpus builders make their corpora available by including a software package with it, and this is increasingly a model which is found on the World Wide Web, where users interact with a corpus via a website (see Chapters Three, Four and Six for examples). In other cases, if we only have access to the text files which constitute the corpus, we need to obtain software ourselves in order to conduct an analysis.

While there are numerous software packages available for download via the internet, two popular tools that I used when writing this book are WordSmith created by Mike Scott and AntConc created by Laurence

Anthony. Both are regularly updated (at the time of writing I use version 5 of WordSmith and version 3 of AntConc). WordSmith has a wider range of functions, and tends to be faster at processing very large corpora containing millions of words, although users must pay a fee to gain access to all of them, while AntConc is free but more limited in terms of functionality. As AntConc also has a simpler interface I would probably recommend it for beginners, who might want to consider WordSmith as they become more proficient (I use WordSmith in Chapter Five, while AntConc was employed in Chapter Seven).

Corpus tools can perform calculations and statistical tests on corpus data, although analysts are limited to the capabilities of the software and there may be cases where additional tools are needed. I often find that I need to refer to more specialist statistical analysis software when working with corpora. One option is to use the open source programming language and software environment R (see Gries 2009). R requires users to learn a programming language, while other statistics software, like SPSS,[5] involve entering numbers in tables and then carrying out tests via the selection of options from menus. The popular spreadsheet application Microsoft Excel also allows users to calculate a number of statistical algorithms like the mean, standard deviation, chi-square test and Pearson correlation.

Additionally, there are quick-to-use online calculators which can perform certain tests when numbers are entered into boxes. For example, I sometimes use an online log-likelihood (LL) calculator developed by Paul Rayson[6] to compare frequencies of one word across two corpora (or two words in one corpus), while if I want to carry out a comparison of more than two corpora, I use a web utility for chi-square tests (Preacher 2001). With regard to more basic manipulation of data (such as summing a column of numbers or multiplying each value in a column by another number), I tend to rely on Excel which was used for calculating the Manhattan Distances in Chapter Two. Having spoken to various corpus linguists, there are different preferences for tools, and I have heard strong (and sometimes conflicting) opinions about which are best. I would recommend that beginners try to make themselves aware of the options, but that it is better to use a low-specification tool well rather than a highly sophisticated one incorrectly.

Many forms of analysis in Corpus Linguistics employ some sort of reference to corpus frequencies (the number of times a word, sequence of words or tag occurs, either alone or in the vicinity of a similar feature). Frequencies can be given as raw, for example the word *yes* occurs 58,521 times in the BNC, or as percentages, for example *yes* comprises 0.059525 per cent of the words in the corpus. If we are comparing the frequency of a word across two corpora, particularly if the corpora are of different sizes, then it makes sense to give both raw and percentage frequencies in order for comparisons to be more easily made. However, because many words are relatively rare and will have small percentages that can be difficult to visualize, it is often common for another form of proportional data to be used, writing that a word appears x times per million words. For example, we could write that *yes* appears 595.25 times per million words in the BNC – this proportion is somewhat easier to understand than 0.059525 per cent. Frequencies are examined most closely in this book in Chapter Four.

Because corpora often contain samples of language from many different sources, it is important that we take into account the extent to which linguistic patterns in the data are realized across the whole corpus or just parts of it. For example, the term *lady doctor* appears 13 times in the BNC. Although this is relatively rare, if all 13 cases occurred in different texts (and across a range of different genres or registers) we would have more evidence that this is a more wide-ranging and well-known term than if it was restricted to just one or two texts (I discuss issues relating to distribution in more detail in Chapter Two).

A frequency list is simply a list of the most frequent words (or word sequences or tags) that occur in a corpus, either in order of frequency or presented alphabetically. Frequency lists can be helpful in revealing common patterns or themes in corpora, although many forms of language contain a very high proportion of closed-class grammatical words such as articles, prepositions, conjunctions and pronouns, so such words are often found towards the beginning of frequency lists and may tell us something about language in general rather than the features that are more unique to a specific corpus. For this reason, another measure, called keyness is often used. Keyness is based on carrying out statistical tests on each word in a corpus, by comparing its frequency against a larger reference corpus (or in some cases, comparing two similar-sized corpora together, with each corpus acting as the reference for the other). The reference corpus acts as a standard measure about normal frequencies in language, so any words which occur relatively more often in the other corpus will be seen to be key – having a low p-value when log-likelihood or chi-square tests are carried out on the data. Keywords do not necessarily need to be highly frequent then, just more frequent than expected, when compared against something else. I examine keywords in Chapter Two and a related phenomenon: key semantic tags in Chapter Seven.

A related aspect of frequency is collocation, or the tendency of certain words to attract others, appearing either next to or reasonably close to other words. Collocates can be useful in revealing how meaning is acquired through repeated uses of language, as certain concepts become inextricably linked together over time. A 'strong' theory of collocation indicates that words can act as psychological triggers for certain concepts if they occur often enough and in mutually exclusive relationships. I examine how collocates can reveal discourses around sexuality in Chapter Five and gender in Chapter Six, as well as looking at how we can take into account more complex relationships between words via a look at collocational networks in Chapter Seven.

While the above forms of analysis take quantification as their cornerstone, another commonly employed method of analysis (particularly when using Corpus Linguistics to examine social issues), is concordancing. A concordance is a table containing all the occurrences of a particular linguistic feature (word, word-tag combination, tag or sequence or combination of words or tags) with a few words of the immediate context displayed either side. Concordances enable corpus linguists to conduct a functional qualitative analysis, based on making sense of the contexts and patterns that a word occurs in, and to make this task easier, concordances can be sorted alphabetically, either to words that are to the left or right of the word (phrase, tag, etc.) being searched on.

As an example, Table 1.1 shows a sample of concordance lines of the word *feminist* and its plural taken just from newspaper articles in the BNC. Although only a small amount of context is provided for each case, I have emboldened a number of words which appear to refer to similar concepts – *axe-grinding, blame, irk, vociferous, battle-cry, vehemently, enraged, militant, outraged* and *outrage*. Together, most of these words appear to access a *discourse prosody* (Stubbs 2001: 65) of feminists as belligerent. Negative stereotypes about feminists have been found in attitude research (see Goldberg et al. 1975) and Williams and Wittig (1997) suggest that they can hinder feminist self-labelling. The examples in the BNC then, are an indication of how journalists can collectively contribute towards negative stereotyping by tying two concepts (feminism and anger) together repeatedly, helping to fix the association in the minds of readers.

TABLE 1.1 *Sample of* feminist(s) *from the press section of the British National Corpus.*

the important thing is the play, not any	feminist	**axe-grinding**. I've really no ambitions
has caused this terror of female flesh?	feminists	can't **blame** it all on men – since time
[with-a] brain.' Most likely to **irk** the	feminists	is 'F O long blonde hair', referring to
defined by a tiny, **vociferous** group of	feminist	leaders, is in direct contradiction to
was a justifiable **battle-cry** of the	feminist	movement and that ambition was
'native races'. Most seriously, the only	feminists	of any note who were not **vehemently**
restore their 'caring' image among the	feminists	they **enraged** by opting out of Europe's
this type of dotty left-wing and **militant**	feminist	thinking,' she said. 'Now they want to
of sexual harassment years earlier, and	feminists	were **outraged** when the court rebuffed
remarks which caused **outrage** among	feminists	He admitted his language was

In cases where a word is particularly frequent in a corpus, eliciting hundreds or thousands of concordance lines, we may want to look at a random sample of lines, or only take into account lines which also contain the most frequent or salient collocates. This method is one which I took in Chapter Five when I examined representations of gay men. Concordancing constitutes a form of down-sampling, in that we focus on a smaller amount of data in the corpus, in this case only the data that contain a particular linguistic item. However, another way that down-sampling could be incorporated could be to select a smaller number of texts that are viewed as especially typical of the corpus. For example, we might elicit a list of keywords from a corpus of 1,000 newspaper articles and then decide to carry out a more detailed qualitative analysis on a smaller number of articles which contain the highest number of keywords. Another way of down-sampling would be to use word frequencies in order to identify common topics or concepts in a corpus and then focus on a more detailed analysis of texts that refer to that topic or concept. This was a technique I used in an earlier project when I examined British newspaper articles about Muslims. An initial analysis of word frequencies indicated that certain topics like 'women who wear the veil' were popular, suggesting areas for closer examination, see Baker et al. (2013). Hopefully, it can be seen then that Corpus Linguistics offers a range of ways to interrogate texts, from those that involve statistical testing of frequency, to those which direct analysts to texts (or parts of them) which contain features that are especially representative, for qualitative analysis.

Having discussed some of the main features of Corpus Linguistics then, this chapter ends with an outline of what is covered in the rest of the book.

Overview of the book

The two chapters after this one both address the issue of identity and language usage, although each takes a different approach. It is useful at this point to outline a distinction made by Tognini-Bonelli (2001), between *corpus-driven* and *corpus-based* investigations. The former uses the corpus as the data and the patterns in it are noted as a way of expressing regularities (and exceptions) in language. The researcher takes a 'naïve' stance towards the corpus data, not imposing any pre-existing categorization scheme but using computational procedures based around frequency in order to allow the corpus itself to drive analysis along. For example, the direction that the analysis takes might be based around a list of keywords which could not be predicted in advance. A corpus-based investigation, on the other hand, employs a corpus more as a way of checking research intuition or examining the frequency and/or plausibility of the language contained within a smaller data set. Researchers may have a set of hypotheses and have decided beforehand which words or phrases they are going to examine in order to test those hypotheses.

As with the distinction between specialized and reference corpora, it is probably easier to view corpus-based and corpus-driven research as extremes of a gradated scale rather than a binary choice. For example, McEnery et al. (2006: 8) point out that it is difficult to approach a corpus from a completely naïve stance, while it is also hard not to impose some sort of categorization scheme on language data (even a naïve process like keywords requires the adoption of a 'word' as a linguistic category). Chapter Two of the book takes a largely corpus-driven approach to the issue of linguistic gender differences, surveying previous research undertaken by corpus linguists before carrying out a comparison of the male and female speech in the BNC. I ask whether the differences between these two sets of data is greater than the difference if we divide just the male speech or just the female speech into two random groups and compare them together. I also try to explain some of the findings from other researchers who have looked at the BNC and postulated gender differences. To what extent are such differences actually generalizable?

Chapter Three continues with the issue of language usage and gender, but in an effort to move away from studies which pit males against females, I instead focus only on the speech of female academic supervisors, examining how they express one form of language – disagreement. Some theories of language and gender have proposed that women are stereotypically more likely to engage in co-operative, non-threatening forms of speech, and the speech of women in positions of power is therefore of interest because in order to be successful in these contexts, women are required to go against the stereotype (and may face censure for doing so). As other researchers have noticed, this can sometimes result in quite complex forms of language use, as women managers and leaders negotiate what are sometimes perceived as competing identities. This chapter therefore takes a corpus-based approach, in that I decided to explore a particular form of language (disagreeing) in advance of examining a corpus. I develop a categorization scheme in order to class disagreements in terms of whether they involve some form of politeness which takes the hearer's face into account. Additionally, this chapter looks at the issues that arise when we move away from searching for simple words in a corpus and instead want to find all the cases where someone expresses disagreement – a much more variable phenomenon.

Moving away from how women and men use language to instead focus on how they are represented through language, Chapter Four considers the usefulness of frequency information when making enquiries of a large diachronic reference corpus of American English stretching back to the early nineteenth century. I discuss how we can compare the frequencies of gendered pairs of words like *man/woman* and *wife/husband* in order to gain evidence for male bias within language. Charting how these frequencies change over time can help to demonstrate whether attempts to counter linguistic sexism or implicit bias have been successful. I discuss a number of cases which warn against over-interpretation, so for example – the word *chairman* does not necessarily always refer to men, and *father* doesn't always refer to men who have children, while a word that is highly frequent doesn't necessarily indicate that people consider that identity to be powerful (*wife* is more frequent than *husband*). As well as looking at frequencies of individual words, I also examine word order – so do people write *men and women* more often than *women and men*, and what do exceptions to this rule tell us? The chapter ends with a look at gender neutral terms like *police officer* and *Ms* – have such terms made an impact into American language use in more recent years?

   In Chapter Five I stay with the idea of representation to consider how gay people are written about in a corpus of articles by the popular British newspaper *The Daily Mail*. Along with other researchers, I argue that it is difficult to understand discourses around gender without also taking into account sexuality. Earlier in this chapter I referred to Butler's heterosexual matrix, an example of this being that terms like *man* and *woman* are often implicitly assumed to indicate heterosexuality, and as Connell has argued, a key element of hegemonic masculinity is based around 'the dominance of heterosexual men and the subordination of homosexual men' (1995: 78). In an earlier piece of published research (Baker 2005: 60–92), I examined how in the period 2001–2 the British newspaper the *Daily Mail* contained a high proportion of references to gay people which negatively constructed them as promiscuous, shameless and shameful, violent and politically militant. In Chapter Five, I revisit the newspaper to see whether changing social attitudes have impacted on the way that gay people were represented in 2008–9. I also revisit the methodology I had employed in the earlier study, which had involved identifying collocates of the words *gay* and *homosexual*, then reading concordance lines containing those collocates in order to posit evidence for discourse prosodies. I reflect on whether this method still involved some form of 'cherry-picking' (e.g. whether I originally found mostly negative patterns because I was expecting to find them). Finally, I consider the advantages of analysing expanded concordance lines which enable the identification of features that can run over multiple sentences, such as legitimation strategies.

   Chapter Six takes a more in-depth look at collocates by addressing different methods of collocation and considering questions like how large the collocational span should be, and whether a confidence-based or hypothesis-testing technique (or both) ought to be used. Having surveyed some key corpus-based studies which have used collocates to examine issues of gender representation, I then investigate how collocates can be automatically grouped according to grammatical patterns, using an online tool called Sketch Engine. Using a large corpus of text taken from British web pages, I compare collocational relationships for the words *boy* and *girl* (and their plurals), in order to identify similar and different ways that these identities are consistently constructed. For example, boys are more likely to be modified by collocates which evaluate their behaviour as either good or bad, while *girl* (but not *boy*) is often used to refer to adults. The chapter ends with a discussion of issues surrounding interpretation, explanation and critical evaluation of such results.

The last analysis chapter (Chapter Seven) ties together the previously addressed themes of gendered usage and representation, by examining three small corpora of male personal adverts taken from the website Craigslist. I use this chapter to first exemplify some issues that corpus builders are likely to encounter if they decide to build their own corpus, such as downloading data from the internet, removing boilerplate, identifying and removing unwanted files and duplicates and tagging files. I also address a couple of contentious matters to do with analysis – how to compare three or more corpora, when most corpus analysis software currently only allows two corpora to be compared, and ensuring cut-off point consistency when working with corpora of different sizes. Another aim of this chapter is to explore the extent to which different kinds of corpus analysis techniques will produce different types of results. To this end, the analysis involves a triangulation of methods on the same data sets, incorporating analyses of key semantic tags, collocational networks and concordance lines.

Finally, in the conclusion chapter I summarize the main findings of the book, reflecting on the research outcomes in the individual chapters, critically evaluating the different methods used, and attempting to address potential limitations of the corpus method to analyse gender. The book ends with a consideration of some of the future directions that corpora and gender research could take.

CHAPTER TWO

Gender difference redux: Do women really say 'lovely' more than men?

Introduction

In this first analysis chapter of the book, I want to use corpus techniques to address one of the older debates within the field of Gender and Language that I referred to in Chapter One – the issue of whether men and women use language differently, and if so, to what extent and in what ways? As described earlier, such a belief is popular in both the news media and in relationship advice books aimed at a popular audience, although within academic research, it is increasingly common to read criticisms of the 'gender differences' paradigm.[1] For example, a meta-analysis by Hyde (2005) of several hundred studies of verbal and behavioural gender differences concluded that most of the studies found that the overall difference made by gender was either very small or close to zero. Only two phenomena – accuracy of spelling and frequency of smiling showed moderate effects of gender. Johnson (1997: 11) writes that 'many linguists have become so preoccupied with the need to uncover statistically significant gender differences that they frequently seem to overlook one important fact: the two sexes are still drawing on the same linguistic resources.' Eckert and McConnell-Ginet (2003: 2) note that the linguistic difference paradigm took place within a 'wider context of psychological difference' and explain that such research was sometimes used as a way of challenging male norms, although 'it also appealed to a popular thirst for gender difference. And in the end, this research is frequently transformed in popular discourse – certainly to the horror of researchers – to justify and support male dominance.' Similarly, Sunderland (2004: 16) reports that gender differences are 'enthusiastically embraced by undergraduate students of linguistics' who are often disappointed if their transcripts of mixed sex talk do not find any differences.

The difference paradigm is perhaps most clearly critiqued (from a linguistic point of view) by Cameron (2008) in *The Myth of Mars and Venus*. Cameron writes (ibid.: 3) 'The idea that men and women differ fundamentally in the way they use language to communicate is a myth in the everyday sense: a widespread but false belief. But it is also a myth in the sense of being a story people tell in order to explain who they are, where they have come from, and why they live as they do.' Thimm et al. (2003: 531) make a useful distinction between the 'sex-dialect hypothesis' which assumes that gender-specific language use exists and the 'sex-stereotype hypothesis', which assumes that people *believe* that gender-specific language exists. Even if we do not agree with the former, there is a great deal of evidence for the latter.

However, not all academic research on Gender and Language has eschewed gender differences. Locke's *Duels and Duets* (2011) posits that men engage in verbal duelling with each other, allowing them to compete for status and sex, while women's speech is more like a verbal 'duet', achieving goals through sharing intimate thoughts and feelings. Locke uses biological and evolutionary arguments to explain such differences, although his research does not make much use of empirical linguistic data. Indeed, a problem with some of the gender difference or male dominance research is that it bases its findings on inappropriate or unconvincing sources. So Tannen (1990) uses examples from fiction to illustrate her claims about gender differences while studies that have used empirical data, like Lakoff (1975) have tended to rely on small numbers of speakers, who tend to be drawn from quite narrow populations (such as white, middle-class Americans). This sparsity of naturally occurring, fully representative data raises a question over the validity of such research, even if the findings intuitively appear to confirm expectations. Perhaps though, they confirm expectations because we are primed to think about societies in terms of gender differences. If only there was a way that very large amounts of naturally occurring linguistic data, encoded for sex, could be analysed in a relatively objective way. What would such data be able to tell us about language use and its relationship to sex?

Corpus approaches to sex difference

While there is enormous potential for corpus-informed research on spoken language and gender differences, this is not currently reflected in the amount of research that has been done to date. Many researchers in the field of Gender and Language favour qualitative analyses of smaller collections of texts, while within Corpus Linguistics there is not a great deal to report on gender either. This may partly be due to issues of practicality. It is difficult and expensive to create large, balanced, representative spoken corpora due to issues around finding participants, setting up recording situations, addressing ethics and transcribing and encoding spoken data. Perhaps the best example of a large spoken corpus is the spoken section of the BNC. Collected in the early 1990s, the BNC has served as a model for a large-scale spoken corpus, containing circa 10 million words of transcribed speech of over 5,300 speakers who were tagged for sex, age, social class and region. Speech was also tagged as demographic (private conversations) and context-governed (public talk).

The spoken part of the BNC can make a good claim for being a representative, balanced sample of speech, although it is somewhat disconcerting to note that at the time of writing, 20 years on, there have been no attempts to replicate it, and it is already an 'historical corpus'. In some ways, the task of collecting the corpus might now be easier, due to improved recording and storage technology, but present-day spoken corpus builders would need to address ethical issues that were somewhat fudged during the collection of the BNC (see McEnery and Hardie 2012: 68). Additionally, there is no information about the sex of about 1,500 speakers in the BNC, and even for the demographic information that does exist, once it is broken down into more fine-grained categories combining sex, age and social class, the amount of information available becomes scant – there is only full information about these three factors for 362 people (7% of the speakers) in the BNC.

Despite such issues, a number of researchers have examined the BNC, attempting to uncover whether and/or in which ways males and females use language differently to each other. Schmid (2003) created a set of topics and linguistic features that he categorized as stereotypically male or female (such as relationships, work, questions, minimal responses), based on claims and findings made in earlier studies. He then identified sets of words and phrases for each category and examined the sex-tagged spoken data in the BNC in order to see whether there were statistically significant differences for sex. For example, 'food and drink' words were initially categorized as more typically used by females, and Schmid found that the female speakers were indeed statistically more likely to say *dinner, tea, lunch, eggs, wine, milk* and *steak*, although males were more likely to say *pint, pizza* and *beer* (which perhaps feeds into a stereotype of beer-drinking men consuming easy-to-prepare food). So for some of the categories that Schmid examined, it did appear that males and females were using language in stereotypically gendered ways – males were more likely to exploit a lexicon associated with public affairs, abstract concepts and sport while females used more words referencing clothing, colours and the home. In other categories, such as hesitators/hedges, the sexes were found to use different terms (so females said *well* and *really* more often while males said *maybe* and *perhaps*) but it was difficult to attribute the category itself to either sex.

Schmid's research addressed whether our stereotyped thinking about linguistic gender differences are borne out, but one question we could ask is whether such a method allows us to consider features we may not have considered. If we begin an analysis with a predetermined set of linguistic phenomena to investigate then our analysis cannot go beyond them. More important differences may exist but will not be uncovered. A corpus-*driven* approach was taken by Rayson et al. (1997) who only used the spoken demographic part of the BNC (the part where private conversations were recorded), comparing around 500 male and 500 female speakers who contributed about five million words of speech in total. Rayson et al. calculated word lists for each sex and then used chi-squared tests to identify which words showed the greatest preference by one particular sex (in essence this was a keyword analysis). They reported 26 words that were 'most characteristic of male speech' and 25 words 'most characteristic of female speech'. The 'female speech' words included the reported speech marker *said*, the pronouns *I, me, she, her, him*, the co-ordinators *because* and *cos* and words that functioned as discourse markers or forms of evaluation: *oh, lovely, nice, mm, really*. Male speakers used the strong swear word *fuck/ fucking* more, as well as a different set of discourse markers: *yeah, aye, right, okay, yes, ah* and numbers *two, three, four, hundred, number*. Unlike the 'topic' differences identified by Schmid, these categories indicate more generalizable uses of language that could be indicative of actual differences. So female first and third person pronoun use suggests that females talk about themselves and other people more often while their higher use of *because/cos* suggests they are more likely to be interested in explanations or accounts. The greater focus on numbers in male speech could indicate more concern with exact quantification. Additionally, both sexes use discourse markers that have a range of functions, although these markers appear to be gendered to an extent, with the male discourse markers indicating agreement and acknowledgement while the female ones seem to be more focused on positive evaluation or signalling interest.

While the amount of corpus research on differences between female and male *speech* is small, the literature on writing is larger, particularly if we take into account a wealth of research which positions itself using terms like *stylometry, authorship identification* or *text categorization* rather than corpus linguistics per se. Koppel et al. (2002) also used a corpus-driven approach with the BNC, this time focusing on the written texts that had been marked for sex and genre. They compared 1,081 linguistic features across 566 documents. These features included 405 function words (like *the, to* and *from*), as well as common part of speech tags, occurring alone, in pairs or triples (e.g. a common triple was a preposition followed by an article followed by a noun). Automated text categorization techniques were able to identify certain features as more commonly used by males or by females which meant that when presented with a new text, Koppel et al.'s algorithm was able to identify the sex of the writer about 80 per cent of the time. Indicators that a text was likely to be written by a male included noun specifiers such as determiners, numbers and modifiers, while females were more likely to use negation, pronouns and certain prepositions. However, they also found that there was a greater difference between fiction and non-fiction texts than between male and female writing, and their algorithm was able to correctly identify whether a new text was fiction or non-fiction 98 per cent of the time.

In another study, Newman et al. (2008) analysed 14,000 text samples (93% comprising written texts), using a tool called Linguistic Enquiry and Word Count which compared text samples to a dictionary containing 2,000 words in 74 categories. They found that women used more words related to psychological and social processes while men referred more to object properties and impersonal topics, although they also found that in cases where constraints were placed on language use, the gender differences were generally smaller.

A newer form of automatic authorship identification has utilized the ease with which texts can be harvested in online contexts. For example, Cheng et al. (2011) used three machine-learning algorithms (support vector machine, Bayesian logistic regression and AdBoost decision tree) to identify the sex of writers, based on training corpora of 6,769 Reuters newsgroup messages from 1996–7 and 8,970 emails from the company Enron (these emails had been made public due to an investigation over accounting fraud). Cheng et al. classified 545 features, grouped into five categories (character-based, word-based, syntactic, structure-based and function words). The support vector machine algorithm performed best, being able to correctly predict author sex in 76.25 per cent of news articles and 82.23 per cent of Enron emails. Perhaps predictably, the researchers found that all three algorithms performed better on longer texts, or when they were given more texts to train on, and that when only one of the five sets of features was employed, accuracy was lower (ranging from 59.08% to 74.81%) than when all five sets of features were combined. They conclude that 'there are significant differences between men and women in personal writings such as e-mails, and gender differences also exist between authors of news articles even though neutral language is dominant there' (Cheng et al. 2011: 86).

The 'gender differences' paradigm is not confined to English. Olsen (2005) carried out a diachronic comparison of French writing, comparing 18.5 million words of texts by female authors with 27 million words of similar texts by male authors, dating between 1500 and 1960. Olsen compared the frequency ratios of these words, noting which ones had higher male or female ratios. He found that the female texts contained more words favouring a personal style (pronouns, emotive, internal or subjective states and relationship terms), while male texts contained more abstract concepts and nouns.

Thus, on the whole, the corpus-driven approaches have tended to find and report on linguistic gender differences, in written, spoken and online contexts. Newman et al. (2008: 233) conclude that their analyses 'demonstrate small but systematic differences in the way that men and women use language' while Koppel et al. (2002: 410) write that their paper has found 'convincing evidence of a difference in male and female writing styles'. So while corpus research and related fields like stylometry have tended to agree that difference exists, this is at odds with the meta-research by Hyde (2005) and thinking within Gender and Language scholarship. Can this divide by explained or resolved?

Measuring similarity

Much corpus-informed reportage of linguistic differences between the sexes confirms popular understandings about gender, and helps to strengthen the belief that males and females use language differently. However, a potential problem with some methods within Corpus Linguistics is that they put researchers in a 'difference' mindset, privileging findings that reveal differences while backgrounding similarities. Take, for example, keyword analysis. If I look at the top 50 keyword lists when comparing the female and male speech in the BNC, the female lexis does indeed appear to imply a more reactive and emotional use of language than male speech which comes across as formal and technical – female keywords include *oh, yeah, well, nice, like, lovely, ooh, really, dear, alright* and *yes*, while male keywords include *point, minus, terms, number, percent, particular, hundred, Mr, question, fact* and *example*.

However, the focus on these short lists of words only tells us about differences, not similarities. Another story about gender differences could be that males and females are more alike than they are similar. Yet to people who are working within a 'difference mindset' such a story is perhaps not as interesting, and it could even constitute a 'non-finding' that is not worth reporting (as I have found when journalists have contacted me about gender differences and language). Meehan and Janik (1990) report that people tend to ignore information that contradicts stereotypes, while having better memory access for information that is consistent with the stereotype. There are plenty of commonly used words in the BNC where there is hardly any difference in frequency between the sexes: pronouns (*everybody, nobody*), nouns (*child, sun, hands*), verbs (*expect, write, pull, read, notice, spend, realize*), yet such words tend not to be reported on in quantitative research on language and gender. Newman (2008: 231) is an example of 'good practice', giving a table which not only shows which gender differences were statistically significant, but also which were *not*: gendered usage of questions, oppositions (such as *but*) and justifiers (like *because*).

An alternative way of looking at gender differences would be to ask to what extent do differences outweigh similarities? There are a number of ways to approach this question once we have found a way of defining what we actually mean by a difference. For the purposes of this chapter, in order to be able to compare my findings to Rayson et al. (1997) and Schmid (2003), I will focus on word frequencies only, although this is only one measure out of many that are possible, so the findings discussed below cannot be generalized beyond word frequency. This chapter therefore does not aim to definitively show whether males and females use language 'differently' but to identify ways in which corpus linguistics approaches can begin to approach this question in more productive ways.

One way that other researchers have tried to identify similarity between corpora is to use the Spearman rank correlation statistic test. For example, Hofland and Johansson (1982) attempted to identify which of the 15 genres of writing in the (Lancaster, Oslo and Bergen) LOB corpus (one million words of written British English from 1961) were most similar to each other. They took the 89 most frequent words in the corpus overall and then obtained rankings of these words within each of the 15 genres. Each of the genres was then compared against each other, to find out which ones had the most similar frequency rankings. The Spearman test produces a number between 1 and –1 for each pairing, with 1 signifying perfect correlation, 0 being no correlation and –1 being perfect negative correlation. With the genres in the LOB corpus this method produced results that appear to make intuitive sense – the genre pair with the highest correlation (0.97) was general fiction and romantic fiction while the pair with the lowest correlation (0.28) was adventure story and government documents. I used this test in (Baker 2009) to compare LOB and three other corpora of British English from 1931, 1991 and 2006 (basing the correlation on the rankings of the 20 most frequent words in the 2006 corpus). I found that as the time distance between the corpora increased, the amount of correlation decreased. So the 1931–61 and the 1961–91 pair both had correlations of 0.99, while the 1931–2006 corpus had a lower correlation of 0.93.

Carrying out a Spearman rank correlation test on the most frequent 20 (male) words in the male and female speech in the BNC results in a correlation of 0.93. This is the same amount of correlation I found in the study reported above for writing in 1931 and 2006. It is not difficult to imagine how such a finding could be reported in the media: 'men and women are as different from each other as people from 1931 and 2006!' However, such a headline would obscure the fact that the measure is only based upon the most frequent 20 words, which comprises only 34.1 per cent of all of the words that people tend to say, and it only examines frequency, not context of use. So the measure does not consider linguistic phenomena like word order, meaning or prosodic aspects of speech like intonation. Additionally, the headline would also overlook that a correlation of .93 is very high –

close to perfect correlation. The true 'story' is that the similarities hugely outweigh the differences.

A problem with the Spearman rank correlation test is that it is based on *rankings* of frequencies rather than frequencies themselves, so if two equal-sized corpora both have the word *the* as their most frequent word, but in one corpus *the* occurs 1 million times and in the other, *the* only occurs 500,000 times, then this huge difference will be overlooked because both corpora still have *the* as their top word. Another similarity measure, which does take actual frequency into account, is the Manhattan Distance (MD). This measure is named after the grid system of streets in Manhattan, and computes the distance that would be travelled to get from one place to another if a grid-like path was followed. For example, the journey from the intersection of 3rd Avenue and 86th Street to 5th Avenue and 90th Street would mean travelling 2 avenues in one direction then 4 streets in another – giving a MD of 2 + 4 = 6.[2]

Similarly, when using the MD to compare the frequencies of words in two corpora, we first sum all of the 'distances' (actually the differences in proportional frequencies to take into account the fact that corpora are often of different sizes) between each word as they occur in each corpus. The higher the resulting number of the added distances, the greater the lexical difference in terms of frequencies. Table 2.1 shows a worked example, using two very small 'corpora', containing only six word types. The MD is the number in the last column of the last row: 33.31.

The MD was used by Juola (2012) to compare written British and American English (based on the Google Ngram Corpus) at various points in time between 1900 and 2005. Juola found that MDs gradually rose over

TABLE 2.1 *Worked example for the Manhattan Distance.*

Word	Frequency Corpus A	Frequency Corpus B	% Corpus A	% Corpus B	%A–%B converted to a positive number
the	20	55	33.33	36.66	3.33
I	16	30	26.66	20	6.66
you	12	15	20	10	10
and	8	25	13.33	16.66	3.33
a	4	20	6.66	13.33	6.66
to	0	5	0	3.33	3.33
Total	60	150	100	100	MD = 33.31

time and argues that rather than British and American English becoming more lexically similar to each other over the twentieth century, they have actually being growing further apart.[3]

The MD thus offers an attractive way of comparing corpora together, and it would also allow us to establish norms about what amount of difference could be expected among two corpora. Before comparing the male and female parts of the spoken BNC together, I decided to begin by comparing various corpora that were clearly very lexically different from each other, to obtain a benchmark of what a high Manhattan Difference would be. First, I compared the French and English sections of *le corpus BAF*, a parallel reference corpus containing about 4,000,000 words in each language consisting of translations of institutional texts, scientific articles, technical documentation and fiction. Here, the MD was 175.6 (rounded to the nearest decimal point).[4] This figure is a useful baseline, telling us how high the MD would be if two distinct languages were compared. However, I also decided to compare some different varieties of English together, in order to see how much that would reduce the MD. I compared a small corpus of Shakespeare plays with a set of newspaper articles taken from the 'A' section of the AmE06 Corpus (containing written American English from around 2006). This time the MD was 108.8. What about more similar varieties? As a third comparison I used the Frown and (Freiburg Lancaster-Oslo/Bergen) FLOB corpora (American and British written English both from 1991). Here, the MD was 29.7.

Bearing these figures in mind, what is the MD for the male and female speech in the BNC?[5] Interestingly it is 31.3, a figure quite similar to the difference between American and British written English published at around the same time period of the collection of the BNC spoken data. While this score is clearly lower than the Shakespeare-American news comparison, would there be much less variation if we randomly split the male speech from the BNC into two equal-sized halves and then compared them together? When I tried this, the MD was only slightly lower at 29.3. When the female speech was split in half and compared, the MD was 34.2 – even higher than the male speech compared against the female speech. However, these figures may not be typical because there are lots of different ways of splitting up a corpus, and some splits may produce extreme cases of similarity or difference. It would make sense to split the corpora up into smaller chunks in order to carry out multiple comparisons. Therefore, I randomly split the male corpora into four equal sized parts (labelled as M1, M2, M3, M4), and did the same to the female corpora (F1, F2, F3, F4). Table 2.1 shows the MDs when these eight corpora were compared against each other. The 12 grey-shaded cells in the table are comparisons of same-sex corpora (e.g. M1 vs M3 or F2 vs F4) while the 16 white cells are comparisons of opposite-sex corpora (e.g. M1 vs F2).

How should we interpret Table 2.2? The comparisons among different sets of male speakers reveal MDs which range from 18.5 to 28.7 (the mean is

TABLE 2.2 *Manhattan Distances comparing different sets of speakers in the British National Corpus.*

	M1	M2	M3	M4	F1	F2	F3	F4
M1		28.7	24.7	18.5	36.6	27.0	27.1	29.3
M2			21.1	28.0	54.2	40.4	40.2	44.6
M3				23.3	47.5	35.1	32.5	37.2
M4					36.8	26.5	24.9	27.4
F1						23.2	26.5	22.0
F2							20.5	19.7
F3								18.5
F4								

24.0). For the female-only comparisons the MDs are between 18.5 and 26.5 (mean 21.7). So both sets of same-sex comparisons show similar ranges and spreads of difference. The mixed-sex comparisons have an MD of between 24.9 and 54.2 (mean 35.4). Here, the amount of difference between each group is higher in general, but also there is more variation in the amount of difference, for example the M4–F3 comparison yields a MD of 24.9 which is similar to some of the same-sex comparisons (such as M1–M3 or F1–F2). However, the M2–F1 comparison yields a much higher amount of difference (54.2). The four pairs with the highest MDs are all mixed-sex pairs (M2–F1, M3–F1, F4–M2 and F2–M2) while the four with the lowest MDs are single-sex pairs (M1–M4, F3–F4, F2–F4 and F2–F3).

At this point then, it we could say that the general picture for the spoken BNC is a greater amount of lexical variation between male and female groups than male–male or female–female groups. However, it is important to note that this pattern is a *trend* rather than an absolute, with some of the same-sex comparisons showing more variation than the opposite sex comparisons.

Does Table 2.2 give *strong* evidence that the males and females in the BNC are 'lexically distinct'? To an extent, it appears that generally, the lexical distance between males and females is higher than for same-sex comparisons, but Table 2.2 tells us that there is also variation within the sexes. We should additionally bear in mind the caveat that our conclusions only apply to spoken British English that was collected in the early 1990s. We cannot directly conclude anything about language use in other places or time periods. And once we start to consider the context that the BNC spoken data was collected, we find an explanation for the trend towards sex difference, which raises a question about the validity of such differences.

Take for example the comparison between groups M2 and F1, where the MD was highest. A keyword comparison of these groups results in top 50 keywords like *county*, *settlement*, *council*, *terms*, *policy*, *percent*, *report*, *government* and *committee* for the M2 group and *mum*, *mummy* and *daddy* for the F1 group. More detailed exploration of such keywords indicates that the M2 males were recorded more often in work-based contexts (such as meetings of local government) while the F1 females appear to have been more likely to be recorded at home, sometimes looking after children. Consequently, an analysis of the types of speech in the F1 and M2 groups bears this out more clearly. Of the 320 speakers in the F1 group, 261 (81%) had their conversations recorded in private settings (being tagged as 'demographic' as opposed to 'context governed' which was used for public and workplace settings). For the M2 group, of the 618 speakers, only 18 (3%) are from private settings. The larger F1–M2 difference then, is more likely to be telling us more about how people speak at work, as opposed to at home, rather than actual male–female differences.

Compare the above proportions to the comparison between F3–M4 – the two opposite-sex files which had the lowest MD and were therefore the most similar lexically. Here, F3 consists of 349 speakers, of which 108 (31%) had their speech recorded in private settings, while M4 had 620 speakers, of which 266 (43%) were recorded in private settings. Here the proportions of speakers in private settings is much more similar, perhaps explaining why F3–M4 has a lower MD. Even so, the larger number of male speakers at work still results in work-related keywords appearing for the M4 speakers like *county*, *chairman*, *product*, *employment* and *bid*, while the F3 keywords are domestic ones like *kitchen*, *children*, *buggy*, *potty* and *baby*. Unsurprisingly, people tend to talk differently when given different roles to perform, and so such lexical differences should not be viewed as telling us anything essential about a particular sex, instead these differences are circumstantial. As Coates (1998: 295) observes: 'the "me" that changes a baby's nappy or mashes a banana for a toddler is a different "me" from the one who participates in a committee meeting or who poses as life model at the local art school.'

Table 2.3 shows the total amounts of male and female speech (in words) for the demographic and context-governed sections in the BNC. There is more than twice as much male context-governed speech as there is male demographic speech, while the reverse pattern is true for females. In other words, males were more likely to be recorded in public contexts, while females were more likely to be recorded in private ones. Clearly then, if we compare the male and female speech together, our analysis is likely to be skewed by this public/private imbalance.

Is it therefore worth just considering the private 'demographic' data by itself, which is what Rayson et al. (1997) did in their research? Even here

TABLE 2.3 *Total amounts of male and female speech.*

	Male	Female	Both males and females
Demographic	1,454,344	2,264,094	3,718,438
Context-governed	3,495,594	1,026,475	4,522,069

we are likely to find 'gender differences' that are a function of *role* rather than sex. So at home and in private, the females who were recorded for inclusion in the BNC seemed to have been more likely to have been involved in non-paid work of a domestic nature, looking after children, cooking, cleaning, etc., whereas males who are recorded in private contexts appear less likely to be involved in such tasks (recall that the BNC spoken data was collected in the early 1990s), so we would still expect many of these 'private' differences to be related to role.[6] Hence, when we compare male demographic against female demographic data, the female demographic keywords include *kitchen, school, children, home* and *shopping*, whereas male ones are more concerned with topics like sport and transport: *player, rugby, goals, game, speed, traffic*. Hochschild and Machung (1989) have coined the phrase 'the second shift' to refer to the fact that responsibilities of childcare and housework tend to be disproportionately borne by women, in addition to paid labour.

Despite these topic keywords appearing, the overall picture for male and female speech when in private settings is one of similarity – the MD for just the demographic part of the corpus for male and female speech is 17.4, the lowest MD we have seen so far. A random split of the male demographic speech into two equal-sized halves resulted in an MD of 15.3, lower than the difference between the male and female demographic speech, but only by a small amount. The female demographic speech, when split randomly into two, gave a smaller MD of 12.7. These smaller figures suggest that when people are placed in similar situations, their language becomes similar. This finding may appear blindingly obvious, although it tends not to be part of 'gender differences' narratives.

Comparing the female and male context-governed conversations only, also results in gendered keywords which are related to role, with female context-governed keywords being concerned with healthcare, childcare and pregnancy (e.g. *bleeding, nursery, midwife, nurses* and *treatment*) while male context-governed keywords relate to mathematical and scientific terms (*gradient, curve, fraction, dioxide, hydrogen, acid*), which are more likely to tell us about roles that males and females took in the workplace (e.g. nurse vs scientist) at the time when the corpus was being collected. However, again, the overall picture of lexical difference is quite low – an

MD of 22.1, not as low as for the demographic data, but still lower than many of the other comparisons carried out in Table 2.1. Comparing two randomly split halves of male context governed speech together gives an MD of 19.0, while this figure is 20.8 when the female context governed speech is split in half and compared.

Table 2.4 summarizes the MDs for the various comparisons carried out so far.

So when context is taken into account (albeit in the rather blunt way of distinguishing between private and public speech), the amount of lexical difference between speakers (of any sex) tends to decrease. The opposite-sex comparisons start to produce very similar results to the equivalent same-sex comparisons, especially for the context-governed part of the corpus. Clearly, the differences for the opposite-sex comparisons are higher, but they are not much higher, and none of the comparisons of the BNC spoken data result in MDs which are close to the distinction between Shakespeare and American news. At the lexical level, at least, it is somewhat of an exaggeration to suggest that males and females speak different 'genderlects'.

TABLE 2.4 *Manhattan Distances for different corpus comparisons.*

Corpus 1	Corpus 2	Manhattan Distance
French written texts	English written texts	175.6
Shakespeare plays	American news articles 2006	108.8
Half female speech	Half female speech	34.2
All male speech	All female speech	31.3
American 1990s writing	British 1990s writing	29.7
Half male speech	Half male speech	29.3
Male context governed	Female context governed	22.1
Half female context governed	Half female context governed	20.8
Half male context governed	Half male context governed	19.0
Male demographic	Female demographic	17.4
Half male demographic	Half male demographic	15.3
Half female demographic	Half female demographic	12.7

Making the atypical stereotypical

Even considering this large difference between public/private contexts, we need to be careful in assuming that the extent of lexical difference we are seeing applies to all speakers, or even the majority of speakers. The way that some features are written about in academic papers could indicate a somewhat binary view of language use. For example, Koppel et al. (2002: 407–8) write '. . . the function words that consistently appear in the final iteration training on fiction are: male features – *a*, *the*, *as*; female features – *she*, *for*, *with*, *not*. When training on non-fiction we find: male features – *that*, *one*; female features – *for*, *with*, *not*, *and*, *in*.' While both males and females use all of these words, the higher frequency of usage by one sex is enough to label such a word as a male or female feature. Let us take a couple of the keywords and explore their dispersions in some detail.

Consider the word *lovely*, a classic 'female' keyword (it is the twelfth strongest word most characteristic of female speech in Rayson et al.'s 1997 BNC comparison) as well as being a widely cited example of one of Lakoff's 'empty adjectives'. In the BNC, *lovely* occurs 2,093 times, its frequency per million words is 433.97 for females and 134.35 for males, so we could conclude that females say *lovely* about three times as much as males – quite a large difference. However, let us consider the data for *lovely* in another way by thinking about how it is dispersed. In total, 318 out of 1,360 female speakers (23%) used this word, while 251 out of 2,448 male speakers (10%) said it. So while *lovely* could be seen as a 'female' word, it would be equally true to say that the majority of males and females in the corpus did *not* say *lovely*, at least during the data collection period. Furthermore, the word is not distributed equally across the speakers. For example, speaker PS0DY (a woman called Ann aged between 45–59) who contributed 1,974 words of speech to the corpus, says *lovely* 27 times in this short period. In the excerpt below, she uses *lovely* three times during a conversation with friends:

Ann:	Have a *lovely* day!
Antony:	Go out and have a look at outside <unclear>
Graeme:	Yes, yes we'll do that!
Ann:	Have a *lovely* time!
Sarah:	Well it's not till <pause> Aug -- Aug --
Graeme:	So
Sarah:	July, so <pause> <laugh>
Ann:	Well, by then you'll have the *lovely* we -- weather by then.

On the other hand, Kathleen, who recorded a much larger amount of speech (39,423 words), only says *lovely* once, and there are many more female speakers who never said it. In fact, over half of the female utterances of *lovely* were made by just 36 speakers (or 2.6% of the female speakers in the BNC). So here we have a pattern where a relatively small number of females are using *lovely* often, but their high use of *lovely* is not typical of all females. The typical picture is that this is a relatively rare word for both males and females, with a few atypical females using it a lot.

Similarly, *fucking* is a 'male' word (actually the top 'male' word in Rayson et al. 1997), spoken 1,724 times in the corpus, with a frequency per million words of 282.43 for males and 99.07 for females (in other words, almost three times as frequent in male speech). But only 89 out of 2,448 males (3.63%) used this word, and 57 out of 1,360 females said it (4.19%). A few male speakers contributed many of the cases of *fucking* in the corpus, including for example, Mark, an aircraft engineer aged between 25 and 34 who said it 274 times during 26,068 words of speech. Here he relates an anecdote about how someone stood on his foot, using *fucking* five times within a 76-word stretch, in order to emphasize his anger at the incident:

> I'm sort of standing there like this up against the counter waiting to be served, suppose to be coming back right, stood right on the [unclear] foot, it hurt, but I thought ok it's a busy shop he won't [unclear] so I'd turned around, sort of he was there, so I sort of went to him like that [pause] and he was [unclear] looked at me and *fucking* looked back, so I said are you gonna apologise then, getting right *fucking* pissed off cos I [unclear] about three o'clock that day, hang over and being dragged up and down the town all *fucking* day ain't my idea of fun you know, ri -- right in a bad mood anyway, and he said no in a real *fucking* why don't you try and make me [unclear] sort of attitude, so I'm just about to *fucking* say something to me, like, how [unclear] out the shop and everything, and she said what's the fuck, what's the matter with you then?

In all, just five speakers contributed over half of the male cases of *fucking*. As with *lovely*, *fucking* may appear to be a gendered word, but its frequency is largely due to a minority of male speakers who used it a great deal more than everybody else.

It could be argued that as we are only looking at one word, we are not taking into account an overall picture. Perhaps the true pattern is that males swear more but they use a wider range of swear-words, so a few say *fucking*, a few say *bastard*, a few say *shit*, etc., which collectively would result in a more robust pattern of dispersion over speakers. Let us examine this hypothesis by considering a set of swear-words together: *fuck, bastard, shit*, *cunt*, *bloody*, *bugger*, *arse* and *piss* (and related forms like *fucking*, *pissed*, etc.) Will this set of words be more likely to be said be males or females?

The results showed that of the 7,023 cases of these words in the corpus, they are relatively equally distributed between males and females. Males say them 888.3 times per million words while females say them 828.29 times – quite a small difference. What about dispersion? Of the 1,360 females, only 250 (18.3%) use these swear words, while 381 of the 2,448 males (15.5%) use them. Again, this is quite a small difference, although it is also interesting (and perhaps unexpected) that these words are relatively more widely dispersed among female speakers than males. And the 'overlooked' pattern here is that the majority of both males and females *did not swear*, at least when their speech was recorded for the corpus.

Table 2.5 examines dispersions of the top 10 male and female keywords in Rayson et al.'s study (in terms of chi-square scores). These 20 words all indicate what are perhaps the strongest lexical differences in terms of frequency between males and females in the BNC. Information on dispersion, based on the proportion of males and females who used the word at least once, and the proportion of males and females who contributed half the mentions of that word, are also added. It was decided to focus on these two measures because they both give different but complementary ways of thinking about dispersion. The first measure – the proportion of people in the group who use a word at least once, is indicative of whether a word is avoided by a certain group. The second measure – the percentage of people who uttered half of the mentions of a word, gives an indication regarding whether a word is atypical of language usage of a particular group. If only a very small proportion of speakers contribute half of total the mentions of a word, then we would not consider such speakers to be typical of the group.

It should be noted that the concept of a 'word' is slightly unusual here. In order to tag the corpus for grammatical parts of speech, some words were split in two, so a word like *can't* is split into *ca* and *n't*, which are counted as instances of *can* and *not* respectively.

Perhaps what is most telling about Table 2.5 is how *similar* most of the columns are for male and female speakers. If a word is frequent, it is likely to be used by most of the male and female speakers, although infrequent words like *aye*, *fucking* and *fuck* tend to be restricted to very small numbers of speakers. However, even for the very frequent words like *the* and *is*, over half of the occurrences of these words are collectively spoken by ten percent or less of the speakers in the corpus. In some cases, the figures in the data run counter to expectations. So *yeah*, *aye* and *right* – male keywords, are actually used proportionally more by females than males, while *I*, *and* and *to* (female keywords) are used by more males.

There are a few cases where the dispersion differences are larger. The male keyword *hundred* is used by 37.17 per cent of males and 25.58 per cent

TABLE 2.5 *Dispersions of top 10 male and female keywords derived from Rayson et al. 1997.*

	Keyword	% of males who used word	% of females who used word	% of males who used half of cases of word	% of females who used half of cases of word
Male keywords	fucking	3.63	3.23	0.16	0.36
	er	74.40	66.02	5.88	4.85
	the	93.79	90.00	10.00	7.20
	yeah	49.22	58.16	3.10	4.11
	aye	12.37	13.82	0.98	1.61
	right	60.53	60.73	4.86	5.14
	hundred	37.17	25.58	3.67	2.35
	fuck	2.61	1.61	0.28	0.51
	is	83.61	80.14	8.21	6.25
	of	88.72	83.38	9.02	6.91
Female keywords	she	34.31	51.17	2.98	3.67
	her	27.84	40.29	3.34	3.67
	said	51.96	54.11	3.92	2.86
	n't	80.18	82.64	6.33	4.41
	I	97.95	88.67	7.59	5.44
	and	90.56	86.61	8.49	6.32
	to	91.01	88.89	9.76	6.69
	cos	34.43	45.00	3.63	3.60
	oh	48.65	62.86	3.02	3.75
	Christmas	8.37	15.88	1.42	1.32

of females, while the female keyword *she* is used by 34.31 per cent of males and 51.17 per cent of females. There are similar patterns for the words *her*, *cos*, *oh* and *Christmas*. The fact that *she* and *her* are used more in female speech is reminiscent of Coates (2003: 121), who, in her qualitative study of men's speech, noted how women featured much less than men in male narratives. The corpus data, while not presenting such an extreme conclusion, does indicate that males generally do not appear to use female pronouns as much as females, both in terms of overall frequency and distribution, although again, the difference is one of gradience rather than exclusivity. So it would be stretching the truth somewhat to label *oh* as a 'female' word, considering that almost half the males in the corpus say it at least once, while over half of the female instances of *oh* are spoken by only 3.75 per cent of the females in the corpus.

A potential problem with the last two columns in Table 2.5 is that they imply that these keywords are only ever used by small numbers of people. However, as indicated above with the discussion of Ann and Kathleen, there is considerable variation in the amount of speech that different speakers contributed to the BNC. Across the corpus, 13 speakers (who were tagged for sex) contributed over 40,000 words of speech each, while around 285 speakers contributed under 100 words each. With many speakers only being represented by a few utterances, it is perhaps not surprising that the speakers who used more than half of the cases of a word are likely to come from the small number of people who spoke the most. In order to compensate for this disparity, Table 2.6 shows data for the 50 males and 50 females who contributed the most speech in the corpus, based on whether they used the top male and female keywords. The top 50 male speakers each contributed between 11,884 and 41,294 words each while the top 50 female speakers contributed between 12,864 and 70,154 words. The results regarding dispersion of male and female keywords are similar to that of Table 2.5. Almost all of these 'prolific' speakers use the frequent grammatical words, while the strong swear words *fuck* and *fucking* are mostly limited to a smaller number of both males and females, both in terms of speakers who actually say the word at all and number of speakers who contribute half of all uses of the word.

The most notable difference is *Christmas*, which was used by 40 out of 50 of the most prolific female speakers and only 25 out of 50 of the most prolific male ones. A second notable difference in Table 2.5 concerns *aye*, which, although a male keyword, seems to be distributed more narrowly among the top male speakers, with only 16 males using it and only 2 of these contributing more than half the uses. Female use of *aye* is spread over half of the top speakers, although again more than half the cases are limited to just a very small number: 4. A third word which appears to show a difference is *oh*, which is spoken by all of the top male and female speakers, although only 9 males contribute to half of these uses, compared to 16 females. This would indicate that *oh* usage is better spread out over female speech, whereas with males, high usage seems to be concentrated among a smaller sub-population. Again though, to label *oh* a female word would be to overlook those male speakers who do use it frequently.

TABLE 2.6 *Keyword use for the top 50 male and female speakers in the corpus.*

	Keyword	Number of top 50 males who used word	Number of top 50 females who used word	Number of males who used half of cases of word (top 50 male cases only)	Number of females who used half of cases of word (top 50 female cases only)
Male keywords	fucking	9	10	2	2
	er	43	48	9	10
	the	50	50	18	14
	yeah	42	47	9	13
	aye	16	25	2	4
	right	50	50	10	12
	hundred	48	46	7	7
	fuck	7	7	2	2
	is	50	50	17	15
	of	50	50	17	16
Female keywords	she	50	49	11	12
	her	49	50	12	13
	said	50	50	7	9
	n't	50	50	15	14
	I	50	50	14	14
	and	50	50	18	14
	to	50	50	18	15
	cos	41	47	10	9
	oh	50	50	9	16
	Christmas	25	40	4	6

It is worth taking a closer look at the word *Christmas* as it was both identified as a keyword, and a word which had a wider distribution among female speakers in general, and the most prolific female speakers in the corpus, compared to their male counterparts. There are 1,148 female mentions of *Christmas* in the BNC across 229 speakers, and common grammatical patterns include prepositions which suggest discussion and planning: *for Christmas, at Christmas, after Christmas* and *before Christmas*. *Christmas* is also a frequent L1 modifier of *dinner, pudding, shopping, party, fair, card, present* and *tree*. An examination of concordance lines suggests that women talk about Christmas more than men because they appear to be more closely involved in the organization of this holiday period, buying gifts, writing cards, cooking the dinner and setting up the tree. The concordance analysis suggests then, that this is a practical, role-based keyword, similar to words like *children, home* and *kitchen*. The frequency profile of this word therefore tells us more about division of domestic duties in British households in 1993 rather than speech differences per se.

The value of a third corpus

I have argued that a problem of using a function like keywords is that it forces us into a 'difference' mindset because we directly compare two corpora together and are given a list of words that are more statistically significantly more frequent in one corpus when compared against the other. However, it is also possible to use the keywords function to focus on similarity by using a third corpus as a reference corpus. For example, imagine the two corpora we want to compare are called A and B. Rather than comparing A and B directly, we use a third corpus, C, and first compare A with C and then compare B with C. With the two sets of keywords that are produced, we can see whether there are similarities or differences between them. Table 2.7 shows such a comparison of the male and female spoken demographic sections of the BNC, using the 1 million word FLOB corpus as a reference corpus. FLOB was chosen because it contains British English from the same time period that the BNC was collected, but is made up of written rather than spoken texts. The table only considers the strongest 100 keywords that were derived in each list and indicates whether that word was key in just the female corpus, just the male corpus, or both. If there really was a large difference between male and female speech, we would perhaps expect that the male and female keywords would be quite distinct from each other, with not much overlap indicated in the last column of the table. As noted earlier, some words in the BNC were split for example *we'd, I'm, gonna, dunno* (which was split into three *du n no*), *gotta, I've, won't*. Additionally, speech that was unclear or gaps in recording were marked with the tags <unclear> and <gap>. As these tags did not occur in FLOB, they appear as keywords and for the purposes of this exercise I have left these two tags in the table.

Eighty eight out of the top 100 keywords are identical to each list. A closer inspection revealed that the actual ordering of the keywords in each list is very similar. For example, the ten strongest female keywords (when using FLOB as a reference) are, in order: *s*, *I*, *you*, <unclear>, *yeah*, *it*, *oh*, *do*, *got* and *ve*. The equivalent male keywords are *s*, <unclear>, *I*, *you*, *yeah*, *it*, *oh*, *do*, *er*, *got* and *ve*. There are only minor differences between these two lists which indicate the strongest differences in male and female speech with writing of the same period and location.

Table 2.7 does show a few differences though – numerals seem to be a more distinctive feature of male speech, while females appear to use indicators which suggest reported speech (*said*, *says*) as well as the female pronoun *she* and the word *lovely*, although as we have already seen, dispersion patterns may not mean that differences in frequency are typical of all females. Indeed, a study by Harrington (2008) examined the issue of whether females engage in more reported speech than males. She found that on the face of it, her analysis of a small spoken corpus did indicate

TABLE 2.7 *Male and female keywords in the BNC demographic section, using FLOB as a reference corpus.*

Female keywords	Male keywords	Key for both male and female
all, coming, dear, lovely, my, off, round, said, says, she, thought, went	du, eight, fifty, four, fucking, hundred, one, six, thirty, three, two, ya	actually, ah, alright, anyway, aye, bit, bloody, can, come, cos, d, dad, did, do, does, doing, done, down, eh, er, five, <gap>, get, go, goes, going, good, got, ha, have, he, here, I, if, it, just, know, like, look, lot, m, me, mean, mm, mum, mummy, n, na, name, nice, nine, no, now, oh, okay, ooh, put, re, really, right, s, say, see, so, something, sort, ta, that, them, then, there, they, thing, think, twenty, <unclear>, up, ve, want, we, well, what, why, wo, yeah, yes, you, your

that females tend to report speech more. However, a dispersion analysis revealed that a small number of female speakers were responsible for the overall high rate of reported speech among women while the majority of female speakers in her corpus had similar levels of reported speech to males. Additionally, some of the differences here are more likely to be due to the unequal context-governed/demographic distribution of male and female speakers. Consider Table 2.8, which gives a breakdown of relative frequencies of *she*.

The table indicates that *she* is over 5 times more common in the private demographic context of the BNC, compared to the public context-governed context. Additionally, males are more likely to use *she* in private contexts than females will use it in public contexts. I would argue that the distibution of *she* tells us more about the role (and absence) of women in the workplace and public affairs in the United Kingdom in the early 1990s than it does about linguistic gender differences.

Conversely, numbers are more commonly found in context-governed contexts than demographic contexts, although in both genres it is males who use them the most (Table 2.9). Koller (2007: 126) has noted the presence of numbers in corporate discourse, referring to the phenomenon as 'number-dropping' and suggesting that it involves a kind of linguistic impression management which 'clearly shows the corporate world's obsession with size'. The fact that males use more numbers than females, even in 'at home' contexts could indicate that numeral use is a more clear-cut 'male difference', although it could be that this is associated with a form of speaking which is learnt in the workplace, and then carries on over into the home.

TABLE 2.8 *Occurrences per million words of* she *in the BNC.*

	Male	Female	Both males and females
Demographic	4838.61	10073.35	8025.95
Context-governed	1081.08	2671.28	1442.04

TABLE 2.9 *Occurrences per million words of numbers (tagged CRD) in the BNC.*

	Male	Female	Both males and females
Demographic	20777.07	15097.87	17319.10
Context-governed	22417.36	17651.67	21335.59

Conclusion

It is possible to draw a number of conclusions from this research, bearing in mind that we can only generalize to what was happening in the United Kingdom in the early 1990s and that we are only considering lexis rather than other aspects of language such as grammar or prosody. First, when male speakers are compared against female speakers the amount of lexical difference is generally larger than when two groups consisting of just males or just females are compared, although there is also a large amount of similarity between male and female speakers and, as shown in Table 2.7, it could be argued that the similarities are actually more extensive than the differences.

But a focus on just the differences does not reveal the full picture – we also need to take into account the fact that *any* group of speakers that are compared (including men vs men or women vs women) will produce differences, as shown in Table 2.2. Additionally, the sex-based differences can be partially explained by gender *roles* – men being recorded more in workplace contexts, women more in 'at home' contexts where they were engaged in domestic unpaid work. When males and females are compared in similar settings, the amount of difference reduces and is only slightly larger than comparisons of single-sex groups, although even when 'at home', females tend to use more words which relate to domestic duties. Second, some of the words which most clearly appear to articulate gender differences do not reflect typical uses for someone's sex, but as with *lovely* and *fucking*, are instead due to smaller numbers of atypical speakers using such words much more than everyone else.

Yet somehow, the atypical has become stereotypical. Gender is such a central way that people make sense of society and human relationships, that we are apt to assign more importance to the linguistic behaviour of people who act in ways that place them at one end of a gendered continuum. Rather than seeing such people as unusual, they tend to be viewed as perfect representatives of their gender, with their behaviour viewed as applying to everyone of their sex.

Cameron (2008: 164–6) discusses an online tool called the Gender Genie, based on a simplified version of the algorithm developed by Koppel et al. (2002) who examined the speech in the BNC, discussed earlier in this chapter. The Gender Genie allows users to paste some text into a box, and then it uses the algorithm to try to predict the sex of the author of that stretch of writing. Cameron examined a user forum on the Gender Genie website, to see how people reacted to having their own writing (sometimes incorrectly) assigned to a gender. Most of the forum posters assumed that the judgement said something about them, rather than the Genie itself. People whose gender had been incorrectly assigned tried to form explanations for why this was the case, based on aspects of their own lives, such as a woman who said she had being brought up in a boys' school, while males joked that it might mean they are gay. Nobody tried to explain the outcome when the Genie successfully predicted their gender. Cameron (ibid.: 165) writes that 'We have a tendency to treat any generalization about men and women as a source of information about "normal" male or female behaviour, which therefore has implications for how we ourselves should behave.'

Eckert and McConnell-Ginet (2003: 13–4) argue that biological differences become exaggerated by social norms. So, on average male vocal tracts are longer than female vocal tracts, resulting in a lower pitch for males. However, even by the age of four to five years, boys have learnt to use a deeper pitch than girls. Another explanation for gender differences at the lexical level, then, is that (some) people act in ways that they feel is typical of their gender, possibly through observing other people who have engaged in extreme gender performances. Such performances are thus replicated over time, resulting in gender differences becoming a self-fulfilling prophecy. Similarly, Deaux and Major (1987) and Deaux and LaFrance (1998) have argued that gender only impacts on situations where factors such as task type or conversational topic are associated with stereotypes about women or men.

It is not the aim of this chapter to 'blame' the popular perpetuation of the gender differences paradigm on a conscious patriarchal plan to ensure male hegemony, although it could be argued that the types of gender differences that are viewed as 'real' are more likely to result in an expectation that males take dominant roles in society and relationships, as well as being taken more seriously in public life. Evidence from psychological studies of cognition and stereotyping suggests that our brains work in a way which makes it easy for many people to accept the difference paradigm. This phenomenon could be viewed as a confirmation bias (Nickerson 1998), a tendency in human thinking to favour information that confirms existing beliefs or hypotheses. If we intuitively believe that men swear more than women, then we tend to notice male swearing more and then report on cases of male swearing, thus influencing the opinions of others that males swear more than females.

This does not mean that we should accept this situation as inevitable. Whatever its origins, to uncritically accept the gender differences paradigm is to condone the limitation of choice and potential in everyone, male or female. The gender differences paradigm creates expectations that people should speak at the linguistic extremes of their sex in order to be seen as normal and/or acceptable, and thus it problematizes people who do not conform, creating in- and out-groups. The result is inequality.

Rather than being critical of quantitative methods per se, this chapter has hopefully shown a danger relating to the *type* of quantitative methods that we employ to research language. We are primed to notice and report difference, and this may mean that we superficially interpret quantitative findings, over-focusing on differences while under-playing similarities, as well as generalizing differences as being representative of an entire group, rather than perhaps being due to the behaviour of outliers within that group. The danger here is not with the measures themselves, but the way that human analysts choose to prioritize certain measures over others, and the way that the results are interpreted. The keywords facility puts us in a 'difference mindset', although other statistics, such as the MD help us to take into account what is similar between two corpora. Additionally, the dispersion facility of corpus tools like WordSmith and AntConc, allows us to probe cases which look like difference, to determine the extent to which such differences are typical of a population, or due to smaller numbers of speakers. Concordancing, though not a measure, allows us to check contexts of usage so that explanations for apparent differences can be found, as in the case for female uses of *Christmas*. It is recommended that when we use keywords, wherever possible we should employ a third reference corpus in order to uncover similarities as well as differences, otherwise we only obtain a partial story. Within Corpus Linguistics, it is recommended that tools are developed which do not send researchers down paths where only difference awaits them.

Additionally, it is advised that we get to know our corpus well before we start to extrapolate conclusions from it. The fact that the male and female data in the BNC is skewed so that the sexes were not recorded in the same contexts in similar proportions indicates that any linguistic gender differences that we do find, need first to be related to context and role, before we can argue that they are indeed essentially gendered differences.

An advantage of a corpus-driven approach is that once we begin to analyse our data in detail, more interesting questions are sometimes raised, which would not have been considered at the start of the analysis. For example, the analyses of dispersion made me question why a relatively small number of men used *fuck* and *fucking* a lot, while others did not. Is it the case that such men are simply 'heavy' swearers and in most situations they are in they will swear, compared to most other men, who swear relatively less. Or was their swearing more due to the context they were in – perhaps they were being recorded in very informal settings with other young males and no females present, and swearing was a way of demonstrating masculinity in that group in relation to other men. Perhaps the majority of males in certain circumstances will swear a great deal? The comparisons of work-based vs home-based conversation indicates that context is an essential factor of language use, and it would be fruitful to carry out further research comparing the speech of mixed-sex and same-sex groups as well as more fine-grained distinctions between the demographic/context-governed binary. Another question which arose was due to the ways that words are actually used and responded to. Two groups of speakers may use a word or phrase with similar frequency but that word may actually hold very different meanings and others around them may react to it in different ways. A more detailed qualitative analysis of concordance lines would help to shed light on these more nuanced differences, and this issue is addressed in the following chapter.

CHAPTER THREE

Nope, good guess though: How do female academics signal disagreement?

Introduction

As indicated in the previous chapter, much Corpus Linguistics research which has taken a 'usage' perspective to look at gender has tended to be focused around the 'gender differences' paradigm, based on identifying differences between males and females or at least testing the hypothesis that differences exist. The studies cited in the early part of Chapter Two tended to take a corpus-*driven* approach in that specific differences were not identified in advance, but they emerged from a large-scale analysis of different phenomena (such as comparing word frequencies or grammatical categories) in a corpus. In this chapter, I will focus more on corpus-*based* research, or studies that have instead selected a small number of linguistic features in advance and then compared their frequencies (and sometimes contexts of usage) across male and female speakers. There are advantages to conducting corpus-based studies which focus on a particular phenomenon, although an aim of this chapter is to demonstrate how it can be difficult to fully uncover all of the examples of certain uses of language in a corpus, as well as reflecting on the pros and cons of various identification strategies.

Additionally, in contrast to Chapter Two, I wish to show how it is possible to conduct corpus research on gender by taking an alternative approach to 'gender differences'. Rather than carrying out another study which compares male and female uses of language, I will instead concentrate only on women's language in a specific context – a university setting. It is therefore unwise to generalize the findings from this study to say that they apply to all women, but I would hold instead that the findings tell us something interesting about the extent to which any study of gender differences can be generalized. A key question that I wish to explore in this chapter is – if we pick a particular usage of language, can we say that women in a university context will be reasonably consistent with each other in how they use it? In other words, is there evidence that such women use language in a reasonably similar way? A second question is: how do the findings from this chapter relate to other studies about how women use language, particularly in terms of some earlier claims about women as co-operative and avoiding confrontation?

Corpus-based studies on gender:
Still difference

If we move away from corpus-driven gender research, which has tended to report on the differences between males and females, do we find that corpus-based gender research is less interested in outlining or examining gender differences? Generally, corpus-based research has also oriented itself around gender differences, focusing on a small number of features where it is normally hypothesized in advance that some sort of gender-based difference will be found. Collectively, such studies are perhaps revealing about the amount of value placed on different sorts of findings in scientific research – a large or statistically significant difference is likely to be viewed as 'finding' that is worth reporting on and publishing, whereas a less dramatic difference, or a similarity is perhaps not seen to be as noteworthy.

For example, Iyeiri et al. (2004) used the Corpus of Spoken Professional American English (CSPAE) containing recordings of speech from 1994–8 in different professional settings, to examine sex variation in the use of *different from* and *different than*. The former is generally seen as the more formal 'correct' use of English, while the latter tends to occur more in informal contexts and is much more frequent in American English than British English. The researchers reasoned that it would be 'interesting, therefore, to investigate the natural speech interactions of professional or academic people compiled in the form of the CSPAE, especially paying attention to gender differences, since "hypercorrect" forms are often and traditionally regarded as one of the characteristic features of women's language' (ibid.: 31). In the four different speech settings in the CSPAE, they found that men were more likely than women to use the more informal *different from*, and the difference tended to be more pronounced in the most formal setting (White House press conferences) and least pronounced in the least formal setting (national meetings on reading tests). They postulate a somewhat generalizing explanation for these differences as 'women tend to be more uptight than men' (ibid.: 32). It is perhaps problematic to conclude that women will use more hyper-correct language than men in general, based on the analysis of a single linguistic feature as there could be other cases where men use more 'hyper-correct' forms.

Murphy (2009) used a small corpus of 20 informal Irish conversations containing either all-male or all-female speech, focusing on the use of swearing. The age of the speakers was also marked, with conversations occurring between people either in their twenties, forties or seventies/ eighties. Having identified that *fuck* and its related word forms was the most frequent swear word in her corpus, Murphy found that the term was used both by the younger speakers and the male speakers more often. In subsequent interviews with the speakers, she notes that female speakers in their forties viewed *fuck* as a 'coarse word' which they felt gave a negative impression of a woman as either uneducated or belonging to a lower social class, although acceptable in certain circumstances (e.g. with close friends or to release emotional tension). The female speakers in their seventies and eighties noted that they rarely heard the word when growing up, and to use it would have gone against their Catholic beliefs. On the other hand, the males in their twenties said that they felt expected to use coarse or taboo language in their interactions. Murphy suggests that its usage by this group facilitates male bonding and a way that a particular type of masculinity is constructed. While Murphy's corpus is small, her study demonstrates how familiarity with a corpus and access to the people who contributed towards it can help to yield insights which help to explain the linguistic patterns found (expectations about language use and identity were cited as important). Murphy's study is also notable because rather than considering simply all males vs all females, she notes how gender interacts with other factors like age and religious belief to produce a more detailed account of difference.

Another corpus study of swearing and gender was carried out in a different context by Thelwall (2008) who collected computer-mediated communication from over 9,000 American and British home pages of the social networking site MySpace. Thelwall used categories employed by the BBC (a British public service broadcasting corporation) to rate strength of swearing. Like Murphy, he found that use of *fuck* decreased with age (he considered ages between 16 and 40), and while there was a gender difference in general, with more males swearing than females, for the younger speakers in the United Kingdom, this difference was lessened. Thelwall suggests that this pattern could be due to the popularity of 'ladette' culture in the United Kingdom (but not the United States), as outlined by Jackson (2006), and involving young women being more likely to take on attitudes and behaviours more typically associated with males in the past.

A written corpus was employed by Nevalainen (2000) who examined the Corpus of Early English Correspondence (consisting of letters written between 1417 and 1681). Nevalainen focused on three processes of supralocalization (cases involving the geographical spread of linguistic features beyond the region that they originated, resulting in dialect levelling). The three process (ibid.: 39) were '(1) the generalization of the object pronoun form *you* in the subject function, (2) the diffusion of the suffix -(*e*)*s* in the third person singular present indicative, and (3) the replacement of multiple negation (negative concord) with single negation and non-assertive indefinites (*any*, *ever*, etc.).' Nevalainen had initially hypothesized that there would be changes in the development of supralocalization over the period covered in the corpus and that women would be involved in these changes. However, his analyses found that while women led the change to the generalization of *you*, neither gender appeared to be strongly associated with the change around the suffix -(*e*)*s*, and the disappearance of multiple negation was led by men rather than women. In explaining this mixed set of findings, Nevalinen (2000: 53) suggests that 'the role of women in language change must also have changed in some important respects between the sixteenth and the twentieth centuries. Women were not in the forefront of the professionally led change away from multiple negation in Early Modern English. This gender difference may be best explained in terms of the two sexes' differential access to education in general and to professional specializations in particular.'

A study by Bijeikiene and Utka (2006) of both language usage and expectations about usage involved the analysis of two corpora each containing about 279,000 words of male and female speech from politicians in the Lithuanian parliament. The researchers presented extracts of the speech to students, finding that in only about one in three cases were students able to correctly identify the sex of the speaker, even though the majority of the students had earlier indicated that they thought male and female parliamentarians used language differently. As part of the same study Bijeikiene and Utka conducted a corpus-based analysis, focusing on phenomena which is generally believed to be typical of either male or female speech. Phrases associated with politeness (seen as being connected to 'female' speech) were actually used more by males, although the researchers only examined a small number of short phrases (such as *ačiū* (*thank you*) and *prašom/prašau/prašyčiau* (*sorry*)), and it is possible that politeness could be expressed in a large range of other ways. Similarly, male speakers were found to use polite terms of address like *gerbiamasis minister* (*honourable minister*) more often. However, in congruence with beliefs about gender differences, males used more words relating to the concepts of logic and essence, as well as phrases relating to opinion and thought. The speakers also confirmed expectations with regard to topics of discussion, with men talking more about business, economics, security and oil, and women mentioning social matters, health and medicine. The study therefore confirms some gender stereotypes while refuting others, although there is still the central premise of comparing men against women.

For the analysis in this chapter, I would like to take a somewhat different perspective from most of the corpus studies of gender and language use that are described above. Rather than carrying out another study which compares male and female language use, I instead focus on female speech alone. In not weighing female speech against that of males, there is an immediate freedom to reformulate the research paradigm along alternative lines, although over the course of writing this chapter, like Taylor (2013), I have reflected on how easy it is to gravitate back towards a difference paradigm, for example, by formulating research questions like '(How) do women of different ages or social classes use language differently?' While these sorts of questions are valid ones to ask, particularly in that they help to emphasize differences *among* women, I want to instead demonstrate how corpus techniques can be used in ways other than those which take difference as the primary focus. I could have conducted an analysis on only men, rather than women, but during the course of background reading around this chapter, I noted that other researchers had identified an interesting 'site' of analysis, involving the speech of women in the workplace, and I felt that it would be useful to approach this topic from a corpus perspective, to see what insights such a perspective could offer.

Identifying complex interactional phenomena

A second focus of this chapter, which aims to provide a different perspective from Chapter Two, is to move away from analysing linguistic phenomena which are relatively easy to identify. The studies described in the section above all involved the identification of a small number of words or phrases which could easily be located via concordance searches using a tool like WordSmith. In some cases, such forms would have been chosen by the reader prior to engagement with the corpus, either through introspection or through reading-related research. However, sometimes during the process of corpus research, further terms are elicited, which may not have been considered previously. The attraction of carrying out research on specific words or phrases is understandable – there is little chance of false positives (cases where the search term elicits unwanted examples) or false negatives (cases where the search term misses a relevant example). A fixed phrase like *different from* is reasonably easy to locate, while even with a phenomenon like swearing, once we have created a list of swear words or phrases, we have a good chance of obtaining relevant examples, although we may miss variant spellings especially if using a corpus that contains non-standard orthography, for example computer-mediated communication. There may also be difficulty in identifying newer forms of swearing if we are unaware of them, or more localized cases which are specific to a particular social group. Carrying out background research or interviewing representative members of that group may help, while looking for examples where swearing is remarked on in the corpus itself (e.g. searching for terms like *swear, bad language*, etc.) could also yield additional cases.

Another way of maximizing recall is to search for lemmas of words or use wildcards. A lemma is the canonical or citation form of a word, and searching on it will yield related grammatical forms. For example, in the BNCweb interface, lemma searches are achieved by putting a word in curly brackets. A search of {fuck} will produce all instances of *fuck, fucks, fucking* and *fucked*. Using the * symbol, which functions as a wildcard for any sequence of characters, at the end of fuck*, also produces those cases, plus 34 other rarer forms which include *fuckface, fuckwits, fuckery* and *fuckin*, all of which are helpful if we want to carry out a full analysis around this word.

However, imagine our focus is not necessarily linked to a small number of short lexical items but comprises a more nebulous form of language which may be exhibited via an extremely wide range of word and phrase combinations. Features of interaction such as agreeing, joking, telling a story, engaging in conflict, being self-deprecatory, boasting, giving advice and apologizing may be much more difficult to identify via a few concordance searches, and are very likely to result in many false positives and false negatives. Some of these phenomena can stretch over several conversational turns and may be rendered obliquely, requiring a detailed understanding of shared knowledge between speakers. Corpus analysts who do not have access to the original sound transcriptions may encounter difficulties identifying more nuanced phenomena, and even when we expand concordance lines to take into account how other speakers orient to earlier utterances, this may only get us so far. For example, a joke may be followed by laughter from other participants, so we might decide to identify jokes by looking at all the places in a spoken corpus where laughter occurs. However, some jokes may not cause laughter (just as many cases of laughter will not be the result of jokes) and as a result, an analyst may not be able to identify all cases of jokes in a corpus using this method.

How do we resolve the problem of identifying interactional or pragmatic phenomena in a corpus? Below I consider a number of potential solutions, along with their potential pros and cons. First, we could use a corpus where such phenomena has already been helpfully annotated by other researchers. Such corpora are becoming increasingly available. For example, The Engineering Lecture Corpus (containing transcripts of lectures), has been marked for features which include humour, stories, summaries and definitions of technical terms (Alsop et al. forthcoming). The SPICE corpus, which contains spoken transcripts of conversations which took place in Ireland, is annotated for nine speech acts which include directives, commisives, expressives, declaratives and social expression. Additionally, words and phrases like *just, you know* and *yeah-yeah* have been marked up if they function as discourse markers, and their position in each utterance is also noted (Kirk et al. 2011). The sex of the speakers in both these corpora has also been annotated. Using such corpora with tools like WordSmith or AntConc, it is possible to count and retrieve instances of particular tags or word-tag combinations.

However, many corpora are not marked up for such features, while those which are annotated may not be tagged for the features that we are interested in. Additionally, if we are able to exploit someone else's annotation scheme, we are relying on their abilities, and it is probably worth carrying out some initial checks to obtain an idea of their accuracy and consistency before commencing.

A second solution would be to simply read the entire corpus and identify all the cases of a feature in a more qualitative manner. This was a solution implemented by Hasund and Stenström (1997) who examined instances where speakers engaged in conflict in a 40,000 word corpus containing the speech of teenage girls. They focused on cases where a speaker verbally opposed the utterance of another speaker by 'disagreeing, refusing, objecting, contradicting or critically evaluating it' (ibid.: 125). Such conflicts were identified by carefully reading the whole corpus and using principles associated with Conversation Analysis, to determine whether an utterance was in opposition to a previous utterance. The identification of conflict could therefore not be made by simply reading a single utterance, but needed to be considered in relation to what had been said by other speakers, prior to that utterance.

With 40,000 words, it is feasible (although still a lot of work) to read through a corpus to isolate a small set of features in this way. However, working with over a million words may prove to be beyond the limits of some time-pressed lone researchers. In that case then, would it be feasible to simply read a sample of text? This option was used by Mauranen (2003: 23) who used the Michigan Corpus of Academic Spoken English (MICASE) which contains about 1.8 million words of transcribed academic speech occurring at the University of Michigan. Mauranen wanted to identify cases of meta-discourse or discourse reflexivity, noting that 'categories like expressing criticism are more elusive because they have not been charted in too much detail in academic speech . . . A more workable solution . . . is to sample transcripts of appropriate speech events, and proceed manually at first, taking note of recurring expressions in contexts of criticism.' So she first read some transcripts of doctoral thesis defence sessions and then selected some items to be searched across the whole corpus.

To what extent would carrying out numerous concordance searches in the hope of catching most of the true positives (examples of the phenomena that we want to find) be effective? The answer would be dependent, to an extent, on the phenomenon that is being investigated. With a feature like apologizing, we might want to define it (for the purposes of our study) as a form of language which is intended to function as an apology and also contains one or more of the following words or related forms (*apology*, *sorry*, *forgive*). A corpus search would catch cases like 'I'm sorry', 'If I offended anybody, I apologise' but not 'I'm at fault' or 'I regret the pain I caused' (unless the search is expanded to include words like *fault* and *regret*). However, the corpus search would also produce false negatives like 'I'm not sorry' or somewhat questionable cases where *sorry* is used by a speaker as a preface for expressing an opinion that someone else might find disagreeable, for example 'I'm sorry but that's outrageous'. If false negatives can be weeded out and ambiguous cases can be noted, then as long as the analyst is clear about what her definition of an apology is for the purposes of that research, then that at least will enable replicability and consistency. Swales (2005) provides an overview of how to conduct concordance searches in order to find cases where people make suggestions in the MICASE Corpus. He notes how he first assembled a list of 14 candidate phrases (including *I suggest*, *my recommendation is* and *how about* . . .) and then carried out concordance searches of those phrases, a process which took about 10 hours in total. This is a method which I wish to follow here, although I also aim to evaluate its effectiveness by comparing it against Hasund and Stenström's (1997) 'read the corpus' approach.

For the purposes of this chapter, rather than look at apologies or suggestions, I have chosen to investigate disagreements. I have chosen this aspect of interaction because disagreements could be considered to be a form of language which other researchers have identified as being more typical of 'male speech'. Holmes and Stubbe (2003: 574) provide a list of what they call the 'widely cited features' of male and female interactional styles. This list notes that men are seen as direct, confrontational, competitive, autonomous and dominating public talking time with aggressive interruptions. Women, on the other hand, are seen as indirect, conciliatory, facilitative, collaborative, giving supportive feedback and making minor public contributions.

Research on gendered strategies surrounding disagreement appears to fit in with ideas about male and female interactional styles. Pilkington (1998: 263) who recorded all-male and all-female groups in informal conversation, noted that a feature which characterized her 'male data that was not present in the female data was the occurrence of frequent, direct and repeated expression of disagreement or hostility. The men often openly disagreed with one another.' She observes that the women avoided disagreement instead (ibid.: 267), a finding which is also noted by Holmes (1995), who suggests that levels of tolerance of disagreement may vary according to different norms for men and women. Research on children has also found gender differences regarding disagreement styles. For example, Van Alphen's (1987) study of Dutch children reported that girls avoid disagreements while boys challenge each other, and Goodwin (1990) found that among African-American children, boys tend to be more aggressive in their disagreements, while girls use a more rhetorical way to disagree. Coates, in her comparison of two large-scale studies looking separately at talk among men and among women, notes that '[c]ertain themes are typical of men's stories – heroism, conflict, achievement – but not of women's stories' (2003: 37) indicating another way that conflict appears to be central to male discourse but not women.

Workplace contexts are a potentially interesting site to examine disagreements because the requirements of a professional role may come into conflict with expectations about gender. Thimm et al. (2003), who interviewed male and female professionals about their workplace styles found that women were more likely than men to view themselves as more relationship-oriented, co-operative and consensus-oriented in conflict behaviour (all three differences were statistically significant). A poll of a small number of women taken by the authors indicated that they reported popular conflict-resolving strategies as being co-operative and avoiding confrontation. There is potentially a double-bind for women managers, in that interacting in non-confrontational ways may be seen as a form of weakness, whereas if a woman uses more powerful and assertive forms of language she could be viewed negatively or as 'trying to be like a man'. Eckert and McConnell-Ginet (2003: 101) note that a staple of gender stereotyping is that 'men argue, women quarrel or bicker', thus when a women engages in a form of interaction normally associated with men, she could face criticism.

Research by both Holmes and Schnurr (2006) and Baxter (2011) indicates that some female managers appear to be more linguistically versatile and aware of their language use than their male colleagues. For example, Holmes and Schnurr show how female managers employ a range of different 'masculine' and 'feminine' strategies, sometimes using irony and parody in order to contest masculine workplace norms, while Baxter (2011), who analysed linguistic data from senior management meetings and follow-up interviews in seven multinational UK companies, found that women managers engaged in more 'double-voiced discourse', whereby they monitored and regulated their language use in order to avoid being negatively judged. Double-voiced discourse is a form of intertextuality which involves referring to and anticipating what someone else has said or might say. Managers who were anxious about how they were perceived were more likely to be self-reflexive in their language use. However, Baxter (2011: 243) notes that double-voiced discourse strategies place greater demands on time, effort and energy, and may even dilute the impact of the words spoken, offering a linguistic reason why women struggle to top positions in industry.

On the basis of such studies of reported or perceived female interactional styles, I felt that it would be interesting to examine how women actually engage in disagreements in the workplace from a corpus-based perspective. The corpus I chose to work with was the MICASE Corpus described above (Simpson et al. 2002). Using the corpus search facility at the University of Michigan's website, I had access to 1,848,364 words of transcribed speech events. The online search facility allows users to either read entire transcripts or carry out concordance searches, restricting the search by various factors including sex, speech event type and academic discipline. Initially, the MICASE Corpus was going to be annotated with various pragmatic features, including disagreement, although the pragmatic tagging appears to have been scaled-back, and currently is restricted to an accompanying handbook which identifies the files that have higher than average salient pragmatic features.

I wanted to identify cases where female academics expressed disagreement with another speaker, with the aim of examining (and quantifying) the various ways that such disagreements could be expressed, and I was particularly interested in cases where women were supervising a class or group and were required to indicate that an answer that a student had given was either incorrect or inappropriate in some way. Such cases are potentially face-threatening acts (FTAs) (Brown and Levinson 1987) in that they could damage the positive face of the hearer. Many of interactions in the MICASE Corpus take place in semi-public contexts, with others present to witness the disagreement, which raises the impact of the FTA. Academic supervisors may need to find a balance between ensuring that students are aware of the right answer to a question and encouraging them to actively engage with the topic rather than feeling too embarrassed to make further contributions. Brown and Levinson's Politeness Theory outlines several types of strategy that speakers can employ when they have the option of making an FTA. These range from 'bald on record', which involves no redressive action to minimize the FTA, through to using redressive action, making the FTA off-record or not doing the FTA at all.[1]

I did not aim to begin with a categorization scheme but instead decided to allow a categorization scheme develop during the process of collecting and analysing women's disagreements in MICASE. I restricted the search of the corpus to exclude interactions marked as service encounters and tours, which I felt were less likely to give me academic-focused speech, but I did include all other types of interactions such as lectures, study groups, office hours, meetings, interviews and advising sessions. I only examined cases where *females* disagreed with someone and I excluded cases of disagreements which took place during informal discussions that were not directly related to an academic task. As well as looking at the speech of academic supervisors I also considered a small number of study groups and project meetings where a group of students were on equal footing without a supervisor present.

First, however, I needed to define what I meant by a disagreement. I included cases where a speaker indicated that she thought another speaker had made (or implied) a factually incorrect statement. This could signify that the speaker thought someone was not telling the truth, not being reasonable in some way, or was simply incorrect. This evaluation could be baldly marked with words or phrases like 'no', 'I don't agree' or 'that's wrong' or by making a statement which was in contradiction to one which another speaker had previously said. Some of the forms of disagreement involved relatively simple cases of 'correcting', where a speaker corrected another person's answer, although others were more complex, involving longer responses or the speaker demonstrating that they disagreed to a certain degree but not fully.

Additionally, I included cases where disagreement was implied but not fully stated, such as a question like 'anyone want to help her out?' or where the speaker reformulated part of someone else's statement as a question, or responded with an utterance which contradicted their statement. I also included indirect cases of disagreement, where the disagreement was clearly implied in some way. I did not include cases where a speaker disagreed with herself or where a marker of disagreement such as 'no' was used in response to a question as in the following case:

Female student: are there no computers?

Female senior undergraduate: not right now

Therefore, I tried to cover cases which involved both explicit and implicit forms of disagreement. In order to locate these disagreements, I decided to employ several strategies. As mentioned earlier, for the purposes of this book, I felt that it would be useful to evaluate the effectiveness of using targeted concordance searches to find cases of a complex pragmatic phenomenon. So I chose first to carry out some searches and read concordance lines, and then follow this up by reading a good proportion of the transcripts in MICASE which involved female academic supervisors. This allowed me to compare the two methods, to see the extent to which there is value in carrying out concordance searches for this type of research.

In order to develop a set of search terms I began by reading two transcripts taken at random and noting the disagreements which occurred. This was a useful exercise in that it confirmed that some of the ways that I thought disagreements might be formed actually did occur, but it was also helpful in providing several cases of disagreements in forms that I had not considered, which were then incorporated into search queries.

Having obtained a candidate list, I first carried out concordance searches of a set of lexical words which I hypothesized would be likely to appear when someone was disagreeing: *wrong, right, incorrect, correct, agree, disagree*. I also conducted concordance searches of negators: *no, not, I don't think* and *nope* (the latter term only having been identified through reading transcripts). Additionally, I searched for hedges and discourse markers: *actually, maybe, well, oh* and adversative conjunctions: *but, although, though, however*.[2] Table 3.1 shows how many cases of relevant disagreements were found from each search, as well as giving an indication of the false positives (cases of unwanted concordance lines that needed to be examined and rejected).

TABLE 3.1 *Search terms and disagreements found.*

Search term	Number of hits (female-only speech, not service encounters or tours)	Number of relevant disagreements found	% of relevant cases	Number of new disagreements found
disagree*	30	4	13.33	4
agree*	151	5	3.31	5
right	4154	20	0.48	19
wrong	191	4	2.09	2
correct	103	1	0.97	1
incorrect	5	1	20	0
actually	1335	7	0.52	5
though	432	3	0.69	3
although	122	2	1.63	2
but	6202	23	0.37	9
maybe	895	3	0.33	1
well	2527	10	0.39	1
oh	2112	8	0.37	5
I don't think	268	4	1.49	3
no	2337	34	1.45	22
nope	42	11	26.19	6
not	4491	26	0.57	4

A search on 17 terms, resulting in 25,397 concordance lines in total produced only 92 cases of relevant disagreements. How many additional cases would be found if I read the transcripts which featured the speech of female academic supervisors? After reading almost all (more than 95%) of these transcripts I only uncovered an additional eight examples which had not already been found by the concordance searches. I am doubtful that I ever could have identified a search term that would have located these extra eight cases. I cannot claim that I found every example of a disagreement via either method, although it was reassuring that the concordance searches at least found a large number of the cases that would have been uncovered by reading the corpus. However, the additional eight cases were interesting in that some of them involved indirect strategies, and so not including them in the analysis would not have presented as accurate a picture of the ways that female academics disagree.

Reading 25,397 concordance lines was not an easy task, particularly for cases where there were more than about 200 lines to look at. The job was made easier by sorting concordances, and so it was often possible to scroll down the concordance and discount many cases which were not involved in disagreements. However, the analysis was made more difficult due to the fact that the concordance lines did not distinguish between multiple speakers, so it was not always easy to identify if a word like *no* was a single utterance by a speaker or made as part of a longer utterance. Additionally, as Table 3.1 demonstrates, the concordance search procedure was one of diminishing returns. A search of *right* produced 20 relevant disagreements, of which 19 were cases that I had not previously encountered when I had looked at *disagree** and *agree**. However, by the time I carried out a search of *not*, even though I found 26 cases of disagreements, I had already seen 22 of these before, so this search only contributed 4 new cases. If time is limited, to minimize the amount of effort spent on this sort of task, I would advocate conducting concordance analyses of the least frequent search terms first, then, when examining the more frequent cases, try to identify longer structures which might be more productive. For example, the word *no* sometimes occurred in a disagreement as part of a repeated string, for example *no, no, no*. It would also make sense to carry out some of the early searches on words which are probably more likely to be closely related to the phenomena you are interested in identifying. Only 0.37 per cent of cases of the word *oh* were true positives while this figure was 13.33 per cent for *disagree**. Another strategy could be to first search on words which have low collocational scores with one another as that would ensure a better immediate coverage of the corpus. If two words are very strong collocates of one another, then a concordance search of the second word is likely to involve the analyst retreading old ground. A related strategy could be to restrict searches so that they do not include cases of previously examined words. This may not be possible with all corpus tools although WordSmith (which was not used here as I was only able to access the MICASE corpus with its web-based interface) allows users to exclude concordance lines if a certain word or set of words appears in the vicinity of the search term.

While the concordance searches were not as effective as reading through the corpus, the analysis of the concordance lines took about a third as long as it took me to read most of the relevant corpus files. The fact that the read-through only produced eight more cases might not justify the amount of effort involved for some researchers. Ultimately, what matters here is whether the goal of the research is to identify every case of a disagreement in a corpus or a reasonably representative sample. If the latter is the case, then can we argue that the 92 disagreements found by concordancing actually are representative? Within them, a range of different strategies occur, as will be shown in the following section. However, the additional eight cases produced by reading the corpus did reveal examples of relatively rare strategies. Therefore, if we decide to identify a pragmatic feature via concordance searches, it is important to be clear about what the search terms were and to make the reader aware of the extent of the potential for false negatives, perhaps by reading through a sample of the corpus and noting how many additional cases were found via that method. Ultimately, I would advocate that a multi-pronged approach is most likely to produce the most representative set of cases. Additionally, it is worth pointing out that whatever method was used, I found it easier to identify the bald 'on record' cases of disagreement than to spot cases where disagreement was more implicitly signalled. I tried to only collect cases where I could be certain that disagreement was occurring, which meant disregarding a number of ambiguous interactions. A problem with reading or listening to a transcript of a conversation which involves speakers whom you will never meet, is that only a small amount of context is available to the reader – and the speakers may be signalling disagreement in subtle ways that are almost impossible for outsiders to discern. Therefore, the analysis in the following section must acknowledge that it is skewed towards the 'on-record' cases.

Disagreement strategies

Table 3.2 presents information about the contexts that the disagreements occurred in as well as the academic role of the speaker. The disagreements occurred across 34 separate interactions and although it is difficult to ascertain from MICASE whether a speaker could have contributed towards more than one file, the fact that a wide range of topics and situations are represented suggests that this is a reasonably well-dispersed set of examples to analyse with no single speaker making a disproportionate contribution (nobody appears to have contributed more than 10% of the cases). Later in this chapter, for some of the speakers who made a higher number of disagreements, I will consider whether they varied the way that they disagreed or remained fairly constant.

It was decided to develop a categorization system which would take into account the different sorts of linguistic phenomena that occurred when the speakers used disagreements. This system would need to be flexible, bearing in mind the fact that some disagreements involved the use of multiple features and that a particular strategy could be achieved through the use of a wide range of different linguistic features. The categorization system was therefore carried out in three stages. First, I identified the salient linguistic

TABLE 3.2 *Meta-information about disagreements.*

Transcript	Speaker	Subject	Interaction type	Cases
DEF270SF061	Senior Graduate	Artificial Intelligence	Dissertation Defence	1
DIS115JU087	Junior Graduate	Intro Anthropology	Discussion Section	2
DIS150JU130	Junior Graduate	Intro Astronomy	Discussion Section	6
DIS495JU119	Senior Graduate	Intro to American Politics	Discussion Section	4
DIS175JU081	Junior Faculty	Intro Biology	Discussion Section	6
DIS475MU01	Senior Graduate	Philosophy	Discussion Session	1
DIS280SU058	Senior Graduate	Economics	Discussion Session	1
INT425JG002	Junior Faculty	Not applicable	Graduate Student Research Interview	1
LES425SU093	Junior Faculty	Spring Ecosystems	Lecture	7
LEL115SU005	Junior Faculty	Medical Anthropology	Lecture	3
LES215MU056	Junior Faculty	Intro Latin	Lecture	1
LES335JG065	Senior Faculty	Graduate Online Search and Database	Lecture	3
LES445SU067	Senior Faculty	Radiological Health Engineering	Lecture	1
LES320SU085	Senior Faculty	Visual Sources	Lecture	8
LES165JG121	Researcher	Rehabilitation Engineering and Technology	Lecture	1
LES205JG124	Senior Faculty	Intro to Groundwater Hydrology	Lecture	2

TABLE 3.2 *Continued.*

Transcript	Speaker	Subject	Interaction type	Cases
LES565SU137	Junior Faculty	Sex, Gender and the Body	Lecture	1
LES115MU151	Senior Graduate	Archaeology of Modern American Life	Lecture	3
MTG999ST015	Staff	Forum for International Educators	Meeting	1
OFC150MU042	Senior Undergraduate	Astronomy	Peer Tutorial	1
OFC175JU145	Junior Graduate	Intro Biology	Exam Review	2
OFC575MU046	Junior Faculty	Statistics	Office Hours	5
OFC270MG048	Senior Graduate	Computer Science	Office Hours	6
OFC280SU109	Junior Faculty	Economics	Office Hours	1
SGR175SU123	Senior Undergraduate	Biochemistry	Study Group	10
SGR999MX115	Senior Undergraduate	Objectivism	Study Group	5
SGR385SU057	Senior Undergraduate	Math	Study Group	1
SGR175MU126	Senior Undergraduate	Intro Biology	Study Group	4
SGR200JU125	Junior Undergraduate	Organic Chemistry	Study Group	2
SGR175MU126	Senior Undergraduate	Intro Biology	Study Group	2
SGR195SU127	Senior Undergraduate	Chemical Engineering	Group Project Meeting	1
SGR565SU144	Senior Undergraduate	American Family	Group Project Meeting	1
SEM340JG072	Junior Graduate	Graduate Public Policy	Seminar	1
SEM495SU111	Senior Faculty	Politics of Higher Education	Seminar	5

features in the utterances where someone was disagreeing – asking, what actually made this utterance a disagreement? This could involve a word or phrase, or relate to sentence form, such as use of questions. Secondly, I grouped similar features together, based on how they appeared to function as part of the disagreement. The categorization of features was refined over time, with earlier disagreements needing to be revisited to check that any new strategies had not been previously missed. The third stage was to then group the different sets of functions together as contributing towards an overall disagreement style. In part, I referred to Mauranen (2004) who had identified various hedging strategies in MICASE. Table 3.3 lists the different types of features that were used. It should be noted that the last column does not add up to 100 (the total number of disagreements I collected) because many disagreements contained more than one type of feature.

Table 3.3 indicates that by far the most commonly used feature involves the explicit signification of disagreement by making a clear statement such as *no* or *that's not right*. This sort of structure occurs in over half of the disagreements found in the corpus.

File LES320SU085

Senior Faculty: does anybody know where this is?

Student 4: Amsterdam

Senior Faculty: no

Another, relatively frequent aspect of disagreements includes the use of an adversative such as *but* or *though*, which generally either signals that a disagreement is to come, or marks an earlier part of an utterance as such, as in the following case, where Student 1 is leading a Study group and has just asked the others how to spell the word *acetyl*:

File SGR175SU123

Student 3: this isn't English class

<Student 2: *LAUGH*>

Student 1: you have to know how to spell them though

Two other frequent features of disagreements include either making a statement which contradicts the speaker, or gives the correct answer, as in the following two cases:

File LES425SU093

Junior Faculty: what's going on with the stamens just, you know, observationally?

Female student: Wild Geranium?

TABLE 3.3 *Linguistic features used in disagreements.*

Feature	Examples	Number of disagreements where this strategy occurred
Straightforward statement of disagreement	no; that's not right	53
Adversative	actually; though; but; well	23
Gives the correct answer	Grand Canyon	23
Makes contradictory statement but does not give the correct answer	that sounds like politics	21
Hedge	I think; I mean; perhaps; might	19
Gives reason for disagreement	and that's because . . .	15
Gives positive evaluation	good guess	12
Asks speaker a question	did you ever . . .	9
Uses an agreement marker first	yeah; okay	9
Hesitation marker	um; uh; er; erm	8
Indication of uncertainty	I don't know	6
Asks whether others agree	do we agree with her	4
Meta-comment on answer	I knew you'd say that	2
Shows sarcasm	yeah right	2
Provides excuse for wrong answer	it's a pretty complicated one	2
Uses directive	take a look	2
Repeats only the correct part of the answer	an X	1
Directs same question at someone else	what's politics? Mark	1

Junior Faculty: it's not Wild Geranium . . .

File LES115MU151

[The supervisor has asked the class what the most visited tourist site in the United States is]

Male Student: L-A

Senior Graduate: Grand Canyon. it's the Grand Canyon Williamsburg, and then uh maybe Disneyland and New York. something like that.

I categorized these four frequent cases as representing 'on record' ways of disagreeing, either through marking the disagreement with a word like *no* or *but*, or by providing an explicit evaluation of an answer as incorrect or giving the correct answer. It is therefore interesting that this strategy of disagreement emerges as the most frequent, although perhaps it could be argued that in an academic context, students are not necessarily expected to always know the right answer and therefore there may be less of an imperative to use indirect strategies.

A range of softening strategies occurred in the disagreements, however, including the use of hedging which involves weak modality or phrases like *I think*, indicators of uncertainty like *I don't know*, the use of hesitation markers like *um* or *er*, or starting the disagreement with a word which normally indicates agreement or at least acknowledgement like *yeah* or *ok*. The questioner sometimes tries to reduce loss to the student's face by providing an excuse for the student, such as noting that the question was difficult. Further softening strategies involve providing a reason why the answer is incorrect, or giving some sort of positive evaluation to the incorrect answer, as shown in the next two cases.

File DIS150JU130

[the supervisor has asked what a line represents]

Student: the horizon?

Junior Graduate: nope and that's because the celestial equator is about here so farther up in the sky. and i'll tell you in a minute why i know that.

File LES425SU093

Junior Faculty: okay this is kind of a tricky one. what the heck is this?

Male Student: Solomon's Seal?

Junior Faculty: no, although that's a good guess.

I classified a third set of disagreement strategies as involving indirectness. These include asking questions, either to the student, to check if they are certain of their answer, or asking others in the class if they agree or disagree with the student's answer. In one case, the supervisor ignores the student's (somewhat facetious) answer and asks the question again, picking on a different student.

> File DIS495JU119
>
> Senior Graduate: so what's politics?
>
> Student 1: stuff, that's political.
>
> <LAUGH>
>
> Student 2: (thoughts and stuff?)
>
> Senior Graduate: what's politics? Mark?
>
> Student 3: um political culture, part of our political culture is freedom.

Other types of indirectness involve using a directive statement, for example asking the student to look at something again, or in one case, the supervisor repeats part of the student's answer, but only repeats the correct part, thus indicating to the student that the rest of the answer is incorrect.

> File OFC175JU145
>
> Junior Graduate: on the X, right. so when i set up a Punnett square . . . and i'll put the male's gametes up here. what are the male's gametes? what what could they potentially have? what should i put up here at the top?
>
> Student: a X-Y
>
> Junior Graduate: an X
>
> Student: X-R
>
> Junior Graduate: big-R, or he could pass on a Y gamete to make a son. and the female?

A fourth, rather rare, strategy involves using humour or sarcasm to comment on the student's answer, as in the case below. Such a strategy might be seen as a form of positive politeness as if the supervisor makes a joke about the student getting an answer wrong, it is implied that the relationship between the two is reasonably warm.

> File DIS175JU081
>
> Junior Faculty: okay so remember, you have to start out diploid in meiosis, but after meiosis one you have two daughter cells that're haploid already. mkay? those two daughter cells, undergo a further reduction division to produce four haploids. okay?
>
> Student: uh- generates two haploid cells from a diploid meiosis one. i don't, nope.

Junior Faculty: okay she sounds confident.

<Other Students: *LAUGH*>

Therefore, the different linguistic features in Table 3.3 can be collapsed into four different strategies of disagreement: bald-online, downtoners, indirectness and positive politeness, although it should also be borne in mind that any disagreement may involve two or more of these strategies. I examined the 100 disagreements again, noting what combination of strategies occurred in each (shown in Table 3.4).

From Table 3.4, it is clear that no single strategy combination occurs in over half the cases, although three relatively frequent strategies count for 91 per cent of cases – bald-online by itself (occurring 43 times), using downtoners to soften a bald-online strategy (38 cases) and using indirectness (10 cases). The use of humour and sarcasm categorized as positive politeness,

TABLE 3.4 *Combinations of different disagreement strategies.*

Number of strategies	Strategy combination	Number of disagreements
1	Bald-online only	43
	Downtoners only	1
	Indirectness only	10
	Positive Politeness only	1
2	Bald-online + Downtoners	38
	Bald-online + Indirectness	2
	Bald-online + Positive Politeness	1
	Downtoners + Indirectness	2
	Downtoners + Positive Politeness	0
	Indirectness + Positive Politeness	1
3	Bald-online + Downtoners + Indirectness	1
	Downtoners + Indirectness + Positive Politeness	0
	Bald-online + Downtoners + Positive Politeness	0
	Bald-online + Indirectness + Positive Politeness	0
4	All four strategies	0

only appears in three disagreements, being rare but still a possibility. There are also a number of combinations of strategies (such as downtoner and indirectness) which are also rare.

As no single combination of strategies represents a majority case (occurring in more than half of the disagreements), it is doubtful that Table 3.4 could be used to argue that there is a female academic style of disagreeing in the MICASE Corpus. Instead, it appears that the female academics make use of a range of combinations of strategies, of which two (being explicit or being explicit with downtoners) are more common than the others. However, even from 100 disagreements, there are 10 different combinations of the 4 disagreement strategies which occur (at least once), and that does not take into account the fact that each of these strategies can be achieved via a wide range of linguistic forms.

Differences among women

If it is difficult to conclude that female academics express disagreement in similar ways, would it perhaps be easier to identify individual women as having a consistent personal style? As Table 3.2 indicates, there were 34 speakers, although some of them only disagreed once or twice, making it infeasible to make any claims that they were consistent. I decided to look only at the nine speakers who had made five or more disagreements in the corpus, and then identify which combination of strategies they used.

It emerged that some speakers did incorporate reasonably consistent styles of disagreeing (at least for the short period that the interaction was being recorded). For example, the speaker in transcript DIS150JU130 mainly used a combination of bald-online disagreements that were softened with downtoners (five times), plus a further case where bald-online was softened with a downtoner and indirectness. A look at her disagreements indicates that not only did she use the same strategy, but she also employed a similar form of language (*good guess*), as illustrated in the following three cases.

File DIS150JU130

Junior Graduate: if we look over here to the southwestern part of the sky, about here, there will be a very, bright object, that's larger than any star that you'll see in the sky, any guesses on what that would be?

Student: Jupiter

Junior Graduate: nope not Jupiter

Student: oh

Junior Graduate: good guess

File DIS150JU130

Student: Saturn?

Junior Graduate: not Saturn, good guess

File DIS150JU130

Junior Graduate: okay these, three stars here, make up Orion's head. and what is he wearing on his head? guesses, he's a hunter.

Student: a helmet

Junior Graduate: helmet nope good guess though another guess?

A number of other speakers tended to mainly use bald-online strategies with no other type of strategy. For example, the speaker in file LES320SU085 made eight disagreements which were all bald-online, although one also contained a downtoner and another contained indirectness.

File LES320SU085

Senior Faculty: cuz i've gotta, i know we've gotta have slides

Student: you can put it on like the wall or something.

Senior Faculty: no. no way Jose. and especially after i've done all this (xx)

File LES320SU085

Student: Germany

Senior Faculty: nope. no

File LES320SU085

Student: isn't this like sitting too close to the television screen.

Senior Faculty: no it isn't.

<BACKGROUND CONVERSATION>

Senior Faculty: lemme show you another one

However, while five of the nine speakers who made five or more disagreements demonstrated a clear preference for one combination of strategies, the other four speakers were much more variable, and it was not possible to identify any particular strategy that they clearly preferred. For example, the speaker in file DIS175JU081 used five different combinations of strategies, including the cases below.

File DIS175JU081

Student: crossing over, can occur i put meiosis one and two. actually,

Junior Faculty: wanna take something back?

Student: um, not meiosis two.

Junior Faculty: mkay, yeah just meiosis one.

File DIS175JU081

Junior Faculty: yeah, if you're a germ cell and you're gonna become a sex cell, you undergo meiosis. mkay, if you're another type of cell in the body you undergo mitosis.

Student: right so they never go through, like all three.

Junior Faculty: um actually germ cells do

File DIS175JU081

Junior Faculty: yeah okay what's the ploidy of this cell? *<PAUSE WHILE WRITING>*

Student: three-N equals

Junior Faculty: i knew you'd say that.

Student: it's wrong?

In the first case above, the supervisor uses a question *wanna take something back* as a form of indirectness to disagree. In the second case she makes a bald statement of disagreement *actually germ cells do*, prefaced with a hesitation downtoner *um*, while in the final example she responds to the student's incorrect answer by telling her *I knew you'd say that*. Publicly implying that the student was expected to give an incorrect answer could be seen as a very face-threatening act, as it implies that the supervisor has little confidence in the student's abilities. Yet having read the full transcript of this utterance and getting a better feel for the tone of the interaction, I have characterized this as a form of humorous positive politeness (although I acknowledge that some readers may simply view the supervisor as impolite).

Although we need to limit the extent of any conclusions by keeping in mind the small amount of data under analysis, it is pertinent to note that some supervisors appear to have a reasonably consistent style of disagreeing as they conduct a single class while others appear to vary their disagreement strategies, even over a short period of time. Ultimately, again there is little evidence to suggest that there is any sort of generalizable pattern about women's disagreement to be made – even the amount of variance is variable.

Conclusion

At this stage, it might be tempting to conduct the same sort of analysis on the male disagreements in the MICASE Corpus, in order to carry out a comparative study of gender differences or similarities. While such a study is possible, it would recast the above research in terms of an exploration of 'gender differences', while I believe there is value in considering women's language use in its own right, rather than as always needing to be compared against men's language use. Additionally, had I found evidence that the female academics in MICASE had a reasonably consistent and similar style of disagreeing, then I would be more open to the idea that there was such a thing as a 'female style', at least within MICASE. However, the amount of variance among speakers and even among some individual women does not support the argument that there is a typical 'female' way of disagreeing in this context. Instead, I would argue that the form of the disagreement is more likely to be influenced by many other factors, some relating to the person who makes the disagreement, some relating to quite specific aspects of context, such as the relationship between the supervisor and the student or the type of class being taught and the topic under discussion. For example, in some of the classes (particularly science subjects), discussions around course materials required students to give an answer that could be clearly identified as correct or not. However, other classes (particularly those in the social sciences) tended to result in student contributions that were more personal or opinion-based, and such cases tended to be less likely to attract short on-record responses like 'that's wrong'. Additionally, the way that the student initially provided an answer could impact on the way the supervisor expressed disagreement. For example, the answer 'stuff, that's political' in response to the question 'what's politics' resulted in the supervisor ignoring the answer and asking the question again. Such a strategy suggests that supervisors may reserve more indirect or humorous ways of disagreeing for less straightforward cases of a student getting something wrong. A multidimensional analysis might be able to take into account the ways that all of these factors interact together, but we would need to be certain that we had taken into consideration all of the relevant factors. It is easy to consider observable phenomena like sex and academic seniority as factors, but other factors such as the speaker's overall mood that day or whether she liked the person she was disagreeing with are much more difficult to ascertain.

As stated earlier, we cannot generalize the findings from this small number of speakers to claim that it tells us something about the ways that women disagree all over the world. However, we can make a better argument for saying that the findings tell us something about the ways that female academics (at least in an American context around the period that the corpus was collected) make disagreements. It is notable that I found little evidence to suggest that any combination of strategies emerged as preferable, although the strategies that are more likely to be stereotypically associated with women – the use of indirectness and downtoners, were present but not the most frequent. If any pattern does emerge from the data, it is that the female academics are most likely to use a bald-online disagreement with no other strategy, although even this does not represent the majority of cases.

Context is key though, and it could be hypothesized that in an academic environment, a female supervisor in charge of students may not feel the need to use a lot of stereotypically 'feminine' downtoners or indirect strategies when disagreeing. But on the other hand, unlike say, women who are CEOs of companies that may be otherwise male-dominated, she may not feel that she has to act in ways that are more stereotypical of men either. Additionally, there was little evidence of double-voiced discourse (which Baxter (2011) characterizes as occurring in female manager's speech) around the disagreements (although the case in DIS175JU081 where the supervisor responds to an incorrect answer with 'I knew you'd say that' could be classed as double-voicing).

In academic contexts, supervisors are generally *required* to indicate that students have made errors, on a reasonably frequent basis. Indeed, the ways that the women disagreed did not appear to cause 'trouble' (from a Conversational Analysis perspective) in the interactions, interrupting the flow of conversation and requiring repair. Instead, the other participants oriented to them briefly, accepting them at face value rather than challenging them or otherwise indicating that they appeared unusual. Mullany (2007) has argued that management strategies can be dependent on the community of practice in a particular institution, while Baxter (2010) theorizes that whole corporations are gendered (e.g. in male-dominated corporations female leaders face prejudices about their competence while in gender-balanced or gender-multiple corporations, women tend to be valued better). Baxter (2011: 235) suggests that 'micro-linguistic practices, contextual factors and wider corporate discourses may contribute to positioning women differently and unequally within business leadership roles and discursive practices.'

In the academic context examined for this chapter then, the analysis indicates that when disagreeing with students, female supervisors need not engage in softening strategies designed to save face, act in stereotypically gendered ways or pay extra attention to their language use by using double-voiced discourse. While universities are not free of sexism, I would conceptualize academic communities of practice as being closer to a gender-balanced or gender-multiple institution than many other institutions. And if women placed in an academic context can disagree in a range of ways that are appropriate to the situation, but not in ways that especially link them to stereotyped notions of gender, then that again supports the idea raised in the previous chapter, that linguistic gender differences which are found in other studies, are likely to be due to context, namely role expectations and specifically gendered communities of practice, rather than anything essentially male or female.

I would not advocate that studies on linguistic gender differences are abandoned, although I am wary of the way that engaging with such research can lead one towards a reifying 'difference mindset'. Instead, studies which take a more fine-grained approach to difference, examining differences among women or among men, and considering dispersion patterns, will help to introduce checks and measures so that over-generalizations are avoided. Moreover, I hope that this chapter and the one before it have shown that findings need to be interpreted and explained in relation to context – if a gender difference is found, it is likely to be telling us something about the ways that gendered *discourses* shape interactions. As Eckert and McConnell-Ginet (2003: 85) write, 'Stereotypes are the starting point of much research on language and gender for a reason. First of all, any research begins with a focus or a hypothesis, and foci and hypotheses have to come from somewhere. If gender stereotypes are part of our sociolinguistic life, they need to be examined – not simply as possible facts about language use, but as components of gender ideology.'

Rather than introspection or a small-scale qualitative-only piece of analysis, I would advocate that a corpus approach towards questions of language usage is more likely to yield robust results by providing larger amounts of data and enabling a more extensive coverage of linguistic phenomena via automatic searches. Clearly though, as this chapter has shown, when dealing with some forms of language, corpus searches do not provide full recall. Of the eight additional disagreements which were found by reading the transcripts, five of them involved combinations of strategies that were quite rare, such as asking a question in order to be indirect. If these cases had been missed completely, it would not have altered the overall picture much, but their inclusion indicates that indirectness, while infrequent, was not as rare as the corpus searches alone would suggest. Therefore, an awareness of the limitations of some types of corpus search is essential, and where necessary, such searches need to be supplemented with other methods. Additionally, while the research in this chapter used a corpus and obtained most of the examples to study via corpus methods, the actual analysis itself did not involve the use of corpus techniques like collocates but instead required the close reading and categorization of each disagreement in a way more typically associated with qualitative methods. Corpus research can be positioned on a cline then, from those studies which purely employ techniques associated with corpus linguistics at every stage, to those which use a combination of different methods. Particularly when dealing with applied linguistic research, I would speculate that most corpus research will fall somewhere on the cline rather than being purely 'corpus-only'.

Building on the idea that linguistic gender differences emerge as a result of gendered discourses, the following three chapters move on to explore how corpus linguistics can be employed in order to study such discourses.

CHAPTER FOUR

Male bias and change over time: Where are all the spokeswomen?

Introduction

While the previous two chapters have considered language usage (how males and females *use* language), this and the following two chapters are concerned with a different but related topic, that of gendered representation (how males and females are *represented* through language). The research in Chapters Two and Three could be categorized under sociolinguistics while the remaining analysis chapters are more easily grouped as discourse-based approaches (although there is considerable overlap between sociolinguistics and discourse analysis). For the purposes of this book, after Hall (1997) I define *representation* as the creation of a mental image of something using signifying practices and symbolic systems (i.e. through language).

In some ways, research on representation can sidestep the criticisms aimed at usage-based research. For example, usage-based researchers could be criticized for making over-generalizations about male or female speech from their research findings if their samples are not representative in terms of size or variety. Additionally, as I have argued in Chapters Two and Three, there can be a temptation in usage-based research to focus on difference rather than similarity. Statistical tests tend to be used to show that males and females use linguistic features with significantly different frequencies, while corpus techniques like keywords, can push the user into a 'difference mindset'. Such research can also over-simplify a picture by dividing people into large social categories based on only one or two variables, while overlooking variation between people in the same group. At its worst, usage-based research based purely on quantification may draw inaccurate conclusions about the function of a particular linguistic item, or identify a 'difference' which is only due to a small proportion of people in a group using a particular item very frequently but does not accurately reflect the typical behaviour of the majority of that group.

Representation research avoids some of these categorization and interpretation issues because we do not have to necessarily compare usage between different groups. Instead we may build or take an existing corpus and treat it as a single entity. The corpus may contain language use from many different speakers and/or writers, but we are often less interested in their individual identities and more concerned with what their language use cumulatively tells us about how gendered categories are understood in the society where the corpus came from. We may need to restrict our conclusions if the texts in the corpus are from quite a narrow source (e.g. a corpus of stories written by children only directly tells us about children's language use), but if we are using a general reference corpus which contains balanced samples of language from hundreds of different sources, then we can be more confident that the analysis reveals something about society's perceptions of gender at large, particularly as the corpus is likely to reflect the sorts of language that large numbers of people will encounter on a daily basis.

There are numerous ways that we can carry out a corpus analysis of gender representation. We may begin by selecting a social group and then explore the frequent and not so frequent linguistic patterns which occur around that group in a corpus. This is the approach I have taken in Chapter Five where I examine representations of gay men in a newspaper. Additionally, we could compare two related (perhaps oppositional) social groups – the approach I take in Chapter Six where I compare patterns of representation surrounding the terms *boy(s)* and *girl(s)* together in a large corpus of text collected from internet sources. When comparing the representation of two groups together, it is a good idea to bear in mind the same issues around comparisons of usage of two groups, that is not focusing on difference only but attempting to take similarity of representation into account too. A central way that we can explore representation is to consider the linguistic contexts that particular social groups are repeatedly found in. Chapters Five and Six both focus on how such patterns can be elicited from corpora by using a combination of collocates and concordance line analysis. This chapter takes a different approach by making frequency its central theme rather than exploring context, although it is often difficult to separate the two concepts. The research in the following two chapters is based around the analysis of a small number of identity-based terms (*gay(s)* and *homosexual(s)* in Chapter Five, and *boy(s)* and *girl(s)* in Chapter Six). The approach taken in this chapter is also somewhat wider than in that I do not focus on any single term, but instead have a broader research question – is there evidence that language use has become less sexist or more inclusive in terms of gender representation over time? This question therefore requires some additional work to be carried out in terms of identifying what sort of language use should be examined, and also which corpora should be used. There are two main comparative aspects of this chapter: (1) how males and females are represented and (2) how such representations alter (or not) over time.

Analysis of frequencies can provide information about the sorts of concepts that are privileged in society, although there is not a perfect relationship between a word's frequency and how important, typical or preferable it is viewed to be in a society. For example, in Baker (2008: 146–8) I demonstrated how words relating to homosexuality are much more frequent than words for heterosexuality in the BNC, because heterosexuality is assumed to be the default norm and preferred state, not needed to be mentioned because it is so pervasive. These frequency patterns aptly demonstrate *heteronormativity* (social practices which presume universal heterosexuality, Warner (1993)) or even what Rich (1980) conceives as *compulsory heterosexuality* (the way that heterosexuality is 'forcibly and subliminally imposed on women', ibid.: 653).

Terms for bisexuality in the BNC are even less frequent than those for heterosexuality though, but this is not because bisexuality is considered to be 'the norm', it is more likely due to erasure of bisexuality in (British 1990s) society, perhaps because bisexuality threatens the appearance of *gay* and *heterosexual* as discrete categories. In fact, references to the concept of monosexuality (desire for only one sex) are even less frequent than references to bisexuality, indicating that British society barely considers sexuality in terms of a bisexual–monosexual continuum – the discourse of 'compulsory monosexuality' is so pervasive that it hardly ever needs to be articulated, and many people may not even be aware of the concept of monosexuality.[1] Thus, as this chapter will demonstrate, frequencies should not be taken at face value but interpreted in relation to our knowledge about society, along with concordance analyses of how particular words are used in context in a corpus.

Corpus analysis on language, sexism and gender equality

There are a number of different approaches that other researchers have taken when using corpora to answer questions about sexist language. One strand of research has focused on comparing different members of the Brown family of corpora together. The Brown family are a series of small reference corpora (approximately one million words in size each) containing published written text across 15 genres. Arguably, the first publically available corpus was the Brown Corpus, (initially referred to as A Standard Corpus of Present-Day Edited American English for use with Digital Computers) created by Henry Kučera and W. Nelson Francis at Brown University.

This corpus contained American English texts that had been published in 1961. An equivalent corpus of British English texts from the same year was later created by researchers at the universities of Lancaster, Oslo and Bergen (referred to as the LOB corpus). Kjellmer (1986) investigated the frequencies of different male and female pronouns as well as the terms *man*, *woman* and their plurals in these two corpora, finding that the male terms were more frequent than the female terms, suggesting an overall bias towards males in written published language. Similar synchronic studies have been carried out on other reference corpora, with comparable results. For example, Biber et al. (1999) examined the Longman English Corpus, reporting that 620 nouns end in the suffix -*man*, whereas only 38 end in -*woman* while Romaine (2001) studied the entire 100-million-word BNC, finding that *Mr* occurs more often than *Mrs*, *Miss* and *Ms* combined and that terms like *chairman* and *spokesman* which erased female participation in such roles tended to prevail.

At later points, additional American and British corpora were added to the Brown family, using the same sampling frame but containing texts from later or earlier time periods, hence the idea of a 'family' of corpora. These additional corpora enabled comparisons to be made across time periods, resulting in a crop of synchronic studies. For example, Holmes and Sigley (2001) and Sigley and Holmes (2002) used the 1961 and early 1990s versions of the American and British Brown family, along with another 'relative', the Wellington Corpus of New Zealand English which used the same sampling frame but contained texts from the late 1980s. They examined the frequencies and contexts of nouns which identified people by their sex (*man*, *woman*, *boy*, *girl*, *lady* and their plural forms), including nouns which contained gender-marking suffixes like -*ess* and -*ette*, as well as nouns which did not mark sex (*children*, *kids*). They found that between the 1960s and 1990s there had been reductions in the frequencies of usage of terms which could be viewed as sexist, such as the pseudo-polite *lady*, generic uses of *man*, and the -*ess* and -*ette* suffixes. However, their analyses of usage found that *girl* was more around three times as likely to refer to an adult than *boy* (although this tendency was less marked in the later corpora), and girls were more likely to be described in terms of their appearance than boys. I expanded some aspects of that study in Baker (2010) by focusing on four British members of the Brown family, in order to compare texts taken from 1931, 1961, 1991 and 2006. This study examined the frequencies of gender-marked nouns along with terms of address like *Mr*, *Mrs*, *Miss* and *Ms*, pronouns, gender-inclusive pronouns (*he/she*) and role-based nouns like *chairman*, *spokesperson* and *policewoman*. I found that over time there only appeared to have been a slight uptake of strategies designed to remove male bias from language such as inclusive pronouns, *Ms* or gender-neutral terms like *spokesperson* but instead noticed an overall decrease in male pronouns, along with a small increase in female pronouns. Similarly, male and female terms of address had decreased between 1931 and 2006, with the male term *Mr* showing the most marked decrease.

There is a danger that researchers can engage in over-interpretation when comparing corpora of different time periods together, even if the corpora are carefully crafted in order to follow the same sampling frame. Millar (2009) examined changes in frequencies of modal verbs by replicating an earlier study on the Brown family (Leech 2003) but instead using a more fine-grained diachronic corpus, the TIME corpus which contained all of the content of TIME magazine from 1923 onwards. Leech's (ibid.) examination of texts from 1961 and 1991 suggested that modal verbs were generally declining in usage, a pattern that was especially marked for 'strong' modals like *must*, *ought* and *should*, and the trend seemed to be led by American English, with British English following. However, Millar was concerned that this analysis did not reveal anything directly about modal usage in the years between 1961 and 1991, and that a snapshot of two points in time might present a partial and thus misleading picture. Indeed, when he compared modals across each decade of the American TIME corpus, he found a more complex picture, which indicated a general *increase* in modal use over time, particularly for *can*, *may*, *could*, *will*, *might* and *should*. Millar cautioned that the TIME corpus only contains text from one source indicating that the results are not properly representative of American English, but notes that the small size of the Brown corpora and the 30-year gap between the two sampling points is also problematic. Leech (2011) addressed these points by updating his study to include five sampling points ranging from 1901 to 2006 based on adding the newer members of the British Brown family, as well as carrying out the same study on two large American reference corpora: the Corpus of Historical American English (COHA) and the Corpus of Contemporary American English (COCA). Again, he found a general picture of modal decline, and argued that Millar's conclusions about modals in the TIME corpus are genre-specific. Two implications of this series of studies are that diachronic researchers should, as far as possible, aim for a high granularity (the number of sampling points divided by the span of years across the corpora being considered) and that they should take care in generalizing their findings beyond the genre(s) of the corpora they examine.

On the basis of these aims, it was decided that for the analysis of this chapter, I would focus on the COHA, a large reference corpus created by Mark Davies at Brigham Young University. The COHA consists of approximately 400 million words, taken from over 100,000 individual texts, covering the period 1810–2009. It is divided into four sections: fiction, magazines, newspapers and non-fiction, from sources which include Project Gutenberg, as well as scanned books, movie and play scripts. The texts have been part-of-speech tagged and categorized according to year and decade, allowing the evolution of a word or phrase in terms of its frequency or meaning to be examined over time. The corpus is freely accessible through a website[2] which also contains a search facility, allowing frequencies, concordances and collocates to be derived. Owing to copyright restrictions, the individual texts are not made available in their full form, although concordances can be repeatedly expanded, allowing analysts to examine longer stretches of language if required.

Choosing terms

A first question to be asked when looking at gender bias in corpora is: what words or phrases are used to refer to gender identity? Perhaps nouns like *man*, *woman*, *boy* and *girl* immediately come to mind. Such nouns often signify other types of identity as well as gender, so *man* is supposed to refer to adult males while *boy* is supposed to refer to male children. However, examination of such words in context reveals that they can also be used in other contexts. Consider, for example the following two uses of *boy* in the COHA:

> FOR A LESSON in good timing, crafty strategy and the virtues of no debt, go no further than John Cassidy Jr., a craggy-faced good old boy from Frederick, Okla.

> The animal was crouching on the ground, looking up, and its eyes were just like fire. Its tail was wriggling just like a snake. Oh boy, I was scared.

In the first example, *boy* refers to an adult male, while in the second case it is used as part of an exclamative and does not seem to refer to an actual boy. Other identity nouns can be used generically, expanding their meaning to refer to almost any person:

> These are the first remains of early man found in this part of the world.

This issue of context of usage is the one that we will address in more detail later in this chapter, but for the moment, let us consider other types of words that refer to gender. As well as considering gender-marked nouns, we may also want to take into account plural forms either alongside or separate to the singular nouns, for example *girls*, *men*. (Single and plural forms combined together are indicated in small capitals, for example WOMAN = *woman* + *women*).

A comparison of the frequencies of WOMAN vs MAN provides an easy way of demonstrating male bias or androcentrism, and the extent to which this bias is changing over time in (American) society (see Figure 4.1).

FIGURE 4.1 *Occurrences per million words of* MAN *and* WOMAN *in the COHA.*

Figure 4.1 shows several important trends – first, in every time period sampled, references to MAN are higher than references to WOMAN. In the earlier sampling points, this ratio is over four references of MAN to every one of WOMAN. While references to both MAN and WOMAN appear to have increased over the nineteenth century, the picture in the twentieth century is notably different, with a reasonably sharp fall in references to MAN between 1900 and the 1990s, which is particularly steep from the 1970s to the 1990s, but may have levelled off. On the other hand, references to WOMAN show a decline between the 1920s and 1960s, but then an increase. The period from around the 1960s to the 1990s reflects an almost inverse relationship between the frequencies of MAN and WOMAN – as the female words increase, the male ones decrease. By the final two sampling points, there is still a gap in frequency with MAN leading, but this gap is at its smallest. In order to carry out a fuller analysis, we would of course need to consider a wider range of terms – other nouns such as GIRL and BOY, terms of address: *Mr, Mrs, Miss, Ms* and pronouns: *him, her, she, he, himself* and *herself.* Ideally, we would like to be able to identify every gendered word in a corpus. For example, it would be useful to include proper nouns such as *Jill* and *John* as contributing towards overall male and female frequencies. While automatic tagging programs are often quite good at identifying proper nouns, assigning sex to them often needs to be carried out by a human analyst.

Another way of considering the extent of bias is to think about any alternative terms which do not mark gender and could have been used in place of MAN or WOMAN. Motschenbacher (2012: 12) notes that 'it is challenging to talk and think about a person not as a female or male person, simply because binary gender is a dominant discourse that structures our ways of constructing people.' Thus, a possible alternative term would be *person/people* (see Figure 4.2).

Figure 4.2 shows that during the twentieth century the frequencies of these gendered terms grew closer to those of the non-gendered PERSON, which suggests further evidence that language use has become less concerned with marking gender over time. However, while PERSON can potentially be used as a replacement for WOMAN or MAN, it can also be used in many other contexts such as to refer to cases where someone's gender is unknown or groups of people which may contain both males and females. Also, there is not a simple binary choice between using say, *man* or *person*. Other terms (*guy, fellow, human being*) may also be used. So while Figure 4.2 is indicative that Americans are more likely to use gender-neutral terms, we would need to consider a wider set of words before we can be certain that this is the case.

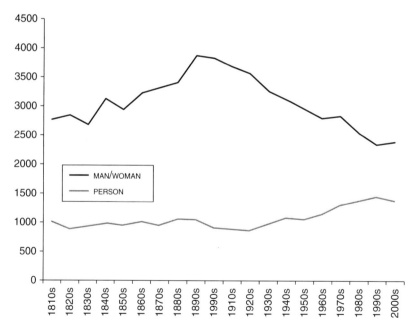

FIGURE 4.2 *Occurrences per million words of* MAN/WOMAN *and* PERSON *in the COHA.*

Functionalization

In the previous section I suggested that if we want to compare the frequencies of gendered nouns, we may also want to take into account relevant non-gendered nouns, although we need to bear in mind that drawing conclusions based on direct comparisons may be problematic. Additionally, *man* and *woman* are not the only gendered nouns we might want to look at, although they are likely to be very frequent. Other nouns or noun phrases could include synonyms (*dude, fellow, bro, lady, the fair sex*) or terms which mark gender via suffixes like *-man, -woman, -lady, -ette* and *-ess*. Such suffixes are often used to refer to the sex of people who perform certain roles or jobs. In order to identify words in a corpus which contain suffixes, it is possible to use a wildcard which stands for any sequence of characters. In the COHA the symbol *acts as such a wildcard. However, we need to take care in assuming that a corpus search of *man will produce only relevant cases. A search of *man on the COHA elicits unwanted words (false positives) like *woman*, *human* and *German*, which are not cases that only refer to males (although we might want to draw a conclusion regarding male bias from the fact that these terms contain *-man* as a suffix). Therefore, a direct comparison of *man and *woman would require checking and removal of false positives.

Van Leeuwen (1996) provides a framework for categorization of social actors, which is useful in helping us to consider the range of possible ways that gendered identities can be differentiated. For example, he notes that one form of categorization is functionalization, or labelling someone with a word which describes what they do (ibid.: 54). Table 4.1 shows the 20 most frequent terms in the COHA which end in *-man* and *-woman* and also refer to gender-marked roles or professions. Cases which refer to nationality like *Englishman*, (usually) inherited status (like *nobleman*) or other states (e.g. *madman*) have been excluded from the table as they do not refer explicitly to roles or professions. To continue the consideration of gender-neutral words, the frequencies of functionalized terms with the *-person* suffix are also included.

Perhaps what is most notable about Table 4.1 are the much higher frequencies for the top *-man* role words, compared to the *-woman* and *-person* roles. Collectively, the *-man* terms add up to 73,206 while the *-woman* ones only amount to 1,844 and there are only 782 *-person* terms. A criticism of this table is that just from looking at words and their frequencies, we cannot be certain that certain jobs refer only to males (or females) who actually perform them. For example, *chairman* might be used generically in some cases to refer to a woman, and the issue of generic usage is explored in more detail below. However, for the moment we should note that in Table 4.1 we cannot definitely conclude that males are represented

TABLE 4.1 *Frequencies of functionalizing* -man *and* -woman *in the COHA.*

	-man	Total frequency	-woman	Total frequency	-person	Total frequency
1	chairman	23,873	spokeswoman	453	salesperson	429
2	policeman	7,646	washerwoman	246	spokesperson	181
3	spokesman	6,542	policewoman	162	chairperson	78
4	statesman	4,292	businesswoman	141	businessperson	23
5	clergyman	3,948	congresswoman	134	newsperson	22
6	congressman	3,437	chairwoman	116	craftsperson	13
7	salesman	3,344	charwoman	90	anchorperson	9
8	foreman	3,151	horsewoman	87	congressperson	6
9	fisherman	2,620	forewoman	62	draftsperson	5
10	businessman	2,306	councilwoman	51	clergyperson	3
11	seaman	1,705	committeewoman	41	repairperson	2
12	watchman	1,662	needlewoman	38	stuntperson	2
13	horseman	1,572	waiting-woman	36	horse-person	2
14	coachman	1,543	serving-woman	33	police-person	1
15	fireman	1,203	washwoman	31	fisherperson	1
16	waterman	1,146	scrubwoman	28	baggage-person	1
17	patrolman	1,045	newswoman	27	committee-person	1
18	footman	998	scrub-woman	24	chairman-person	1
19	doorman	879	anchorwoman	22	busperson	1
20	boatman	795	apple-woman	22	cameraperson	1

more as being 'in work' than females, although even if some of the male words do refer to generic uses, we can still be fairly confident that males are represented as being in work more than females. We can more decisively conclude that when jobs are labelled explicitly as gendered (even if in reality they are held by both sexes), they are much more often shown to be linked to males than females (about 40 times as often).

We may also want to look at the sorts of jobs in Table 4.1 that are most often explicitly gendered. So those ending in -*man* can involve positions of influence and leadership: *congressman, clergyman, chairman, foreman, businessman, spokesman* as well as jobs which relate to the protection of others: *policeman, fireman* or require a form of transport to be controlled: *seaman, horseman, coachman, boatman*, thus involving responsibility for the safety of others. Many of the -*woman* jobs appear to involve service-related tasks, often related to clothing and cleaning: *needlewoman, scrub-woman, washwoman, washerwoman, charwoman, serving-woman, waiting-woman*. However, there are also roles which suggest more powerful positions and appear to be equivalents of -*man* jobs: *congresswoman, councilwoman, forewoman, chairwoman, spokeswoman, businesswoman*. The discrepancies in frequencies, however, suggest that such jobs are historically viewed as 'male', for example: there are 23,836 references to *chairman* and only 116 references to *chairwoman* in the COHA.

Table 4.1 does not show how any of these terms are dispersed over the different time periods in the corpus, and a closer inspection reveals that the more powerful jobs associated with women tend to have occurred since 1980. For example, of the 453 citations of *spokeswoman*, 96 per cent of them occur after 1980. This figure for *spokesperson* is similar at 97 per cent, although for *spokesman* it is much lower, with only 34 per cent of mentions of this word occurring after 1980. Before 1900, the use of the -*person* suffix to describe roles is almost non-existent, with the only case being a reference to a *horse-person* in 1883. This does not mean that there are not other ways of referring to roles in a gender-neutral way that may occur. For example, the term *chair* can be used instead of *chairperson* and in Baker (2010) I note that *chair* (used to refer to people) is more frequent than *chairperson* in the British Brown family of twentieth century written reference corpora, although still much less frequent than *chairman*. Romaine (2001: 163) who examined *chairperson* in the BNC, found that it tended to refer to the office rather than a particular person holding it, although she also noted that there was considerable variation over labelling women who held this role, and they could be referred to as *chairman, chairwoman, chairperson, Madam chairman* or *chairlady*.

With 55,422 instances of *chair* in the COHA, it would be a daunting task to have to read through every concordance line to identify which ones referred to furniture and which ones referred to people. A possible solution could be to examine a sample of the data in detail, say 100 lines, and only look at more data if the pattern does not appear to be particularly conclusive. It is not normally a good idea to look at the first 100 lines in a concordance, or at any consecutive 100 lines because usually concordance lines are not presented in a random order but start at the first file in the corpus and move through to the last file. If we only examined the first 100 lines of every concordance, then we would always be focusing on the first few files in our corpus. So instead, it is preferable to take a random sample.

Some corpus software, such as CQPweb, give the option for analysts to 'thin' a corpus to a specified random number. Such randomized samples are not truly random, however, as they are usually based on the software accessing a pre-set list of random numbers and using this list to select which concordance lines to look at. The KWIC (Key Word in Context – another term for 'Concordance') function in COHA appears to offer a random set of concordance lines, and under the options settings, the number of concordance lines required can be specified. I therefore looked at 100 concordance lines of *chair*, noting those which referred to people taking the role of chair. I did this three times, obtaining a different random sample each time. The first search gave no cases of chairs referring to people, the second search elicited five cases and the third time resulted in none again. Clearly, human chairs do appear in the COHA, although the examination of random samples indicates they are unlikely to be as frequent as *chairman*.

Reporting frequencies can give readers an impression of a trend or difference, but it is often a good idea to carry out statistical tests if we want to present a more convincing argument. Initially, in corpus linguistics the chi-squared test was popularly used to compare differences in frequencies (see, for example, Hofland and Johansson 1982; Woods et al. 1986; Oakes 1998), although this test assumes that frequency data has a normal (or bell-shaped) distribution, which is generally not the case for frequencies based on language. Additionally, the chi-squared test tends to be unreliable when dealing with frequencies under 5 and Dunning (1993) has since suggested that the log likelihood (LL) test is a better statistic to use with corpus data. The LL test compares two frequencies together and produces an LL value which can then be compared against the more familiar p or probability value. A p-value is the probability that we would obtain the results we have observed assuming that the 'null hypothesis' is true. So if we were comparing the frequencies of *chairman* and *chairwoman* in the COHA, our null hypothesis would be that there is no difference in the frequencies of such words in naturally occurring language use (in America between 1810 and 2000). The COHA therefore acts as a 'representative sample' of such language. As well as comparing the frequencies of two words in one corpus, we can also compare frequencies across two corpora – for example, consider the frequencies of *chairman* in the 1990s and 2000s sections of the COHA. We can take each section as a 'sub-corpus' and compare them together.

Entering the numbers in Table 4.2 into a LL calculator[3] gives an LL value of 14.12. Consulting tables which relate LL values to p numbers, we can see that to reject the null hypothesis at the 0.1 per cent level we need a critical LL value of 10.83 or higher, while to reject it at the 0.01 per cent level we need a critical LL value of 15.13 or more. So we can reject the null hypothesis (in this case, that there was no difference in frequency of use of *chairman* between the 1990s and 2000s in American English) at the 0.1 per cent level (but not the 0.01% level).

TABLE 4.2 *Frequencies of* chairman *across parts of the COHA.*

	1990s sub-corpus	2000s sub-corpus
Frequency of *chairman*	1,486	1,366
(sub)-corpus size (tokens)	27,941,535	29,567,390

Some care needs to be taken when writing about p-values in order not to overstate or misinterpret their meaning. A p-value is not the probability that the null hypothesis is true, nor is it the probability that our finding or difference is a fluke or due to chance. Instead, as stated above, it is the probability that we would have obtained the results we found (in our corpus) if our null hypothesis was true.

While Americans appear to be moving away from *chairman* (at least since 1990), we need to take care in interpreting this finding. Although *chairman* occurs less in the 2000s data, we do not yet know anything about the contexts that it occurs in. One question which arises is the extent to which *chairman* is used generically, and whether this tendency has increased or decreased over time. Unfortunately, there is no easy way to answer this question, other than reading through (often expanded) concordance lines and noting the gender of whom (if anyone) is being referred to. Even with just 2,852 concordance lines, this may prove to be a daunting and tedious task for a human researcher to perform, and may also result in errors creeping in. An examination of a random sample of 100 concordance lines of *chairman* did not uncover any obvious cases which referred to females, although most of them clearly referenced males, being marked by male names or pronouns. An examination of a second random sample of 100 lines elicited 2 cases of *chairman* referring to females, so again, while this usage is possible, it appears to be very rare. However, when looking at a smaller, specialized corpus (the 10-million word corpus of written Business English), Fuertes-Olivera (2007: 299) notes that the term *chairman* was used to refer to women who acted in the chair role 28.3 per cent of the time (17 out of 60 cases), indicating the advantage of specialized corpora in eliciting richer data.

Explicitly gendered cases of functionalization are not limited to the *-man* and *-woman* suffixes. Other cases involve suffixes like *-ette* (e.g. *usherette*), *-ess* (e.g. *actress, hostess, seamstress*), *-e* (*artiste*), *-lady* (*landlady, saleslady, charlady*) and *-lord* (*landlord*). Additionally, some suffixes are written as separate words or either with or without a hyphen (e.g. *paper boy, call-girl*). Some of these cases of suffixation involve marking exceptional cases, implying that the 'default' gender of certain roles is male. For example, *hostess* (3,495 occurrences) is morphologically derived from the more frequent *host* (12,491) which must thus implied to be male. On the other hand, it can sometimes be difficult to decide upon a male version of certain words that appear to have been derived via a female suffix. Take, for example, *seamstress* (546 occurrences). The 'morphologically correct' male version is *seamster*, although this word only appears once in the corpus and the term *tailor* (2,563 occurrences) seems to be a more popularly used male equivalent. However, there is also a morphologically derived female equivalent of *tailor*: *tailoress*, which occurs only 44 times in the COHA. The puzzle as to why *tailors* and *seamstresses* are popular but their morphologically related gender-equivalents are not could be explained to an extent by the fact that tailors and seamstresses have many overlapping roles but there are also differences – seamstresses tend to work at creating and sewing a wide range of garments, accessories and upholstery, while tailors usually make, fit and alter custom-made garments only. The preference for *tailor* and *seamstress* over *tailoress* and *seamster* therefore both reflects and constructs an additional level of gender specification in the role of people who work with material for a living.

Another case of marking relates to cases where the sex of particular roles is explicitly marked, often with a preceding noun. Such cases can be found by searching for terms like *male*, *female*, *lady*, *gentleman*, *man* and *woman* and then examining the most frequent role-based collocates that occur one place to the right of those words (see also Romaine 2001: 158). Cases which arose during this exercise are shown in Table 4.3 below.[4]

It should be noted that some of the terms in the first column of Table 4.3 could refer to unwanted cases. For example, *doctor*, *nurse*, *escort* and several other terms can be verbs as well as nouns. A search of *male model* could return cases like 'I want to see a male model this costume'. As the COHA is part-of-speech tagged, it is possible to specify searches to only include words that have been tagged in a certain way. Therefore, the words in the first column only include cases that were tagged as nouns. The syntax in the COHA for this search was escort. [NN*]. The full-stop attaches a grammatical tag to a word, and the tag itself appears within square brackets. The tag [NN*] refers to any noun.

Rather than use LL tests to compare the frequencies in Table 4.3, I have instead used ratios. It would have been possible to carry out LL tests, using the overall frequency of each word (given in the second column) as the 'corpus size' (subtracting the gender-marked frequencies from it first). However, even though the frequencies of the gender-marked cases are quite small, we find that almost all the results in the table indicate significant differences at the 5 per cent level or below. Kilgarriff (2005: 272–3) is critical of using hypothesis testing with corpus linguistics, arguing that 'Language is non-random and hence, when we look at linguistic phenomena in corpora, the null hypothesis will never be true . . . Hypothesis testing is rarely useful for distinguishing associated from non-associated pairs of phenomena in large corpora.' At the time of writing, hypothesis testing still continues to be widely used within corpus linguistics, and hypothesis tests like LL and the T-score are incorporated within techniques such as keywords and collocation in popular corpus tools such as WordSmith and AntConc. In my own experience, while such measures should not be considered as ideal for use with frequencies derived from corpora, they still often help to highlight the most *salient* differences or differences that would otherwise not be noticed, so they have analytical valiency. However, it is useful for corpus linguists to be aware of a range of different ways of comparing linguistic phenomena and with this in mind, Table 4.3 is based on the ratio between cases of gender-marked professions rather than LL scores.

The ratio of difference between the male and female marked versions of each term was calculated by simply dividing the largest number (of the male or female marked term by the smallest number. For example, there are 54 cases of *male/gentleman/man nurse* and only 18 cases of *female/lady/woman nurse*, so the ratio is 54 divided by 18 equalling 3 cases of *male/gentleman/man nurse* for every 1 case of *female/lady/woman nurse*. The table has been ordered in terms of this final column so it is possible to see where the most extreme differences lie. The break some way down the table shows the point where the preference for marking switches from male to female.

The second column of Table 4.3, containing relatively high numbers, shows that in all these cases the typical behaviour is *not* to explicitly mark gender at all. None of the role words in the table contain explicitly male or female marked morphemes (such as *actress* or *landlord*) so they do not appear to imply that they are typical of one gender over the other. However, the cases where these words are marked with a preceding gendered noun tell us something about society's expectations regarding who normally carries out these roles. For example, people explicitly note when a model is male 33 times but only do this for female models 8 times. The fact that people mark models as male over four times as much as females indicates that we are more likely to expect models to be female so there is more need to make this clear when it is not the case. Conversely, in the corpus, nobody in the corpus notes when a reporter is male, but this is pointed out 59 times for females.

It is therefore interesting to consider the words in Table 4.3 to see what exceptional gender-marking tells us about norms relating to roles in (American) society. For example, roles that involve arousing desire in others: *escort*, *prostitute*, *stripper*, *model* tend to be exception-marked as male, indicating that they are usually taken to be carried out by females. Added to this are more caring, 'secondary' roles like *secretary* and *nurse* (as opposed to *boss* and *doctor*). That is not to say that there are not less powerful jobs that are normally assumed to be male, as attested by the higher prevalence of female marking of *clerk*, *attendant* and *assistant*. However, there are other female-marked roles which indicate an assumption of male power: *doctor*, *physician*, *politician*, *producer*, *teacher*, *author*, *boss*. Table 4.3 therefore suggests that some roles which are not usually explicitly marked

TABLE 4.3 *Exceptional gender marking in roles in the COHA.*

Non-marked term	Frequency	Preceded by male/man/ gentleman	Preceded by female/ woman/lady	Ratio
prostitute	802	11	1	11
escort	3,031	11	1	11
stripper	213	5	0	NA[5]
model	15,910	33	8	4.12
nurse	13,378	54	18	3
dancer	2,819	62	22	2.81
servant	14,951	239	95	2.51
secretary	38,998	28	21	1.33
officer	36,955	17	29	1.70
teacher	22,845	23	41	1.78
author	34,929	7	13	1.85
boss	11,398	7	14	2
clerk	13,055	14	29	2.07
operator	5,397	4	9	2.25
attendant	3,953	18	41	2.27
guard	22,607	6	15	2.50
burglar	1,684	3	11	3.66
politician	5,324	3	11	3.66
assistant	6,529	6	25	4.16
singer	4,056	6	32	5.33
artist	18,853	6	36	6
physician	10,703	3	37	6.16
doctor	61,815	12	86	7.16
athlete	1,860	4	29	7.25
novelist	3,384	4	30	7.50
producer	5,370	1	9	9
reporter	9,255	0	59	NA

for gender do not need to be – because of a shared societal understanding that they *are* gendered anyway.

Relational identification

Van Leeuwen (1996: 54–5) notes that one way that social actors can be identified is through relational identification, which involves making reference to someone in terms of their relationship to someone else, for example *mother*, *friend*, *co-worker*. Fuertes-Olivera (2007: 226) gives two contrasting examples of how professional men and women are typically referred to in the Corpus of Written Business English:

> Patti Manuel, President and COO, Long Distance Division Sprint Corp. 'I am a boss, an employee, a friend, a mother, a daughter, and a member of my church and community . . .'

> Andy Pearson has had no fewer than four careers. He has served as a senior partner at McKinsey & Co., as President and COO of PepsiCo, as a professor at Harvard Business School, and as a partner in a management buy-out firm.

In the first example, Patti is quoted as referring to herself with several relational nouns which position her both in terms of her workplace (*boss*, *employee*), her family (*mother*, *daughter*) and her circle of friends (*friend*). Additionally, she uses the noun phrase *member of my church and community* to indicate her relationship to the community she lives in. Patti's workplace identity is therefore indicated to be one of many she possesses. On the other hand, Andy is described only in terms of professional identities: *senior partner*, *President*, *COO* (Chief Operating Officer), *professor*, *partner*. It is worth examining a few relational terms in the COHA, to see whether certain relationships are more likely to be assigned to males or females. Figure 4.3 shows the frequencies per million words of two such terms: *husband* and *wife* in the COHA, indicating change over time.

One notable aspect of Figure 4.3 is that the two lines do not intersect. The word *wife* is always referred to more than *husband* at every time period in the corpus, although the ratio in frequency fluctuates. In the 1880s references to *wife* approaches almost double that of *husband*, while by the 2000s, the gap seems to be closing. It is also worth pointing out the sharp drops in references to both *wife* and *husband* between the 1810s and 1830s, and again between the 1880s and 1910s. We can perhaps be less certain about the representativeness of the 1810 data, because only 1.1 million words were collected from that decade (as a comparison, each decade in the twentieth century part of the COHA contains at least 22 million words at the time of writing). Corpus frequencies can often provide interesting

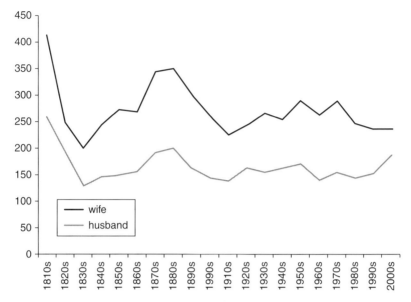

FIGURE 4.3 *Frequency per million words of* husband *and* wife *in the COHA over time.*

patterns but graphs alone do not explain patterns. Sometimes explanations can be found by interrogating the corpus further, for example, by reading concordance lines or the texts in the corpus in order to get a better idea of the context in which words occur. It is also sensible to turn to other sources of information outside the corpus though, and in attempting to explain some of the fluctuations in Figure 4.3, I found it helpful to consider the social and legal status of wives and husbands in American society over the nineteenth and twentieth centuries. For example, in the United States there were attempts to reform marriage in the nineteenth century as many states only granted divorce for a wife's adultery, not a husband's. By the end of the nineteenth century, many states passed laws allowing wives to hold property, sue and be sued. One effect of these changes may have been that women were more likely to be referred to in their own right rather than as wives, and looking back to Figure 4.1 we do see a gradual doubling in references to *woman/women* over the nineteenth century, and we could link this to the fall in *wife* in Figure 4.3 between the 1880s and 1910s.

What about other familial relations? Figure 4.4 shows the combined frequencies per million words for female relational nouns (*wife, mother, daughter, aunt, niece, grandmother, sister, granddaughter*) and male relational nouns (*husband, father, son, uncle, nephew, grandfather, brother, grandson*). This figure differs rather dramatically from Figure 4.3 as collectively, the male terms appear to be slightly *more* frequent than the female ones in the majority of the time periods sampled. It appears then,

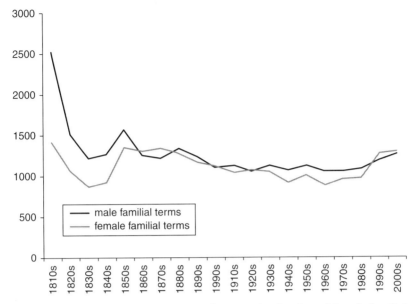

FIGURE 4.4 *Collective frequency per million words of male and female familial terms in the COHA over time.*

that the pattern for *wife* and *husband* may be exceptional, and further searches of the COHA bear this out: *father* is generally more frequent than *mother*; *son* is more frequent than *daughter*, and *brother* is more frequent than *sister* (see Table 4.4).

It is always worth checking concordances, however briefly, in order to ensure that we are measuring what we think we are measuring, so for example, *father*, *mother*, *brother* and *sister* can refer to religious roles rather than familial ones. One way of identifying the extent that such roles interfere with frequencies is to carry out a more specific search. In this case we could look at cases of *father* or *mother*, followed by a proper noun. In COHA, the search syntax would be father *.[NP*]. While there are 205,592 cases of *father* across the corpus, there are 12,991 cases of *father* followed by a proper noun (about 6.3%). The proportion of cases of *mother* followed by a proper noun is smaller: about 2.7 per cent, although I noted several non-religious cases of *mother* like *Mother Nature*, *Mother Goose* and *Mother Earth*. While these cases should still be discounted (if we are only strictly interested in cases of familial relations) because they do not refer to literal mothers in the corpus, they demonstrate the utility of corpus analysis in providing cases that the researcher may not have considered beforehand.

Why is there a different frequency relationship for *wife* and *husband* compared to other familial terms where the male term is generally more frequent? In Table 4.4, *wife* is the only female term which is more frequent

TABLE 4.4 *Gendered familial equivalents in the COHA.*

Female term	Frequency	Male term	Frequency
mother	186,903	father	205,592
wife	107,730	husband	64,770
daughter	52,015	son	80,232
sister	47,320	brother	65,222
aunt	38,739	uncle	44,666
grandmother	11,237	grandfather	13,964
niece	3,887	nephew	5,274
granddaughter	1,335	grandson	2,654

than its male equivalent. I would suggest that Table 4.4 shows two types of male bias. First, the general rule is that males receive more attention than females in society, so they will normally be written about more than females. However, *wife* is the exception that proves the rule. At the time and place when the corpus data was created, *wife* and *husband* indicated a close familial relationship between two opposite-sex adults. Therefore, at every period in the corpus, women are more likely to be identified as being in this relationship than men. This pattern is so strong that it over-rides the first rule about male terms being more frequent. *Wife* is so frequent because it implicitly refers to a man.

Male firstness

Another type of gender bias is described by Freebody and Baker (1987: 98) who refer to 'male firstness'. In their analysis of 'Peter and Jane' (not 'Jane and Peter') children's books, they note that in cases where a writer or speaker has attempted to be inclusive, mentioning both sexes, one must come first, and generally the male form is given precedence. This appears to be borne out in the COHA, as Table 4.5, which examines the order of gendered binomial pairs which are marked with either the conjunction and/or demonstrates (Motschenbacher forthcoming also finds similar results for the BNC). As well as searching for both types of conjunction, further searches needed to be carried out in order to take into account cases which included articles (e.g. *the*, *a*) like the ones below:

She is a perfect enigma both to the women and the men.

They have two children, a boy and a girl.

TABLE 4.5 *Evidence for male firstness in the COHA.*

Female term first	Frequency	Male term first	Frequency
woman and/or (a/the) man	135	man and/or (a/the) woman	3,689
women and/or (the) men	44	men and/or (the) women	11,593
girls and/or (the) boys	364	boys and/or (the) girls	2,835
girl and/or (a) boy	183	boy and/or (a/the) girl	1,148
females and/or males	14	males and/or females	234
female and/or (a/the) male	47	male and/or (a/the) female	1,471
mrs and/or mr	0	mr and/or mrs	51
madam and/or (a/the) sir	3	sir and/or (a/the) madam	16
she and/or (a) he	101	he and/or (a) she	1,587
her and/or (a) him	55	him and/or her	609
mother and/or (a/the) father	1,504	father and/or (a/the) mother	3,509
mothers and (the) fathers	211	fathers and (the) mothers	377
wife and/or (a/the) husband	75	husband and/or (a/the) wife	1,562
wives and/or (the) husbands	61	husbands and/or (the) wives	344
ladies and/or (the) gentlemen	1,545	gentleman and/or (the) ladies	210
Total	4,342	Total	29,235

Even armed with knowledge about sexism in language, Table 4.5 indicates a surprisingly high amount of male firstness in American English. For example, in COHA, people are 263 times more likely to put *men* before *women* than the reverse order. In all cases but one, the preference is to put the male term before the female one. The only exception is *ladies/gentleman*. The terms *ladies* and *gentlemen* are polite ways of referring to women and men respectively (Sigley and Holmes (2002: 140) refer to *lady* as pseudo-polite), and it appears that when people are attempting to be polite, they use these forms and put the female term first. Wider social knowledge of this practice is demonstrated, for example, by an American television panel series in 1951 which was titled by the aphorism *Ladies Before Gentlemen*. However, it appears that the practice of putting ladies before gentlemen is another exception to the general rule of male bias. Generally, males come first about six-and-a-half times more than females come first.

An interesting case of male firstness combined with a relational bias is found in the phrase *man and wife*, which occurs 607 times in the COHA. Not only is the female term second, but the woman is referred to in terms of her relationship to a man, while the term for the male is not marked for such a relationship. Alternative ways of expressing this phase are either extremely rare (e.g. *wife and man* occurs only twice in the COHA) or non-existent (there are no cases of *woman and husband* or *husband and woman*). A salient case of this phrase occurs in marriage vows, where it is common for the person who conducts to ceremony to say 'I now pronounce you man and wife'.

Does it matter who comes first? Evidence about the frequencies of other binomial pairs in American English suggests that powerful identities tend to come first. For example, in the COHA we are more likely to see the orderings: *parent and child, teacher and pupil, master and slave* than their opposites. Additionally, preferable states also tend to come first: *good and bad, happy and sad, rich and poor*. When we encounter binomial pairs, it could be argued that people are primed to consider the first element of the pair as being the preferred one, due to the vast amount of prior experience they have had of language.

Perhaps the situation is starting to change though. Figure 4.5 shows the frequencies over time for the pairs *women and men*, and *men and women*.

The figure shows a changing pattern of frequency for *men and women*, which begins quite low and gradually rises until the 1920s before declining quite steeply again. There has been a smaller rise since the 1960s, although

FIGURE 4.5 *Change over time for male firstness (frequency per million words).*

this may not be as long-lasting. On the other hand, the frequency of *women and men* has barely moved above 0 occurrences per million words until the 1960s, when it starts to make a small impact. While it is tempting to argue that language use was most sexist around 1920 (when the difference between the two terms is largest), it is important to consider this figure in conjunction with some of the information that we have already seen. For example, Figure 4.1 indicated that there were very few references to *woman/women* at the start of the nineteenth century, and that such references had almost doubled by the end of that century. Therefore, it is likely that we saw fewer references to *men and women* at the start of the nineteenth century, simply because there were fewer references to women per se. As such mentions grew over the nineteenth century, it seems that they became more likely to be tagged on as an afterthought, to men, although this practice began to decline over the twentieth century, with women more likely to be referred to as separate from men. That is not to say that 'equality was achieved' by the end of the twentieth century. Figures 4.1 and 4.5 still indicate male bias, even for the final decades examined.

Genericization

Another aspect of male bias which has been discussed by Cooper (1984) is the generic use of male terms (in particular). Such cases extend a term's meaning to make them refer to any or all humans or living creatures. Hellinger and Bußmann (2001: 10) argue that the 'asymmetries involved here, that is the choice of masculine/male expressions as the normal or "unmarked" case with the resulting invisibility of feminine/female expressions are reflections of an underlying gender belief system, which in turn creates expectations about appropriate female and male behaviour.'

Meyerhoff (1987) found a decline in the use of androcentric generics in New Zealand English while Holmes (2001: 124) only identified a small number of cases of *man* used as a generic, also in New Zealand English. Fuertes-Olivera (2007: 227–8), found quite a high rate of generic *man* in the Corpus of Business English (79 out of 208 instances of *man* were generic) but he also argues that the practice is relatively rare in the corpus, that the majority of generic references involved the word *person*, and that dual gender references such as *man and woman* were also quite frequent (although see the section on male firstness above). As noted earlier, it can be difficult to tease apart different usages in very large corpora, and so in order to examine the use of generic *man* over time, rather than reading through all 588,572 occurrences of *man* in the COHA, I decided to examine 100 random concordance lines from each of the 20 decades in the COHA (resulting in an examination of 2,000 lines). It was not always easy to immediately identify when *man* is used generically, and I strived for consistency across my own classification. Cases which referred to a specific man could easily be discounted:

> ... Young man," he added, turning to Charles.

Additionally, cases where men were contrasted against women were not viewed as generic because even though referred to men as a class, such cases did not use *man* as a synonym for any human being, women included:

> If a woman is mild and forgiving, a man must be just in governing himself, his family and all ...

However, cases where *man* referred to humans as a class, and a word like *person* or *anyone* could just as easily have been used, were viewed as generic:

> There appeared to be no place for man or beast ...

> It would reduce society to an infantile condition. Every man actively engaged in agriculture, commerce, or the arts ...

> No other way than by the atonement of our Saviour can man be purified from sin.

Cases where *person* could be used in place of *man*, but were actually referring to a specific group of men, or a specific individual man were not counted as generic:

> The officers have, to a man, come in to the conspiracy.

> 'Infatuated man', said Ellingbourne, after his departure.

Finally, interjections or exclamations like 'Oh man!' or 'Man alive!' were not included as generics as here *man* did not appear to function in its traditional noun sense. Figure 4.6 shows the results of the concordance analysis of generic *man*.

Figure 4.6 indicates that although there are fluctuations from decade to decade, the general pattern is an overall decrease in the use of generic *man*, which peaked in the early nineteenth century and has gradually declined. By the last decade in the corpus, only 6 out of the 100 lines sampled were generic cases of *man*. The figure does not indicate, however, that generic *man* has become extinct. The thin straight line in Figure 4.6 is the trend-line, which shows the straight line which runs as close as possible to all the points on the graph, giving an indication of the overall trend in the data. The equation $y = -1.485x + 37.842$ provides information about the cline of the trend. The fact that the first number, -1.485 is negative, shows that the trend is negative, that is decreasing over time,

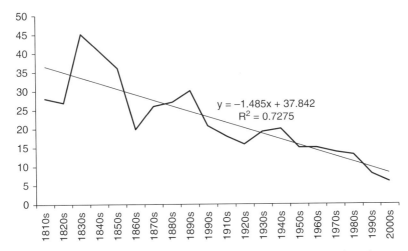

FIGURE 4.6 *Occurrences of generic* man *in the COHA, over time (based on sampling 100 concordance lines for each decade).*

while the amount shown –1.485 indicates the amount (in this case the percentage of times that *man* is generic) which goes down for every unit in the y-axis (every decade in this case). The last number +37.842 simply indicates where the trend line starts, in the 1810s. The R^2 value is given as a number between 0 and 1, where the closer to 1, the more closely the trend line actually corresponds to the actual observed data. The R^2 value is therefore a measure of correlation. Generally, the more points of measurement in a chart, the more reliable the trend line is.

As well as examining random concordance lines of *man* to find generic cases, I decided to carry out more specific searches, involving terms which were identified when examining the concordance lines of *man* referred to previously: *mankind, known to man, early/prehistoric/Neanderthal/primitive/industrial man* and *man* as a verb. However, most of these cases were very rare across all the decades in the COHA, producing frequencies of around 1 per million words. An exception was *early man* which had a relative frequency of between 0 and 0.65 cases per million words for every decade except the 1880s, when it rose to 3.54 cases per million words. However, this rise was found to be mainly due to a single text, a non-fictional book called *The Prehistoric World* which contained 68 out of the 72 occurrences of *early man* in the 1880s and made repeated references to two books: *Early Man in Britain* and *Early Man in Europe*. When a dramatic increase in the frequency of a word or phrase in a reference corpus is due to a single text, then this depletes our ability to claim that its frequency at that point in time is representative, although such cases can still be worth examining as they can tell us about minority discourses or positions. In any case, *early man* and other terms like it (*prehistoric man, industrial man*, etc.)

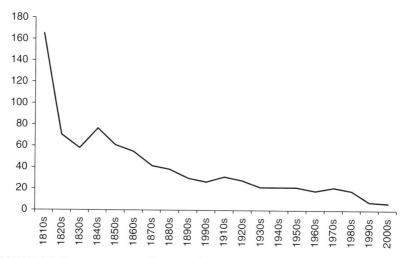

FIGURE 4.7 *Frequency per million words of* mankind *in the COHA, over time.*

are not particularly frequent in the COHA, mainly due to the fact that they are very specific terms which tend to occur in historical non-fiction texts. That is not to say that this is evidence that generic *man* is rare: Figure 4.6 indicates its prevalence, even though it is declining.

A more robust exception was *mankind*, whose pattern of decline over time is shown in Figure 4.7. The pattern for *mankind* is quite similar to that of generic *man*, even showing the slight increase around 1830–40, before the decline.

Pejorative terms

The English language contains numerous negative terms for women, some which suggest sexual licentiousness or prostitution: *slut, floozy, harlot, temptress, hussy, wanton, wench, hooker, bimbo, streetwalker, tramp, whore, ho, tart, skank*; others which indicate physical unattractiveness or an unpleasant personality: *crone, fishwife, frump, hag, harpy*. Women are also sometimes referred to via animal metaphors: *cow, shrew, dog, bitch, cat* or by body parts: *cunt, twat, cooze, pussy* (the latter term also being an animal metaphor). Some terms can be used endearingly, but are often thought of as patronizing, particularly if used outside of the context of a romantic relationship: *honey, babe, sweetie, hotlips*, etc. It is perhaps telling that there are not many male equivalents of these words, and even the equivalents do not have a similar negative force. For example, words describing sexually promiscuous males tend to have positive connotations which suggest virility and desirability: *stud, stallion, lothario, playboy, lady killer*, *rake*. It is notable that a set of male-targeted words which are more insulting in nature: *tosser, jerk, wanker*, label the recipient as someone who masturbates (implying that they are *not* sexually active with anyone else). This sexual double-standard thus punishes women for sexual activity while encourages men to seek partners.

When aimed at men, some sexual words are generally negative: *prick, dickhead*, but they do not seem to be tabooed in the same way as *cunt*.[6] Additionally, some words often aimed at males contain implicit insults to women in them. The term *motherfucker* implicates the target's mother as incestuous and potentially promiscuous, while *bastard* implies that the target's mother was unchaste, having sexual relations outside marriage. Another set of male insults refer to homosexuality: *fag, pansy, mary, poof, queen, shirtlifter, queer, homo*, etc., and are indirectly insulting to women as they imply that homosexuality and effeminacy are linked, and that it is bad for a man to be feminine. Therefore, while female terms insult women only, some male terms have the dual function of being insulting to both men and women, indicating another way in which male bias is incorporated into language.

The terms listed above are typically directed at only one sex, although McEnery (2006: 236) notes cases in the BNC where *bitch* is used on male targets, so there are exceptions to the rule and such cases of insulting someone with a word normally used on the opposite sex could involve additional intent to offend, by implying that the target's gender is being brought into question. There are multiple difficulties when attempting to track the relationship between gender and pejorative terms over time in corpora then. We must first ensure that the term is being used in its pejorative sense (e.g. for *cow* we are not counting occurrences which refer to people rather than literal cows), and we have correctly identified the sex of the target. There is also a danger, particularly when trying to identify patterns of change over long time periods, that any change we witness is more to do with certain words simply going in or out of fashion rather than showing an actual increase or decrease in pejorative constructions of women or men. For example, consider Figure 4.8 which shows change over time for three words relating to female sexual licentiousness.

It might be tempting to note that collectively, words for female sexual licentiousness were high in the 1810s, then declined until around the 1910s, when they rose again, particularly in the case of *whore*. However, we are only considering three words and it is difficult to make any sorts of generalizing claims about words for female sexual licentiousness per se beyond the words in the figure. Also, words can go in and out of fashion (as seen with *whore*, which becomes much more frequent after 1920) and so new words can be coined which help to perpetuate older discourses. The issue here is in ascertaining that we have found every possible word across the time period under question which refers to the same concept, which becomes more difficult if euphemistic references like *she who is no*

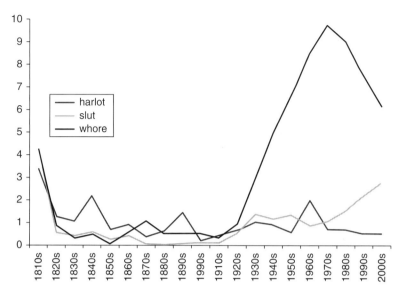

FIGURE 4.8 *Frequency per million words of pejorative terms relating to female sexual licentiousness in the COHA, over time.*

better than she ought to be are taken into consideration. Rising frequencies towards the end of the graph might simply indicate that the researchers are more familiar with current slang or that language users are less likely to rely on a wide range of euphemisms.

A further problem with interpreting Figure 4.8 is that even if frequencies of words remain more stable, as with *harlot*, which retains a frequency per million words between 0.4 and 3.39, the pejorative force of the word may alter over time. To call someone a *harlot* in 2009 is unlikely to be as insulting as to use that word in 1839. Additionally, a concordance analysis of *harlot* reveals that even though it appears in the late twentieth and early twenty-first centuries, it is almost always used in historical senses, particularly historical fiction. We could argue that the historical reproduction of *harlot* contributes towards keeping the word, its associated concept and negative gendered discourses alive, long after the vast majority of people have stopped using it, although there is a danger in assuming an equivalence in force of meaning between such usages over a 200-year stretch.

Additionally, pejorative words can change their meaning over time. From around the fourteenth century, *slut* referred to a dirty, slovenly or untidy woman, not obtaining its association with promiscuity until later. While it is easy to ascertain what is meant when people use *slut* in the COHA in the twentieth century, the earlier references to this word are more ambiguous – the term was still clearly an insult, but perhaps due to different mores around acceptability of referring to sexual topics, the association with promiscuity is harder to identify.[7]

Thus, compared to some of the other ways of examining sexist language use that this chapter has considered, it is more methodologically problematic to attempt to identify a group of pejorative words for women (and/or men) and then track their change in frequency over time. Even if careful concordance analyses identified only the cases that were intended as insults and referred to the appropriate sex, there would still be the question of whether we had identified every possible word, and taken into account changes in force and meaning over time. For that reason, I am disinclined to advocate a simplistic representation of change over time in a figure for such phenomena, but would instead advise a more nuanced and detailed qualitative analysis of the ways that certain words and their meanings fluctuate over time.

Gender-inclusive terms

While the analysis so far does not indicate that linguistic practices that we might consider to be sexist have been completely curbed, the picture since the latter decades of the twentieth century is encouraging with regard to certain linguistic practices. Another way of considering sexism, however, would be consider its opposite. Have people begun to engage in practices that might be considered more inclusive or sensitive? One such practice is the term *Ms* which has been suggested as a way of equalizing the gendered term of address system. While men are referred to as *Mr*, women can be called *Miss* (if unmarried) or *Mrs* (if married). Therefore, *Ms* does not force a woman to declare her marital status. An initial search of *Ms* suggests that it was most frequent in the 1950s, with 1,193 occurrences in that decade in the COHA. However, an examination of concordance lines reveals that most of these incidences are from film scripts where the abbreviation *MS* is used to stand for *Medium Shot*. During other decades, *MS* refers to *Multiple Sclerosis*, *Mississippi*, *milliseconds*, *manuscript* or the word processor package *MS Word*. Therefore, it is necessary to carry out disambiguation before counting frequencies. The tag for the term of address form of *Ms* is NNB, although unfortunately a search of Ms.[NNB] reveals many cases of mistagging, particularly in cases where MS is used in film scripts or plays like:

5. INT. MS Lester and girl on stage.

In the above example, *MS* is erroneously tagged as a term of address as the word after it is a proper noun. In cases like this, it is often quicker to carry out the disambiguation by hand, by looking at concordance lines. In fact, after looking at almost 4,000 occurrences of *ms* across the corpus, only 26 of them were found to refer to *Ms* as a term of address, and 23 of these appeared in the 1990s or 2000s. In contrast, *Mrs* occurs 27,985 times in the COHA and 1,161 times in the 1990s and 2000s, indicating that in American English it is still very common to use a term of address to signify when a woman is married.

What other terms suggest gender inclusiveness? Looking back over some of the previous categories that we have already examined, it is possible to consider additional terms which are alternatives to gendered ones. For example, *firefighter, salesperson, spokesperson, chairperson, supervisor, police officer*. Additionally, cases of generic *man* could be rephrased as follows: *humankind, layperson, average person, best person for the job*. The collective frequencies per million words for these terms are shown in Figure 4.9.

Figure 4.9 curves upwards, although there are two unusual peaks in the 1840s and 1930s which interrupt the smoothness of the curve. These are worth investigating further in order to examine whether something unusual was happening in those decades. The peak in the 1840s section of the corpus is due to a relatively high number of occurrences of *police officer* which are spread over 11 texts. However, almost half of them are located in one single text and removal of this text would bring the frequency per million words in the 1840s down from 4.92 per million cases to 3.30 per million. Similarly, in the 1930s, there are a high number of occurrences of the word *supervisor*, due to the inclusion of a text called *The Office Supervisor* in the corpus at that period. If this text was not included, the frequency per

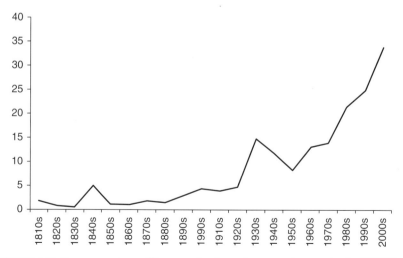

FIGURE 4.9 *Frequency per million words of gender-neutral terms in the COHA, over time.*

million words would be 6.3 per million for the 1930s, rather than 14.59 per million, which would reduce the second peak. As noted earlier, when dealing with especially infrequent terms, it is worth making certain that frequencies are not skewed due to the inclusion of a single, atypical text.

Conclusion

The overall trends that can be gleaned from the analyses in the preceding sections of this chapter indicate an overwhelming male bias in American English, stretching back at least as far as the start of the nineteenth century, although the second half of the twentieth century has indicated a move towards equalization, even though this process appears to be ongoing and incomplete at the time of writing. The male terms are usually (much) more frequent than the female ones, and where there are exceptions, such as *wife/husband*, this can often be explained as a different form of male bias, in this case, to do with identifying women in terms of their relationship to a man. The professions that contain the *-man* suffix are much more frequently referred to than *-woman* ones in the COHA, and tend to be more powerful. The jobs that are exception-marked reveal implicit assumptions about the usual genders associated with them (*male nurse, female reporter*), when females and males are mentioned in quick succession, it is usually the man who comes first and *man* continues to be used as a generic term, standing in for all people, although this practice does appear to be steadily declining, while a look at a few more gender-neutral terms gives evidence that they appear to be on the rise. For feminist researchers, these trends are encouraging, although some of the analyses, such as the continued privileging of *men and women* over *women and men*, suggests that further progress needs to be made.

Methodologically, the examination and/or comparison of frequency data in corpora should encompass an early initial stage of analysis rather than constituting the analysis in itself. Accordingly, we should not make too many assumptions about the frequency counts that we carry out. First, there is a danger in associating a particular phenomenon as being fully represented by the finite number of search queries that we have carried out. Table 4.5 shows 15 pairs of terms which examine male firstness, and while these terms include high frequency pairs like *she/he* and *man/woman*, they clearly do not represent every gendered pair in the English language. If there is a diachronic aspect to our research, then we also need to take into account that terms can change their meaning or the context that they are used in, existing terms can go out of fashion and new ones can be coined to replace them, indicating that while individual words can decline, the discourses they indexed may continue to survive.

While we should ensure that our search terms are at least reasonably representative of the phenomena that we want to investigate, we also need to avoid making the assumption that all of the cases of a search term we find are actually meaningful examples of the linguistic phenomena that we are trying to count. *Father* can refer to a familial relationship or occur as a religious title. We could argue that both uses of *father* are relevant if we are interested in examining male bias in language, but if we are specifically interested in familial relationships, we need to be aware of, and exclude the religious cases. A search of *Ms* produced numerous cases which were not relevant at all and even a reliance on the tagged form Ms.[NNB] proved to be unhelpful due to this word being difficult to accurately tag.

Supplementing our analyses with a scan of concordance lines allows us to check our expectations about the characteristics of words. Additionally, while introspection can help to provide us with a candidate list of terms to carry out searches on, concordances are useful in helping us to spot cases where a word's high frequency is due to its repeated mention in one or two texts, as well as facilitating the identification of additional terms that we may not have initially considered. It was only through looking at concordances of *man*, that I was able to identify some potentially frequent cases of generic *man*, like *known to man*. However, concordances are more valuable than simply enabling a quick verification or providing new ideas, they also enable a much more sophisticated analysis, based on context, as the following chapter will show.

CHAPTER FIVE

Discourse prosodies and legitimation strategies: Revisiting the *Daily Mail*'s representations of gay men

Introduction

In this chapter I continue the focus on representation of gender, by examining how particular discourses can be identified, and to an extent, quantified, in a corpus of newspaper articles. The focus of this chapter is the representation of gay men in a single British national newspaper, the *Daily Mail* along with its Sunday edition *The Mail on Sunday*. Simplistically, it could perhaps be argued that the topic of 'gay men' is better placed in a book on sexuality rather than gender. However, researchers of gender have pointed out how sexuality and gender are strongly interconnected. For example, Cameron and Kulick (2003: 72) note that 'There is no such thing as a generic, genderless heterosexual: rather there are male and female heterosexuals', while McIlvenny (2002: 139) claims that 'gender and sexuality cannot be separated out: doing gender produces heteronormativity, not only gender hierarchy'. Additionally, Remlinger (2005: 133) argues that 'ideologies of gender and sexuality are interdependent. How students believe, value and practice gender in their talk directly connects to how they believe, value and practice sexuality', and Connell's (1995) theory of hegemonic masculinity stresses how ideas about exemplary masculinity are grounded in comparing it to other types of subordinated masculinity: 'Subordination is "the dominance of heterosexual men and the subordination of homosexual men"' (ibid.: 78). It is worth noting how negative stereotypes of gay men have sometimes been centred around adjectival terms like *camp*, *effeminate*, *limp-wristed* and *flamboyant*, which characterize gay men in terms of a supposed 'feminine' gender performance. Additionally, nominations like *sissy*, *queen*, *pansy* and *fairy* also conflate homosexuality and gender by suggesting that gay men are like women. Such terms are generally pejorative although in some cases have later been 'reclaimed' and resignified with more positive meanings (e.g. the term *radical faerie*). However, as I have argued in the previous chapter, the initially pejorative uses instruct us to interpret such constructions as negative because they imply that there is something bad about being (like) a woman. Homophobia is thus connected to sexism, and in particular the view that both women and gay men are inferior to heterosexual men.

Herek (2004) discusses the origins of the term *homophobia*, attributing it to the psychologist and gay activist George Weinberg who popularized it in his book *Society and the Healthy Homosexual* (1973). The use of the suffix *-phobia* in the term associates it with fear, which Weinberg claimed led to great brutality. However, Herek (2004) and others have criticized the appropriacy of the term, for example, arguing that hatred of gay people is based on disgust rather than fear, so the term is misleading (see Olatunji and Sawchuk 2005). Griffin (1998) conceives of a continuum of homophobia, suggesting that there are different forms of which some are more damaging than others. Additionally, bearing in mind the above points about the relationship between gender and sexuality, homophobia can often involve hatred directed at men who are camp or women who are butch, so some people have used terms like genderphobia or sissyphobia to more accurately label this kind of prejudice. Perceptions of homophobia (particularly regarding language use) can be subjective. Issues surrounding production (did the user of the word intend it to be homophobic and can we know this with any certainty) and reception (did I or others interpret the word as homophobic) further complicate definitions.

Despite problems in defining exactly what counts as homophobia, it could be argued that attitudes and behaviours considered to be homophobic are problematic for societies. For example, homophobia can involve verbal and physical violence towards women and men who are (or are perceived as) gay. At the institutional level, homophobia can be responsible for oppressive laws or discriminatory practices. Homophobia can also result in the oppression of gay identities, meaning that gay people may enter into heterosexual relationships or marriages. Such relationships may be stressful, requiring negotiation, compromise or the maintenance of secrecy. Additionally, as argued above, homophobia both reinforces and reflects sexist attitudes and behaviours, thus disempowering women and girls. Finally, gay sportsman and activist John Amaechi (2010) argues that homophobia restricts male heterosexuals, pointing out that men and boys may be wary of engaging in certain behaviours if they become associated with being gay or feminine.

Such behaviours may include being kind and thoughtful, polite to teachers and parents, sexually considerate to women, being interested in academia and not drinking to excess. However, in the long term, such behaviours may actually benefit individual males (by helping them obtain a partner or a good job), as well as those around them and the society as a whole.

The *Daily Mail*

While homophobia can take many forms, I would argue that homophobic practices are enabled through discourses or negative representations of gay men and lesbians which are articulated through language. The analysis of language is therefore an important way of understanding the extent to which a society is homophobic, as well as giving a window onto the nature of such homophobia. The language which occurs in the media is one of most influential ways that discourses can be circulated, maintained or challenged due to the fact that media language both has a large audience and is plentiful (see Baker et al. 2013: 13–17). I have also previously argued that 'newspaper reporting has a cumulative effect. Day after day, many people purchase and read the same newspaper, absorbing its news and also the way that it reports world events. Newspapers are therefore ideal sites where the incremental effect of discourse can take place. A negative or ambiguous word, phrase or association may not amount to much on its own, but if similar sentiments appear on a regular basis, then the discourse will become more powerful, penetrating into society's subconscious as the given way of thinking' (Baker 2005: 61–2).

This research revises and extends an earlier study reported in Baker (2005), which involved a comparison of the representation of gay men in two British tabloid newspapers, The *Daily Mail* and *The Mirror* (and their Sunday equivalents). I had built small corpora of articles which contained the words *gay(s)* or *homosexual(s)* in each newspaper over the period 2001–2. I then examined concordances and collocates of those search terms in order to identify different representations of homosexuality. The *Daily Mail* was found to contain more negative representations, particularly connecting gay men with crime and violence, and constructing them as promiscuous and politically militant. In this newspaper homosexuality was often seen as something to be ashamed of, conceived of as a sexual practice rather than an identity while gay relationships were viewed as transient and unimportant.

In this chapter, I examine a similar corpus of *Daily Mail* and *Mail on Sunday* news articles from several years later (2008–9) in order to investigate whether its representations of homosexuality have altered since 2001–2. Around the period under consideration, the United Kingdom's (New) Labour government introduced legislation to improve the lives of gay men and lesbians. In 2000 British gay people were allowed to serve in the military, while Clause 28 which banned the 'promotion of homosexuality' in schools was over-turned. The following year, the government lowered the age of consent for gay men to 16, bringing it in line with heterosexual people. In 2005, gay people were allowed to form civil partnerships, while in 2007 the government forbade discrimination in the provision of goods and services against gay people. Such changes to the law seem to be supported by the majority of the populace: a 2009 poll by Populus found 61 per cent of people supported allowing same-sex couples to marry and only 9 per cent would reject their own child if they were gay.[1] I was thus interested in examining whether the *Mail* had altered its representations of gay people in order to reflect these recent changes in law and public opinion.

The research in this chapter was also inspired by a high-profile news story which took place in 2009. The death of the pop singer Stephen Gately in October 2009 at an apartment in Majorca was attributed to an undiagnosed heart condition. Gately had spent the previous evening with his civil partner at a nightclub, and they had returned to their apartment with another man. While no evidence of violence, drugs or alcohol was found, there was initially speculation about the nature of the death and the couple's relationship with the third man. A *Daily Mail* columnist called Jan Moir published an article on 16 November 2009 entitled 'There was nothing "natural" about Stephen Gately's death'. She wrote that 'the circumstances . . . are more than a little sleazy' and that Gately's death 'strikes another blow to the happy-ever-after myth of civil partnerships'.[2]

As I had found in my previous analysis of the *Daily Mail*, such articles were not atypical of the newspaper. However, this time the article resulted in 25,000 complaints to the Press Complaints Commission, an independent body which regulates the British press, and resulting in advertisers removing their adverts from the online page which contained the article. The editors of the *Daily Mail* perhaps under-estimated Gately's large fanbase, as well as a softening of public attitudes towards homosexuality. Additionally, they had perhaps not fully considered the way in which social networking sites had recently enabled the large-scale publicization of news stories at a grass-roots level, as well as the ease in which complaints can be made via the internet. For example, the celebrity Stephen Fry used Twitter to convey his disgust at the article, while it was widely discussed on sites like Facebook. As a result, many people who did not normally read the *Daily Mail* were alerted to the existence of the article and went on to complain. The controversy indicates how the concept of a 'newspaper audience' can be extended far beyond the remit of those who choose to buy the newspaper, but may involve anybody with internet access.

As noted, Moir's 2009 article appeared to be congruent with the negative representations of gay men that I found in the *Mail* in 2001–2. However, the day after it appeared, another *Daily Mail* columnist, Janet Street-Porter criticized Moir, writing that she was astonished by the article and pointing out that there should be more focus on deaths of gay men who had died due to violent homophobic attacks instead. While cynically, we could interpret the publication of this second article as 'back-tracking', there is still some evidence that the *Daily Mail* did not have a unified stance on the article, which was another reason to warrant further investigation of the newspaper's general stance.

In 2010 a poll I conducted of the gay social networking site OUTintheUK, asking which British newspaper was thought to be the most homophobic. Of the 62 people who replied, 90 per cent of them chose the *Daily Mail*. While this was a small-scale poll, it is indicative that some gay people view the *Daily Mail* is more homophobic than other British newspapers. However, perceptions can be problematic and I was concerned that my own analysis of the *Mail* in Baker (2005) could have been coloured by researcher bias and my own identity as a gay man. Prior to that research, I had also perceived the *Mail* as homophobic and had gone on to find such homophobic representations in its corpus of articles. However, in reflecting on the research process, I wondered whether I had only uncovered a partial picture, perhaps overlooking representations which could have been more positive. I therefore decided to revisit the 2001–2 *Mail* corpus, as well as comparing it with an equivalent corpus from 2008–9.

From collocates to discourse prosodies

The online newspaper database Nexis UK was used to collect articles about homosexuality from the *Daily Mail/Mail on Sunday*. Nexis UK was used because its search facility allows users to identify articles which contain certain words, and searches can be restricted to particular newspapers and time periods. Once identified, the articles can be saved to the user's personal computer, at the rate of 500 articles a time. This can mean that very large corpora can take some time to build, although the process is faster than copying and saving articles individually. Nexis is not the only newspaper archive in existence but it was one which my university subscribes to and I was familiar with its interface. For people who do not have access to such archives, many newspapers have online editions which allow similar searches to be carried out, although they do not usually enable articles to be downloaded en masse.

The search term I used to locate relevant articles contained the words *gay* and *homosexual*. Nexis UK automatically looks for the plurals of these words too. Two corpora were built, one for 2001–2, the other for 2008–9. When building a corpus about a particular topic, the search term is a crucial factor. It could be argued that all search terms are limiting to an extent because there are many ways of referring to a topic. For example, there may be negative representations about homosexuality embedded in a story about a particular person, even if words like *gay* or *homosexual* never occur in the article. Additionally, it could be argued that articles which exclude gay people in some way or assume that everyone is heterosexual are also contributing towards homophobia. Such cases of heteronormativity (Warner 1993) would be exemplified by a sentence like 'Every woman who ever met Chris seemed to fall under his spell' (which occurs in an article in the *Daily Mail* from 2008).[3] Therefore, to fully capture every reference to homosexuality, we would need to read the entire output of the *Mail* in the time periods under examination. For most people this would be too time-consuming, and probably result in diminishing returns. Therefore, a decision was made to focus the analysis around two commonly used words that are used to refer to homosexuality: *gay* and *homosexual*.

Another decision needed to be made with regard to the exclusion of 'duplicates'. Nexis UK can be instructed to remove any articles that have either a high or exact similarity to each other. The issue of duplicates is relevant here due to the fact that newspapers can sometimes print morning and evening editions of the same issue, or there may be regional varieties of the same newspaper (such as English or Scottish versions of the *Mail*) which contain similar articles. Nexis UK sometimes archives all of these varieties which results in the same article appearing multiple times. Obviously, when conducting a large-scale frequency-based analysis, this can result in a skewed data set, with certain patterns being over-represented. It is advised, where possible, to consider whether the corpus-building facility you are using will result in duplicates and whether these can be weeded out (I discuss ways of finding duplicate texts in Chapter Seven).

For this study, articles with exact similarity according to Nexis UK were not included, although those with 'high' similarity were allowed to remain. This was because there are sometimes cases where articles quote from other articles (a letter about an article from the previous day often reproduced the headline from that article) or may incorporate the same quotation from someone. In terms of enabling an intertextual analysis, it is worth keeping in such cases.

The search terms elicited almost equal sized corpora of approximately 2,100 articles (about 2.2 million words in total) for each time period.

The same method was separately used to analyse each corpus. First, using the corpus analysis tool WordSmith 5, concordance searches of the terms *gay*, *homosexual* and their plurals were carried out. One way of analysing the data would be to simply alphabetically sort and then read all the concordance lines in detail, noting the discourses which occurred in each, but with approximately 9,000 lines elicited in this way, this would have taken a long time. A solution, which has been discussed in other chapters, would be to just look at a smaller, random sample of concordance lines. However, in this chapter I wish to demonstrate an alternative approach, which is based on identifying discourse prosodies via collocational patterns. In this chapter I use a very basic notion of collocates, which is based upon simply counting the number of times that a word occurs near or next to another word. In the following chapter, I use a more sophisticated way of measuring collocates, based around using statistical tests or algorithms to identify more exclusive relationships between words.

For the two *Mail* corpora, a list of all of the collocates of each of the four search terms was derived. Figure 5.1 shows a small part of this list. The two words in each row are a pair of collocates (words which co-occur next to or near each other). For the purposes of this piece of research, I was interested in all words which occurred near *gay(s)* and *homosexual(s)* even if they occurred only once, reasoning that even a single occurrence could contribute towards an overall picture. Therefore, I considered all pairs of words, even if they only occurred near each other once. I used WordSmith's default span setting of five words to the left or right of the search term. After experimenting with different spans, the default setting of five words was felt to be a good compromise (I discuss issues relating to collocational span in Chapter Six).

Figure 5.1 shows how WordSmith gives a detailed breakdown of the number of times a pair of words appear together, along with their positions. For example, line 456 shows that the word *allegations* and *gays* co-occur once (the number in the Total column). However, *allegations* also co-occurs with *homosexual* ten times (line 457), and it occurs with *gay* 18 times (line 458). In total then, *allegations* combines with the search terms 29 times, while other related words like *alleged*, *allegedly*, *alleges* also co-occur with the search terms.

The numbers in the other columns give more information about exactly where the words appear in relationship to each other. So for line 457 we can examine the relationship between *allegations* and *homosexuals*. In the L2 column is the number three, meaning that the word *allegations* occurs

N	Word	With	Total	Total Left	Total Right	L5	L4	L3	L2	L1	Centre	R1	R2	R3	R4	R5
443	ALERT	gays	1	0	1	0	0	0	0	0	0	0	0	1	0	0
444	ALEX	gay	4	2	2	0	1	0	1	0	0	1	1	0	0	0
445	ALIENATED	gay	1	0	1	0	0	0	0	0	0	0	0	1	0	0
446	ALIKE	gay	1	0	1	0	0	0	0	0	0	0	0	0	0	1
447	ALISON	gay	2	0	2	0	0	0	0	0	0	0	1	1	0	0
448	ALISTAIR	gay	1	0	1	0	0	0	0	0	0	0	0	1	0	0
449	ALIVE	gay	1	0	1	0	0	0	0	0	0	0	0	0	0	1
450	ALIVE	homosexual	1	0	1	0	0	0	0	0	0	0	0	0	1	0
451	ALL	gays	8	5	3	3	0	0	1	1	0	0	1	0	1	1
452	ALL	homosexuals	12	10	2	0	1	1	1	7	0	0	1	0	1	0
453	ALL	homosexual	15	10	5	0	4	2	2	2	0	0	2	1	2	0
454	ALL	gay	45	29	16	4	11	2	3	9	0	0	3	5	3	5
455	ALLEGATION	gay	5	3	2	0	3	0	0	0	0	0	2	0	0	0
456	ALLEGATIONS	gays	1	1	0	0	1	0	0	0	0	0	0	0	0	0
457	ALLEGATIONS	homosexual	10	9	1	4	2	0	3	0	0	0	0	1	0	0
458	ALLEGATIONS	gay	18	6	12	1	0	3	2	0	0	1	6	4	1	0
459	ALLEGED	homosexuals	1	1	0	0	1	0	0	0	0	0	0	0	0	0
460	ALLEGED	gay	4	0	4	0	0	0	0	0	0	0	1	2	1	0
461	ALLEGED	homosexual	9	7	2	1	0	1	0	5	0	0	0	0	0	2
462	ALLEGEDLY	gay	7	4	3	0	0	2	1	1	0	0	1	0	0	2
463	ALLEGES	homosexual	2	2	0	0	0	0	0	2	0	0	0	0	0	0

FIGURE 5.1 *Screenshot of collocation table (2001–2 corpus).*

C	Concord

File   Edit   View   Compute   Settings   Window   Help

N	Concordance
1	chief Brian Paddick is unlikely to face criminal charges over drug allegations by his gay ex-lover. Å Å Å The Metropolitan Police
2	January 1997: MP for Harlow, married with two children, faced allegations of gay relationship with teenage Commons researcher
3	Tighe. Å Å Å For as Buckingham Palace is rocked by fresh allegations of gay orgies among servants, Dominic was regaling
4	perverting the course of justice to protect a favourite courtier from allegations of homosexual rape - with the Prince's former wife
5	wife and TV handlers demanded to know the truth about the gay allegations. Å Å Å 'It's not pretty,' said one of the producers. There
6	former gay lover, James Renolleau, has made a series of lurid allegations about him, including predatory homosexual
7	Boy George has a better idea. Upbraiding Cruise for suing over allegations that he's gay on the grounds that homosexuality no
8	measure of honour, and their love for their country, while reading allegations about hushed-up homosexual rape - not to mention
9	questions' about Charles himself. Å Å Å The incident revived allegations of a 'gay mafia' in the royal household which first
10	household which first surfaced in the early 1980s. Å Å Å Then, allegations emerged of a homosexual coterie aboard the Royal

FIGURE 5.2 *Concordance of* allegations *with* gay *or* homosexual.

two words left of the word *homosexual* a total of three times. This means that the pattern 'allegations [something] homosexual' appears three times in the corpus.

Clearly then, there is some sort of relationship between the word *allegations* (and its related forms) and references to gay people. However, the collocation table tells us no more about this relationship than frequency and word position. To find out exactly what the relationship is, we need to carry out a concordance search of *allegations*, looking at the lines which also contain the search terms. This is shown in Figure 5.2.

Normally, it was possible to obtain an understanding of the way that the collocates related to each other by looking at the concordance line, although in some cases, it was necessary to expand the concordance line to look at the entire paragraph or even the whole article, in order to produce a better-informed interpretation. Figure 5.2 demonstrates a potential complication of analysing the words *gay* and *homosexual*: they can function as nouns or adjectives. So these words sometimes modify other words, for example *allegations of a 'gay mafia'* (line 9), but not always, for example *allegations that he's gay* (line 7). The word *allegations* can thus be used to suggest that someone is gay, but it can also be used in other contexts. So line 4 contains allegations about a rape which is described as a homosexual rape, whereas line 1 has a gay person making an allegation that an ex-lover has taken drugs.

If we wanted to argue that the word *allegations* contributes towards a representation of homosexuality as being scandalous or shameful, then we would therefore need to filter out any cases which do not show that. Each case would need to be considered in detail. For Figure 5.2, it was decided to discount line 1 which refers to an allegation about drugs. However, the other cases were viewed as contributing to a 'homosexuality as scandalous' representation because they tended to view some aspect of homosexuality as a scandal, rather than something else like drugs-taking as being scandalous.

Therefore, the number of concordance lines involving the word *allegations*, as it contributed towards a particular way of representing gay people was counted (after discounting the misleading cases). Words which appeared to contribute towards a similar representation were grouped together, and gradually I was able to identify a number of discourse prosodies around homosexuality.

Stubbs (2001) refers to a discourse prosody as a feature which extends over more than one unit in a linear string. So for example, the word *allegations* is suggestive that being gay is somehow a secret or shameful. But other words like *slurs, admission, smears* and *confessed* also seem to work in similar ways in the corpus data, for example:

allegations of gay relationship with teenage Commons researcher (October 1, 2002)

Tom, Nicole and those gay **slurs** (January 20, 2002)

Mr Portillo's **admission** of a gay past (January 7, 2002)

I was upset by the campaign of gay **smears** (October 20, 2002)

She's not **confessed** to being gay or alcoholic (August 22, 2002)

So together, these words all contribute towards the same discourse prosody – that being gay is somehow shameful and needs to be kept a secret. I was able to identify various discourse prosodies, and by counting the number of times that the collocates occurred, I could see which discourse prosodies were more frequent. By comparing the two time periods, it was possible to see which prosodies appeared to be dying out in the newspaper, which ones were being maintained, and which ones were growing in frequency.

Figure 5.1 only shows about 20 pairs of collocates, whereas in reality there were several thousand pairs to consider. In order to make the task more manageable, I needed to be selective in terms of which collocates I conducted concordance searches on. I decided to focus on collocates which contained lexical items only. So I did not look at collocates which were articles, prepositions, conjunctions, determiners, numbers, auxiliary or modal verbs. I instead focused on nouns, adjectives and lexical verbs and adverbs. I mainly ignored proper nouns unless there was a very clear attempt at a particular representation. For example, the proper noun *Mandelson* (referring to the gay Labour MP Peter Mandelson) collocated with *homosexual* twice, although this did not reveal much about a discourse prosody of homosexuality. However, the proper noun *Mandy*, which was used by journalists as a feminizing nickname for Peter Mandelson collocates twice with *gay*. In this case, *Mandy* was felt to be contributing to a discourse prosody of gay men as feminine.

The analysis cannot claim to be *exhaustive* – it is probably impossible to identify every case which contributes towards a discourse prosody, even when using a much smaller amount of data. However, the analysis of collocates should result in a representative analysis and allow comparisons to be made between different discourse prosodies and across the two time periods, particularly if conducted in a consistent way, which is what I aimed for.

Being aware that the original analysis of the 2001–2 corpus was carried out with the view that the *Mail* would produce negative representations of homosexuality, the analysis for this study attempted to address this by seeking to identify positive or neutral representations. As a form of cross-checking, if a set of words which referenced a particular discourse prosody were found in one time period, the same words were also sought out in the other corpus.

The identification of discourse prosodies is, of course, subjective, and as the analysis progressed, it was noted that certain collocates of *gay* and *homosexual* could be viewed as contributing towards two or more discourse prosodies. For example, a phrase like *flamboyant homosexual* could be seen as representing a particular gay man as theatrically camp, but it could simultaneously imply loudness or shamelessness. In categorizing discourse prosodies, I had one category for words which referenced camp/effeminacy (such as *catty*, *effete*, *sissy*) and another which referenced lack of shame (*flaunt*, *notorious*, *outlandish*). I categorized the word *flamboyant* as contributing more to the 'shameless' discourse prosody, but I also noted such overlapping cases. As a result, the picture of representation that I eventually identified had fluid categories, with discourses being linked together or 'leaking' into each other.

The Mail's discourse prosodies

Before describing the discourse prosodies that I identified, however, it is perhaps worth noting what was *not* found in the two corpora. One problem with carrying out any form of linguistic data analysis is in identifying what could have been said or written but was not. It is possible (although sometimes difficult) to identify a minority position if it only occurs a very small number of times, but if it never occurs (or is not identified via the techniques we are using), then we may not know what is missing. Here we may want to rely on other ways of gathering information, including introspection, consulting other sets of data and making comparisons or conducting analyses of other cultures or time periods which may offer alternative perspectives. A combination of some of these methods were used, including comparing the discourse prosodies found in the *Mail* corpora with those found in Brindle's (2010) analysis of Stormfront, a white supremacist bulletin board which regularly discussed homosexuality. Brindle's data contained representations of gay men as disease spreaders and paedophiles, some Stormfront posters expressed the wish to have homosexuality recriminalized or advocated violence towards gay men. Homosexuality was also viewed as being against God, and pejorative terms like *faggot* were regularly used. None of these extremely negative representations were found to be voiced by journalists in either of the *Mail* corpora although below I outline a case of a letter writer who uses a religious argument against homosexuality, and there are instances where journalists report on other people using terms like *faggot*. However, in terms of a 'homophobic continuum', the *Mail* does not appear to exist at the far extreme of what is possible.

What sort of discourse prosodies were found in the corpora then? Table 5.1 shows the prosodies which were relatively more common in the 2001–2 corpus. Obviously, with only two sampling points care needs to be taken in straightforwardly assuming that a change indicates a linear pattern or decline, so the results here are indicative rather than proof of a decline over time.

The figures in the final columns show the total number of times the collocates in this category contribute towards a particular prosody (rather than the number of types of collocates). I define these three discourse prosodies as declining because, out of all of the prosodies I identified, these three had declined the most (in terms of the percentage decline) between the two time periods. In 2008–9 the proportion of times that the discourse prosody of gay men associated with crime and violence is only 12 per cent

TABLE 5.1 Mail *discourse prosodies more common in 2001–2.*

Discourse prosody	Example of collocates	Freq. 2001–2	Freq. 2008–9
1 Gay people are associated with crime and violence	arrested, assault, convicted, crackdown, crime, criminal, dangerous, guilty, illegal, inmates, jail, jailed, killer, offences, offender, outlawed, paedophile, prisoners, psychopathic, rape, violent	218	27
2 Gay people are promiscuous and sleazy	brothel, cottaging, debauchery, grubby, haunt, predatory, trawling, wolf-pack, sauna, stranger, ring, prostitute, brothel, cruising, pick-up, porn, magnet, notorious, promiscuity	206	114
3 Being gay is a secret shame	accusation, admission, allegations, claim, closet, confess, denied, outed, private, repressed, rumours, scandal, slurs, smear, rumours, secret, suspected	363	134

what it was in 2001–2. This is 55 per cent and 37 per cent for the other discourse prosodies in Table 5.1.

Although we need to be cautious about arguing that we are seeing a trend that is likely to continue after 2008–9, focusing just on the differences between the two time periods, we can conclude that these discourses were definitely less common in 2008–9 than they were in 2001–2. It is notable that these three discourse prosodies are among the more negative ones that were found.

Table 5.2 shows discourse prosodies where there is little difference between 2001–2 and 2008–9. While most of these discourse prosodies are also declining, the percentage rate of decline is not as marked as in Table 5.1. Three of these discourse prosodies (gay people wanting access to children or being effeminate, and gay people having their own community) have increased slightly.

It is worth noting how the prosodies identified so far relate to each other. In Table 5.1, the view that being gay is something to ashamed about (3) seems to contradict the view in Table 5.2 that some gay people are shameless about being gay (4). In fact, these two discourses tend to reinforce each other, as the negative construction about people who are not ashamed about being gay implies that that they ought to be ashamed.

Two other prosodies in Table 5.2 also reinforce each other – with homosexuality being viewed as a sexual behaviour or practice (5), and gay relationships being seen as transitory and thus unimportant (6). The prosody in Table 5.1 about gay men being promiscuous (2) could also be related here – they are implied as preferring sex with numerous partners over maintaining lasting relationships.

In my original analysis I had identified one discourse prosody which was based around collocates of gay that referenced collections of gay men like *community, culture, district, fraternity, village, mob, population* and *society*. In Baker (2005) I had labelled this a 'ubiquity' discourse, particularly because some of the collocates like *full of, dominated by* and *packed with* seemed to suggest that there were many gay people in existence. However, when reanalysing these collocates, I concluded that they had a stronger function of representing gay people as having their own culture, rather than there being many of them. Therefore, I have relabelled this discourse prosody in Table 5.2, although acknowledge that this discourse can at times be suggestive that gay men are numerous and thus a powerful force. The view of gay people having a common culture could perhaps be interpreted as a more neutral or even a descriptive discourse, although it could also be argued that such a representation is somewhat homogenizing and separating as it groups gay people together, implying that they have similar interests that are different from heterosexual people.

I also relabelled an earlier discourse originally named in Baker (2005) as 'gay men as proselytising children'. Upon further consideration of concordance lines, I changed this to 'gay men want (access to) children', as

TABLE 5.2 Mail *discourse prosodies, little difference between 2001–2 and 2008–9.*

	Discourse prosody	Example of collocates	Freq. 2001–2	Freq. 2008–9
4	Some people are shameless about being gay	absolutely, declare, extravagantly, flagrantly, flamboyant, flaunt, known, notorious, obvious, openly, out, outlandish, proclaimed, prominent, really, resolutely, seriously, unabashedly, unashamedly, very	226	192
5	Homosexuality is a practice not an identity	act, behaviour, consenting, experience, fantasies, feelings, experimented, inclinations, practising, proclivities, tendencies, tastes	182	126
6	Gay relationships are transitory (and unimportant)	affairs, casual, crushes, lovers, encounters, flings, liaisons, occasional	74	67
7	Gay people have their own culture	community, crowds, culture, district, following, mafia, population, scene, village	119	120
8	Gay people want (access to) children	adopt, child, foster, literature, material, parenting, promote, propaganda, proselytize, teachers	293	330
9	Gay people are politically militant	activists, agenda, bigot, complained, political correctness, demands, demonstration, fundamentalists, intolerant, joyless, lobby, madness, militant, placard, preferential, protesters, radical, rally, rant, sensitivities, spiteful, zealots	200	168
10	Gay people are effeminate	artistic, bitchy, camp, catty, dame, effeminate, effete, feminine, gossipers, hysterically, limp-wristed, Mandy, mincing, pranced, preening, screaming, sissy	39	45

I felt the collocates associated with this discourse were more about gay men wanting to adopt rather than 'turn' children gay, although a case could be made that some readers would assume that the former was indistinguishable from the latter.

A further discourse prosody which I had not identified at all in my original analysis of the 2001–2 corpus was that which represented gay men as effeminate. This was a relatively infrequently referenced discourse (in both corpora), and in my original analysis, some of the relevant collocates had been categorized as contributing to the 'shameless' discourse prosody. However, I felt that there were sufficient collocates to warrant it its own category. A pertinent point about these collocates relates to the sorts of phenonena and people who are represented as effeminate. For example, the Oscar-winning film *Brokeback Mountain* which documented a loving, sexual relationship between two cowboys was described in the *Mail* as a 'camp cowboy movie'. This description of the film as 'camp' is strange (and some might argue, inaccurate). Camp is often related to ironic, mocking and playful humour, and is particularly associated with 'effeminate' gay stereotypes such as the Polari-speaking Julian and Sandy in the 1960s *Round the Horne* radio series. None of the male characters in *Brokeback Mountain* are effeminate, and the film ends in tragedy rather than being humorous.

The *Mail* also referred to two gay men, the Member of Parliament Chris Bryant and the entrepreneur Ivan Massow as flamboyant. While people may disagree on definitions of flamboyancy, from my perspective, neither man seems especially flamboyant in appearance and manner, particularly when compared to say, the gay singer, Elton John who has performed in drag and is well-known for throwing ostentatious parties. Additionally, a gay rights campaigner Ben Summerskill was referred to four times by the newspaper as *Dame Ben Summerskill*. Such instances suggest that the newspaper conflates sexuality and gender together, whereby even gay men who are not especially feminine, are still feminized because they are gay. As with Table 5.1 then, most of the discourses in Table 5.2 indicate a negative stance, although in the case of Table 5.2 these discourses do not appear to be overly more or less frequent across the two time periods.

Table 5.3 shows discourse prosodies which were clearer much more frequent in 2008–9 than in 2001–2.

In general, these are more positive discourses, apart from perhaps the first one which simply links gay people to other 'minority' or oppressed groups such as asylum seekers, black people, bisexuals, disabled people, women and transgendered people (11). A common strategy of the *Mail* in 2001–2 was to use lists of such groups in articles.

The latest piece of tinkering is a reported plan to discriminate 'positively' (i.e. negatively) against white male Parliamentary candidates by parachuting blacks, Asians, gays and women into safe Tory seats. (7 October 2002)

While this discourse prosody is more frequent in the later period, a closer examination of the types of words associated with gay people is worth making. The 2008–9 data tended to link gay people to other sexual groups such as lesbians or bisexuals, rather than ethnic minority groups.

TABLE 5.3 Mail *discourse prosodies more common in 2008–9.*

	Discourse	Example of collocates	Freq. 2001–2	Freq. 2008–9
11	Gay people linked to other minority groups	asylum seekers, blacks, bisexuals, disabled, immigrants, lesbians, ethnic minorities, women, transgendered	278	597
12	Gay people can have positive attributes	admirable, attractive, beautiful, brave, celebrated, charismatic, confident, defiant, doughty, embattled, gifted, gorgeous, happy, influential, nice, prestigious, proud, respected	9	60
13	Gay people have or want rights	achievements, campaign, equal, equality, -friendly, movement, parade, pioneers, pride, rights, tolerance	262	526
14	Gay relationships exist	blessing, ceremonies, civil, couple, household, marriage, partner, partnership, relationships, wedding	319	465
15	Some people claim homophobia exists	abuse, anti-, assault, attack, basher, bigot, bullying, condemned, criminalizing, derogatory, discriminate, hanged, homophobia, hostility, murder, oppression, persecution, prejudice, taunt	127	259

The Belong to Ireland support group, which provides services to gay, lesbian and transgender teens, said it had heard of the two cases in the mid-west. (5 September 2008)

The use of terms like 'gay, lesbian and transgender' could be interpreted as an inclusiveness strategy, whereby the newspaper attempts to acknowledge that some people view 'gay' as associated with males, so it also refers to lesbians as a way of including women, and adds on 'transgender' as a group who may experience similar issues. The above 2008 article (which reports on two gay teenagers who have been abandoned by their parents), is much more positive in tone than the 2002 article, which is disapproving of 'positive discrimination' in the Tory party, and links gay people with a range of other people which are viewed as 'different' and therefore problematic.

Moving on, a relatively small category was used to refer to positive adjectives used to describe gay people (12). I only found 9 in the 2001–2 corpus (and my original analysis of this data set did not uncover any of them), but they had gone up to 60 in the later data set.

Additionally, other discourse prosodies acknowledged that gay people wanted or already had equal rights to heterosexuals (13), the existence of gay relationships (14) and that some people claimed that homophobia exists (15). I had not identified any of these discourses in my original analysis, having originally categorized some of the words as being part of other discourses, for example a collocate like *murder* was categorized as connecting homosexuality to crime and violence, rather than viewing it as part of a discourse which orients to the concept of homophobia.

Having reappraised these collocates though, I felt that they are more accurately classified as referring to gay rights, relationships and homophobia. And comparing their frequencies between 2001–2 and 2008–9, there appears to be an important change in the *Mail's* discourse. Collectively, it uses collocates from these three categories 708 times in 2001–2, while this figure rises to 1,250 times in 2008–9. This suggests that the *Mail* has become more likely to use the *language* associated with more positive discourses about homosexuality. So in reporting on a change to the law which allows gay people to have civil partnerships, the *Mail* has to acknowledge the existence of such partnerships and that gay people want (and are allowed) to express commitment to each other. Such language contradicts the 'transiency' discourse prosody (6) articulated through terms like *liaison* (Table 5.1).

However, it should not be assumed that the *Mail* is necessarily accepting of civil partnerships or other changes in UK legislation that benefit gay people. Instead, it sometimes prints quotes or stories which could be interpreted as being critical of gay equality movements. For example, consider the following two extended concordance lines which show the relationship between the collocates *gay(s)/homosexual(s)* and *civil*.

Loads of gays and lesbians rushed into civil partnerships because it was new and 'cool' without the thought and preparation (emotionally, financially, etc.) that one makes for straight marriage. (Letters, 11 May 2008)

No escaping the town hall Thought Police SORRY about this, but right-thinking people are rejoicing too soon over the case of Lillian Ladele the registrar given a hard time at a Left-wing town hall for refusing to officiate at homosexual civil partnerships. (Opinion column, Peter Hitchens, 20 July 2008)

The first example is a letter from a reader who argues that gays (not gay people) and lesbians do not take civil partnerships as seriously as heterosexuals take marriage. The second is from a columnist who makes a contrast between 'right thinking people' and a 'left-wing town hall', also implied to be 'thought police', because a registrar was found to have broken the law by refusing to officiate in civil partnerships. Both stories therefore appear to focus on negative aspects of civil partnerships. Perhaps it is an indication of the shift in discourse, but in 2008 the *Mail* does not openly state that it believes that civil partnerships are wrong. Instead, its position needs to be more carefully inferred via the types of civil partnership stories that it reports on.

One aspect of the 'some people claim that homophobia exists' discourse prosody in *The Mail*, demonstrates a conflicting set of values in the newspaper, as shown in the following examples.

> POPE BENEDICT'S Christmas assault on gay rights seems outrageous, given the unearthing of never-ending child sexual abuse scandals in the Catholic Church. (2 January 2009)

> That means an end to the increasing toleration of Islamic sharia law as the effective jurisdiction in Muslim areas, which so badly threatens in particular the safety and wellbeing of women, homosexuals and converts from the faith. (28 December 2009)

> For when it comes to gay rights, Jamaica's machismo society is still stuck in the Dark Ages . . . Several top reggae stars have stoked the hatred with lyrics inciting violence against gays and lesbians. One of the most sickening songs, Boom Bye Bye, by Buju Banton, glorifies the act of machine-gunning and hurling acid at homosexuals. (19 September 2009)

> At one point, the BNP policy was to ban homosexuals from holding high public office, and now it merely hopes to return homosexuality 'to the closet'. Mr Griffin himself has called homosexuals 'repulsive creatures' but lived for a number of years with Martin Webster, a gay BNP organiser, who claims that they had an affair. (24 October 2009)

These four cases are interesting because they all appear to defend gay people as being victimized by other groups. The first case is critical of the Pope's 'assault of gay rights', the second is concerned with how Sharia law (and by extension Islam and Muslims) threatens homosexuals, the third disapproves of Jamaican society and reggae stars while the fourth is critical of the British National Party (BNP) who want to 'return homosexuality to the closet'. Some readers may find the idea of the *Mail* being concerned about gay people to be surprising or even amusing, considering how it is perceived as homophobic. One possible reading of such articles are that they are indications of plural voices in the *Mail*, similar to the way that Janet Street-Porter was critical of Jan Moir. But it might also be argued that the *Mail's* concerns about the well-being and rights of gay people are 'strategic', in that gay rights can be used to attack other groups whom journalists do not approve of, or even to create animosity between those groups. The last excerpt indicates a somewhat ambivalent stance because it insinuates that the leader of the BNP is gay himself, therefore also referencing the 'secret shame' discourse prosody (3) described earlier.

At other times, the *Mail* refers to a case where someone has claimed or could claim that something is homophobic in order for the author of the article to disagree with the claim, which is why I have labelled this discourse 'some people claim homophobia exists' rather than simply 'homophobia exists'. The following example demonstrates this kind of denigration.

> WE ARE surrounded by a climate of Political Correctness, in which anyone can declare themselves to be part of a minority and thereby gain whatever they want . . . On the surface it's easy to make allegations of homophobia when gays are refused permission to adopt children. (7 November 2002)

However, again, in cases like these, in having to reject the homophobia, the *Mail* still must acknowledge language surrounding homophobia, along with its associated discourse, in a way which would have been very difficult to achieve in a national newspaper in British society 100 years previously.

Overlapping prosodies

Having discussed all of the discourse prosodies found, it is worth spending some more time discussing how they tend to overlap or reinforce each other. For example, consider the following excerpt.

> It hasn't been easy for Maria, especially this week since downmarket Sunday newspaper splashed across several pages allegations of her husband's sordid gay life. He was said to trawl gyms, saunas, clubs and hotels looking for casual sex. (28 February 2008)

Here, a discourse of 'secret shame' is referenced, particularly with references to 'allegations of her husband's sordid sex life'. However, the allegations are not just about being gay but also about the fact that the husband 'was said to trawl gyms, saunas, clubs and hotels looking for casual sex'. Therefore, the allegations are both about being secretly gay *and* about being promiscuous. The two discourses, both being negative, reinforce each other.

The 'promiscuity' discourse is also linked to other discourses:

> Often clad from head to foot in black leather, Joe revelled in lowlife sleaze, constantly cruising the red-light districts of London in search of anonymous rough-trade sex, returning home to fill his diaries with shocking details of 'frenzied homosexual saturnalia' in public lavatories.

He would proposition any attractive male who took his fancy, myself included, regardless of their persuasion. (4 April 2009)

Here is a construction of a gay man as promiscuous (the playwright Joe Orton, who died in 1967), referenced by words like 'constantly cruising', 'anonymous rough-trade sex' and 'proposition any attractive male'. However, the excerpt also references the shameless discourse. The word 'revelled' indicates how the man seems to enjoy the promiscuous sex, whereas his description of propositioning any attractive male also positions him as without shame.

The shameless discourse can also be interdiscursively linked:

SCREAMING LORD MANDY'S NAUSEATING FLYING CIRCUS
Screaming Lord Mandelson makes jokes about his mortgage fraud. He flaunts his dubious associations with multi-millionaires, for whom he does favours. (18 August 2009)

This article, about the Member of Parliament Lord Peter Mandelson, uses the adjective *screaming* to describe him, in a play on the name of a British politician called Screaming Lord Sutch, a 1960s pop star and the founder of the Official Monster Raving Loony Party (a satirical political party which deliberately had a bizarre manifesto). This linking of Mandelson to Lord Sutch could be interpreted as indicating that the author thinks Mandelson is a 'raving loony', however, the word *screaming* could also be seen as referring to Mandelson's 'loud' (or open) homosexuality (the phrase *screaming queen* occurs twice in the BNC). In the second sentence the verb *flaunt* is used to refer to Mandelson's associations with multi-millionaires. Both words are suggestive of a man who is not ashamed of either his sexuality or his connections. However, as well as being constructed as shameless, there is also a representation of Mandelson as effeminate or camp. He is given the feminizing nickname *Mandy*, while the adjective *screaming* also positions him as outrageously camp.

And finally, effeminate representations can also be connected to political militancy:

WITH his rabid environmentalism and militant gay rights beliefs, Patrick Harvie is a proud cheerleader for fashionable, Left-wing causes. (29 January 2009)

In the above short example, the term *cheerleader* (an activity currently mostly associated with teenage girls and young women) is linked to the gay rights campaigner Patrick Harvie, who is always linked to the words *rabid* and *militant*. The case described above, of referring to another campaigner as Dame Ben Summerskill also connects effeminacy and militancy together.

Therefore, while it was initially helpful in terms of analysis to categorize individual collocates as contributing to a particular discourse prosody, when analysing cases in more context, it becomes more difficult to fully tease the discourses apart from each other. Instead, they appear to be interlinked, contributing towards an overall picture. These associations could mean that when one discourse (such as gay men are promiscuous) is articulated, another one (such as homosexuality is a secret shame) could also be triggered in the minds of readers, due to the fact that in other articles, readers have encountered both discourses occurring in tandem.

Legitimation strategies

Another aspect of the analysis in this chapter, going beyond the analysis I carried out in Baker (2005) involves examining how the newspaper is able to legitimate its negative discourses. Fairclough (2003: 19) defines legitimation as 'widespread acknowledgement of the legitimacy of explanations and justifications for how things are and how things are done'. A legitimation strategy is thus a way of justifying a particular state of affairs or stance towards that state of affairs. Van Leeuwen (2007) identifies a number of legitimation strategies, including authorization (legitimating via reference to some form of authority) and moral evaluation (legitimating via reference to value systems).

While an examination of collocates (often within the context of the concordance lines that they appear in) is often revealing of a particular discourse or stance, it is not so easy to elicit legitimation strategies from simply examining a list of collocates, or even a concordance table. Instead, it is usually necessary to read an expanded concordance line, as well as take into account the title of the article, who wrote it, the type of article it is, and additional contextual information. I demonstrate how this procedure works in the example below.

First, the word *homosexual* was found to collocate with the word *preyed*. This elicited the following concordance line:

> of bisexuality, his closest male friend was a homosexual who daily preyed on young boys, while

This concordance line could be seen as contributing towards several discourses – one of gay men as associated with crime (e.g. paedophilia), or of gay men as promiscuous (the use of the word *daily*), or of gay men as wanting access to children. If we view the *Mail* as generally being negatively disposed towards gay people, then it could be argued that these discourses themselves operate as legitimation strategies. However, with national opinion turning against the *Mail's* negative representation of gay men, we need to consider another level of legitimation strategy – how can the *Mail* justify its articulation of such negative discourses, particularly when it increasingly attracts wide-spread criticism in doing so?

Merely reading the above concordance line does not reveal any clues with regard to this sort of legitimation strategy. Instead, we could expand the concordance line to obtain more context:

> And though he vehemently denied rumours of bisexuality, his closest male friend was a homosexual who daily preyed on young boys, while there is clear evidence that Greene regularly seduced under-age teenage lads on the Italian island of Capri. (19 March 2008)

Even here, there is not a great deal of context, although some analysts may infer that the article is about the novelist Graham Greene. Reading the entire article confirms this, as well as explaining why the article is being written. It is about a new edited collection of Greene's letters which has recently been published. Greene owned a villa in Capri in 1948. Therefore, the negative description of two predatory gay (or bisexual) paedophiles is located in the past. It refers to a man who died in 1991 (and cannot sue), and events which (may have) happened 60 years earlier.

When reading other expanded concordance lines, I was reminded of this article, in that other articles also referenced famous figures from the past who were involved in gay 'scandals'. Relative to other newspapers, *The Mail* often appears to have articles which focus on twentieth-century British history, and in writing about people or events that occurred in the past, it appears to be able to nostalgically refer back to a period which was perhaps more in keeping with aspects of the newspaper's own political stance. The article about Joe Orton cited above fits in with this pattern, and below are two further excerpts from articles about gay people in the period before the decriminalization of homosexuality.

> After the uncovering of the homosexual traitor John Vassall in the early Sixties, MI5 placed a telephone check on four other agents. One of them used to indulge in 'long conversations . . . of a revolting nature' with more than 250 men 'much given to referring to each other by girls' names (Maud, Kitty, Alice and so on)'. (18 October 2009)

> Then, yearning for more intimate company, he decided to visit one of London's infamous underground public lavatories to seek out a gay lover. [John Gielgud] had done this many times before, but this time he was arrested by Scotland Yard's so-called 'Pretty Police' young recruits picked for their looks and stationed in the urinals for the purposes of entrapment. (20 March 2008)

Collectively, such articles serve as a reminder that homosexuality used to be illegal, that a notorious traitor was gay and that famous gay people were sometimes caught in compromising positions by the police, or were alleged to be paedophiles. Therefore, these articles help to reference discourses of shame, scandal, criminality and child abuse around gay people. However, it is notable that the authorial tone of these articles tends not to refer to the treatment of gay men during this period as problematic. Instead, arrests and scandals are usually reported in a matter-of-fact way, with the emphasis on the scandal of the person's sexuality and their behaviour, rather than the intolerance and bigotry of the time. Therefore, it could be argued that one legitimation strategy used by the *Daily Mail* is to uncritically refer to the past, particularly referencing the negative discourses around homosexuality of that period.

A second legitimation strategy involves authorial voice and quotation patterns. Again, such strategies tend not to be revealed simply by looking at collocates or concordance lines, but expanded concordance lines, or the entire article must be read in order to derive them. One strategy involves printing examples of more negative discourses via the reader's letters page:

> It's a travesty of the faith to ring-fence a Christian service and keep it exclusive to one group, especially when one considers that homosexual acts are condemned in the Bible and by the Church. (Letters, 10 January 2008)

The above letter makes a reference to 'homosexual acts' being condemned by the Bible and the Church. This is a point which *Mail* journalists do not usually make themselves, and thus may represent a more extreme condemnation of homosexuality than the editorial voice of the newspaper is prepared to own. However, by printing it as a letter, the newspaper is able to include the position within its own newspaper, without attracting direct criticism: it could argue that it is 'giving a voice' to its readers. Clearly though, newspapers can be selective with regard to which letters they publish, and we do not know the identities of such letter writers and their relationship to the newspaper.

Another type of quotation strategy involves giving precedence to gay people who articulate negative discourses:

> Militant gay madness. I'm A 53-year-old homosexual who has lived through years of real prejudice in my earlier years . . . I do not believe that I am the only homosexual in Britain who fears that if the militant homosexual lobby continues to dominate there will inevitably be a backlash at some point, which could sweep away the reforms which have made life so much better for the homosexual who simply wants to live free from discrimination. (Letters, 8 Feburary 2008)

> 'Gay marriage does not work – men are just too predatory' says Pete Burns (4 May 2008)

The first example above also uses the 'letters' legitimation strategy, but this time, the letter writer identifies as a '53-year-old homosexual'. This choice of *homosexual* over another word like *gay* is interesting, particularly because the former word is often more associated with negative legal, medical and religious discourses from the pre-decriminalization period in the United Kingdom. The letter writer refers to a 'militant homosexual lobby', referencing the 'gay people are politically militant' discourse. Later in the letter, the writer specifically complains about lobby group Stonewall's apparent call for teachers to use inclusive language, particularly when children have two same-sex parents. However, it is worth noting that on 12 February, there are two letters from other readers (not printed here) who are supportive of Stonewall, which indicates that the *Mail* does not always print negative opinions about homosexuality from its readers.

In the second excerpt above, there is a quote from the gay pop star Pete Burns who is claimed to say that gay marriage does not work as men are too predatory. As well as contributing to the negative discourse of gay men as sexually promiscuous, this position is legitimated because it is a gay man who is saying it, rather than the *Mail* itself. The *Mail* could have sought the opinions of many other well-known gay men (or carried out a large-scale survey of all gay men), and it is notable that they chose to report on one gay celebrity who did not approve of gay marriage, in keeping with its own stance.

As with letter writers, a final legitimation strategy must also be inferred by examining the author of the article. In this case it is the use of columnists to articulate more negative discourses. As described at the start of this chapter, on 16 November 2009, *Mail* columnist Jan Moir published an article about homosexuality which was widely criticized. Other columnists, particularly Richard Littlejohn, also reference some of the negative discourses, especially the 'militant gay agenda' and 'promiscuous gay men' discourses.

> Like most things, the homosexual equality movement has been hijacked by hysterical headcases with ever more extreme demands. You can never make too many concessions to them. They just keep coming back for more, hoping to wear down their opponents with a relentless fusillade of vile abuse. (Richard Littlejohn, 15 May 2009)

> [Hampstead] Heath is a magnet for gay men who enjoy sex with strangers. Favourite spots include the 'Vanilla Path' and the 'Yum, Yum Tree'. Don't ask. But far from cracking down, the authorities started hanging free packets of condoms and lubricant from the trees as part of an anti-Aids initiative. (Richard Littlejohn, 22 August 2008)

In order to understand why some of the more negative representations of homosexuality are written by columnists, it is necessary to step outside the corpus and consider other sources of contextual information. At the time the articles were published, complaints to the British press were handled by the Press Complaints Commission (PCC): 'an independent self-regulatory body which deals with complaints about the editorial content of newspapers and magazines (and their websites)'.[4] Both Richardson (2004: 68) and Petley (2006: 56) describe cases where newspaper columnists in *The Daily Express* made comments about Muslims or Islam which received reader complaints to the PCC. Petley points to an article by columnist Richard Kilroy-Silk (16 January 1995) which contained the line 'Moslems everywhere behave with equal savagery'. Petley (ibid.) notes that the PCC responded with 'The column clearly represented a named columnist's personal view and would be seen as no more than his robust opinions.' Richardson relates an article by Carol Sarler (15 November 2001) who wrote: 'every Moslem state in the world today is a cauldron of violence, corruption, oppression and dodgy democracy: the direct opponents of everything a liberal holds dear; yet at your peril do you mention it.' She also referred to The Qur'an as 'no more than a bloodthirsty little book'. However, the PCC responded as follows: 'the article, headed as comment, was clearly distinguished as the opinion of the columnist, in accordance with terms of the Code.'

It appears that during the time period under discussion, opinion columnists had a special status in British journalism, being able to articulate negative positions about social groups, without falling foul of the media's code of conduct. Jan Moir's article was also not upheld by the PCC. Petley (2006: 61) claims that the PCC 'is paid for by newspapers and its Code Committee is stuffed with editors'. It is therefore interesting to note how regulatory structures such as the PCC appear to enable certain journalistic practices, which are taken advantage of by certain newspapers.

Conclusion

Methodologically speaking, it is a useful reflexive exercise to 'revisit' a piece of data analysis and compare the extent to which the two analyses differ. My original analysis of the 2001–2 corpus did not find any positive representations of gay men, but instead focused on the numerous ways that they were negatively perceived. At the time I conducted that analysis, I had expected to find negative representations, and although I did not feel that I was being biased, it is clear from the analysis in this chapter, that I overlooked a small number of cases where gay men were positively appraised. It is often easier to first identify a 'majority pattern', and then find more evidence for it, and while I have argued elsewhere (Baker 2006: 14) that corpus linguistics procedures enable analysts to uncover the 'resistant' or less frequent patterns, I suspect that such patterns are more likely to be identified by experienced analysts.

As well as overlooking a small number of straightforwardly positive representations, my more recent analysis resulted in me reinterpreting some sets of collocates as contributing towards different discourses. To a large extent this was a result of more careful reading of concordance lines, and particularly expanding concordance lines to access more context. It could also be the case that certain discourses are easier to identify if they become more popular in society and are therefore more likely to be 'noticed' by the analyst. My own identification of discourses surrounding the existence of homophobia and gay relationships may be a result of such discourses being increasingly articulated in British society over the first decade of the twenty-first century.

As well as looking at expanded concordance lines in more detail, my more recent analysis also considered other forms of social context, as a way of trying to explain some of the patterns found. Knowing that the PCC does not usually uphold complaints about the opinions of columnists is helpful in making sense of why some of the more negative patterns occurred in opinion columns, while it was useful to consider whether a particular collocational pattern or concordance line was attributed to a letter writer, someone who was identified as gay themselves, or referred to an event which took place many decades ago. While an analysis of collocates and concordance lines alone would have still produced the discourse prosodies, it was only with ·a more detailed analysis of context that I was able to explain why such prosodies occurred.

In light of this, I would argue that while my analysis of the *Mail* is reasonably valid and reliable, I have most likely captured a general picture and that other analysts who conducted the same research would probably produce different frequencies or even different interpretations of the sorts of discourses that are articulated. Another aspect of carrying out the analysis a second time, was that I found the categories of discourse prosody to be much more interlinked and fluid than I had initially conceived them to be. Hopefully I have conveyed this in the analysis – it is clear that the identification of discourse prosodies is very much a subjective matter, and that people who approach the data from a different political stance may notice or interpret different aspects of it to me.

The analysis in this chapter at least has internal consistency, in that the same procedures were carried out by the same analyst at the same period of time on two separate yet related corpora. If we compare the results of the analyses of these two corpora, there do appear to be notable changes in the ways that the *Mail* represents homosexuality over time. Table 5.4 summarizes the 15 discourse prosodies, listing them in order of their frequency in 2001–2. It can be seen that the 2001–2 corpus contains many more negative representations and very few positive ones. The 2008–9 corpus, on the other hand, tends to refer much more to the existence of gay rights and homophobia, and it is less likely to represent homosexuality as

TABLE 5.4 *Summary of* Mail *discourse prosodies around homosexuality.*

Discourse prosody	2001–2	2008–9
Being gay is a secret shame	363	134
Gay relationships exist	319	465
Gay people want access to children	293	330
Gay people and other minority groups	278	597
Gay rights exist	262	526
Some people are shameless about being gay	226	192
Gay people are associated with crime and violence	218	27
Gay people are promiscuous and sleazy	206	114
Gay people are politically militant	200	168
Homosexuality is a practice not an identity	182	126
Homophobia exists	127	259
Gay people have their own community	119	120
Gay relationships as transitory (and unimportant)	74	67
Gay people are effeminate	39	45
Gay people can have positive attributes	9	60

a source of shame, connected to crime and violence and promiscuity and sleaze.

It could still be argued that there are negative discourse prosodies of homosexuality in the 2008–9 corpus, although they are less frequently articulated than in the equivalent 2001–2 corpus, and are more frequently interspersed with positive discourse prosodies. On a number of occasions, in the 2008–9 corpus I found it difficult to characterize a single sentence as being overly positive or negative, but instead it seemed to express a rather conflicted stance. Two further examples should suffice.

Comically, such 'gesture politics' apologies are often made to people who are dead. Thus Gordon Brown's abject apology to Alan Turing – the brilliant wartime Bletchley Park code-breaker, who was also a homosexual and who committed suicide in 1954 after being prosecuted for an act of gross indecency. (16 November 2009)

The country's most celebrated gay campaigner has come out in support of the Irish language poet who was filmed admitting he had sex with 16-year-old boys and likened his situation to the plight of Oscar Wilde. (9 February 2008)

Both excerpts here use positive adjectives to refer to gay people. So in the first article, Alan Turing is described as a 'brilliant' code-breaker, while in the second article, senator David Norris is referred to as 'the country's most celebrated gay campaigner'. Collocates such as *celebrated* and *brilliant* appear to contribute towards a positive discourse prosody of homosexuality. However, the thrust of the first article is that Prime Minister Gordon Brown should not apologize for the treatment of Alan Turing, nor is the article critical of Turing's arrest and subsequent prosecution. In the second article, the 'celebrated gay campaigner' is characterized negatively as supporting someone who had sex with 16-year-old boys in Nepal (which the newspaper notes elsewhere is not illegal). Therefore, these articles express a conflicting stance towards gay people, representing them both positively and negatively.

Additionally, it appears that in 2008–9, there is particular disapproval levelled at one relatively small sub-group of gay men; people who are viewed as 'militant' gay rights campaigners. Such people are regularly described as *bullies*, *bigots* and *spiteful*. This is an interesting development in that it suggests that the *Mail* is focusing its ire on a smaller number of people who are actively campaigning for further changes to the law.

Considering the changes in British laws and social attitudes mentioned earlier in this chapter, it seems that the during 2008–9 *Mail's* discourses on homosexuality are following rather than leading. While the newspaper does not appear to be especially supportive of civil partnerships or equality-based legislation during this period, it must also acknowledge that such legislation has happened, and in doing so, use terms like *gay marriage* and *homophobia*. While there are cases where the *Mail* problematizes such terms, there are also other occurrences where they are used uncritically. As mentioned at the beginning of this chapter, The *Mail* must also acknowledge that the concept of 'audience' is expanding due to the fact that social media enables large numbers of people who are not normally readers of newspapers to be quickly directed to controversial stories. Finally, the fact that the *Mail* occasionally refers to people or other social groups who are homophobic as a way of attacking them, suggests that while gay people may not remain a target in the future, the newspaper still appears to be in the business of telling its readers whom to dislike.

CHAPTER SIX

What are boys and girls made of? Using Sketch Engine to analyse collocational patterns

Introduction

The previous chapter showed how a detailed analysis of concordance lines derived from collocates could be used to identify discourses of homosexuality in a corpus. The method used to identify collocates was based on whether two words appeared near each other within a span of five words. Even if the two words only occurred together once, they were still taken into consideration, as they were viewed as possibly contributing towards a wider picture in terms of discourse prosodies. This method meant that thousands of potential word pairs had to be examined (Figure 5.1 shows only a small part of a much larger table), producing a thorough analysis, but also requiring quite a lot of time. The task could have been reduced somewhat by stipulating a minimum frequency that would need to occur before a pair of words were considered as collocates. Researchers therefore need to decide how thorough they want to be, and some sort of compromise between achieving full coverage and managing time constraints must be made for each project.

However, basing the notion of collocates on how many times two words appear together (with an attendant cut-off point) is only one way of considering collocation. A potential problem with this method is that it can elicit collocates which are simply very frequent words throughout a corpus. For, example, the first column of Table 6.1 shows the ten most frequent collocates of the word *man* in the 100-million-word BNC.[1] As *man* can also be a proper noun (e.g. *Isle of Man*) or a verb (e.g. *to man the lifeboats*)

I only consider cases of *man* as a common noun in this table (although the other grammatical categories of *man* are worthy of commentary from a gender discourse perspective). The collocates in Table 6.1 all belong to closed-class grammatical categories (articles, prepositions, auxiliary verbs, etc.). I have not shown the number of times that these words occur near or next to *man*, but they all occur within the vicinity of *man* at least 3,500 times in the corpus.

Unfortunately, these grammatical words are likely to appear as frequent collocates of many other nouns, so this information generally tells us little about the specific or unique contexts and meanings associated with a word. Other methods of calculating collocation have therefore taken into account the strength of association between two words, for example, by considering the observed number of occurrences of a word pair with its expected number of occurrences.

For example, in Table 6.1, the Mutual Information (MI) measure asks 'how strongly are the words attracted to each other?' (Evert 2009: 1228), yielding collocates that 'are idiosyncratic instances peculiar to [one] corpus' (Clear 1993: 281). The MI measure assigns a score to a pair of words, the higher the score indicating the strength or salience of collocation. As a result, the MI measure tends to produce rather infrequent words as collocates of *man* in the BNC (the words in the column for MI occur with

TABLE 6.1 *Different measures of collocation of* man *(as a common noun) in the BNC, ranked according to highest score.*

Rank by frequency	Mutual information	Log-likelihood	T-score	Z-score
the	Cornerville	a	a	young
a	odd-job	who	who	a
of	Shrestha	young	the	who
to	O'war	old	young	old
and	thin-faced	the	old	tall
who	inhumanity	was	was	inhumanity
was	measureless	woman	with	woman
in	sandy-haired	tall	had	middle-aged
with	born-deaf	dead	his	Utd
that	bobsleigh	with	woman	was

man less than 50 times). The strongest collocate here is *Cornerville* which only occurs 5 times with *man* and is restricted to a single text in the BNC (*Cornerville man* refers to a type of gang member in a text about urban sociology). This is not an especially helpful collocate in telling us about how *man* is typically used.

Another way of considering collocation is to use a hypothesis-testing measure, which tests the null hypothesis that two words appear together no more frequently than we would expect by chance alone, considering their frequency in the corpus and the size of the corpus. Such measures include the LL score, the T-score and the Z-score. Clear (1993: 279–82) notes that while 'MI is a measure of *the strength of association between two words*, measures like the LL score are measures of '*the confidence with which we can claim there is some association*' (original italics), although importantly, these latter measures do not tell us about the strength of collocation.

Looking at Table 6.1 again, the LL method produces much more frequent collocates of *man*, including some of the grammatical words like *the* and *a* which we have already encountered. But it also yields high-frequency nouns and adjectives like *woman*, *young* and *old*. In terms of telling us more about typical contexts relating to *man*, this is perhaps more helpful, although even here, the collocates tend to be of a rather generic nature (quite a few of them are also found in the top ten LL collocates of *woman* also). The T-score (another confidence-based measure) yields similar results to the LL score, giving mainly high-frequency grammatical collocates or high-frequency nouns and adjectives. However, the Z-score measure appears to privilege a much wider range of types of collocates, with some very frequent collocates appearing in its top ten, like *a* and *who*, but also infrequent words like *inhumanity* (in cases like *man's inhumanity to man*) and *Utd* (in the phrase *Man Utd* referring to the football team Manchester United). This collocate actually unearths a mistagging in the BNC as in this case *Man* should have been originally tagged as a proper noun rather than a common noun – serving as another reminder that automatic tagging is not infallible.

An issue with these three confidence-based measures is that they are based on comparing what has actually occurred in a corpus against a model of words occurring in a completely random order across a corpus. However, as noted in Chapter Four, Kilgarriff (2005) is critical of the idea that language data is ever random. Durrant and Doherty (2010: 130–1) make a similar point:

> Grammar, semantics, and real-world occurrences all constrain the construction of real language. It is therefore very common for word pairs to co-occur 'more frequently than random', regardless of specifically collocational relations. Given this, levels of statistical significance are not usually thought to constitute useful cut-off points in identifying collocations. Rather, the statistical tests are used to *rank* word pairs

according to their relative likelihood of being a collocation. (Stubbs 1995: 33; Manning and Schütze 1999: 166)

Within the corpus linguistics literature it is common to find researchers using different measures of collocation, and it would not be surprising if people who are just beginning to use corpus linguistics methods felt unsure about which measure they ought to use. It can also be difficult to decide on how large the span should be (how close together two words have to be before they are considered as candidate collocates) and what the cut-offs are for considering whether a collocate is worth reporting and analysing. Do we just consider a ranking system – for example the top 10 collocates, or do we use some other measure? Hunston (2002: 71–2) reports that anything which has an MI score of 3 or higher is often taken as evidence that two words are collocates, while a T-score of at least 2 is statistically significant. More recently, experiments by Durrant and Doherty (2010) indicate that for 'collocational priming' to occur (whereby we are triggered to think of one word when we encounter another), an MI score of at least 6 or a t-score of at least 7.5 is required. Furthermore, some researchers have only considered a pair of words to be collocates if they score highly on two collocation measures, one which takes into account strength of association, the other which takes into account the confidence with which we can claim an association (e.g. Salama 2011 requires collocates to have an MI score of 3 or more and a T-score of 2 or more).

There are sometimes practical constraints with regard to which measure can be used. For example, WordSmith 5 allows the rank by frequency, MI, MI3, Z-score, T-score, dice coefficient and LL measures to be used when calculating collocation. AntConc 3.2.4 allows rank by frequency, MI and T-score. So the type of software being used to conduct the analysis may limit the type of measure that can be considered. Additionally, real-world time and space constraints may mean that researchers are unable to carry out analyses of all of the collocates that they would like to. Many academic journals require submitted papers to be around 10,000 words in length, which means that the analysis part of a journal article is often only about 4,000–6,000 words. As a result, researchers regularly need to make choices about what to include in their analysis, and so they may sometimes decide to focus on a smaller number of collocates because such collocates enable an interesting analysis or the collocates are especially salient (e.g. scoring very highly on the measure used), or are somehow representative of a larger picture. For example, sticking with the word *man* (common noun) in the BNC, it collocates with 324 words which have an MI score of 3 or higher. Carrying out a full analysis of each word would not only take up a lot of space, but would probably result in repetition as many of the collocates function in similar ways. An initial step could be to group collocates that have related grammatical or semantic properties. For example, a number of the adjectival collocates of *man* reference a certain type of body: *broad-shouldered, stocky, well-built, burly, tubby, portly, plump, muscular, fat, overweight*. These words tend to reference large size (either musculature, frame or weight). Collectively they could be said to endow *man* with a semantic preference for largeness. It is probably not necessary to report on how each one individually is used in connection with *man*, but instead we could give details of the general picture (e.g. are these collocates used positively or negatively, are any of them used in very similar ways or different ways?) We might choose a couple of words, for example *tubby* and *burly* and compare and contrast them, noting which of the other collocates operate in similar ways to either of them. Alternatively, we could choose the most frequent collocate, or the collocate which has the highest MI score from the list for a more detailed analysis.

Another point to bear in mind is that the size of your corpus and the frequency of the word you are interested in are likely to play a role in how many collocates you may have to deal with, which will have subsequent issues for the cut-offs you apply. Tables 6.2 and 6.3 illustrate this point (and it is discussed further in Chapter Seven). Table 6.2 shows the numbers of collocates for a range of different synonyms of *man*, using the MI score and a span of 3 words either side the node word (the node is 'the word or form being investigated' (Stubbs 2001: 29)). Again, as many of these word forms are homonyms (e.g. *guy* can refer to a type of male or can be a proper noun), searches were carried out on the singular common noun form (tagged as NN1 in the BNC). It can be seen that in general, there is

TABLE 6.2 *Number of collocates of* man *and related words in the BNC.*

Word	Frequency in the BNC	Number of collocates (MI > 3)
man	57,589	324
gentleman	5,070	67
guy	2,278	37
fellow	1,573	41
bloke	1,214	19
chap	1,487	31
gent	123	4
swain	11	1

TABLE 6.3 *Number of collocates of* man *in the Brown family.*

Corpus/Corpora	Size in words (approximate)	Number of collocates (MI > 3)
LOB (section A only)	100,000	1
LOB (sections A, B and C only)	200,000	1
LOB (all sections A–R)	1 million	9
LOB + FLOB	2 million	18
LOB + FLOB + Brown	3 million	21
LOB + FLOB + Brown + Frown	4 million	23
LOB + FLOB + Brown, Frown + BE06	5 million	28
LOB + FLOB + Brown + Frown + BE06 + Lancaster 1931	6 million	35

a correlation between frequency and the number of collocates, although the correlation is not perfect (e.g. *fellow* has more collocates than *guy*, despite being less frequent). Words which are quite infrequent in a corpus (occurring less than say, 500 times) might not provide many collocates for an adequate analysis, and it may be better in such cases to simply carry out an analysis of concordance lines or find a larger corpus.

Table 6.3 shows the effect of increasing the corpus size. Here we only consider collocates of *man* (as a common noun) which have an MI of 3 or more. I am using the Brown family of corpora which are reference corpora of British and American published written English from different time periods, each one consisting of approximately one million words of text. As we successively add more texts, the number of collocates of *man* rises.

Additionally, the type of corpus is likely to impact on the number of collocates yielded. If we collect a corpus of newspaper articles and stipulate that each article must contain at least one mention of the word *man*, then this will result in *man* having a relatively high frequency and is likely to yield more collocates of this word. But if we had an equal-sized corpus of newspaper articles about say, insects, then it is likely that we would have fewer instances of *man* to begin with, and so there would be fewer collocates.

There are further ways in which cut-off points can be applied in order to decrease or increase the number of collocates that you can work with. One way could be to alter the span – the window of words either side of the node word. Most software tools are set to a default span, although this can be altered as desired. WordSmith's default is 5 words either side of the node word, while AntConc's default is only 1 word either side. As a rule of thumb, the smaller the span, the fewer collocates that will be produced. Using a small span may be useful if dealing with a very frequent node word and/or an extremely large corpus. A small span is likely to catch collocates which tend to directly modify the node word. So if our node word is a noun, a small span will catch cases like adjectives that occur immediately to the left of the node word (e.g. *burly man*) or verbs which indicate an action carried out by or towards the node word (*man accused*). However, a small span may miss some cases of words which actually do relate to the node word in some way. For example, consider the following sentence from the BNC:

In Vienna there is a man called Schulz, who is a kind of genius.

In this case, we might want to note that the word *genius* is being assigned to a *man*, although as the two words are eight words apart, it is unlikely that the default collocational spans will spot this. On the other hand, there are dangers of making the collocational span too large, as the next BNC example indicates.

We got a dreadful van from a man called Nick the Maltese, down the East End.

It we had set the span to five words either side of the node word, then this example would include *dreadful* as a potential collocate of *man*. However, *dreadful* does not directly modify *man* here, it modifies *van*. We might argue that *dreadful* indirectly modifies *man*, because it modifies something that is owned by the man in question, so there is a kind of 'guilt by association', but if *dreadful* showed up in a list of collocates, we would need to take care to include that the relationship is always one where a *man* is being referred to as dreadful.

Yet another aspect of applying cut-off points is to do with dispersion (see also Chapter Two). If a collocate is reasonably frequent and/or shows a strong relationship with a node word, it conceivably could be because it only occurs in a small number of texts in a corpus and is not especially representative of the way that the node word is used. For example, in the BNC, the words *underground* and *healthy* both co-occur 26 times with *man*. However, this relationship is restricted to only 4 texts in the BNC for *underground*, whereas it occurs across 25 texts for *healthy*. In actuality, 23 out of those 26 collocations of *underground* + *man* only occur in one text and had this text not been included in the corpus, it is much less likely that this collocational pair would have reached our attention. There may be good reasons to consider infrequent and/or poorly dispersed features in a corpus – for example, they may point to a 'minority' representation or discourse in a small number of texts in a corpus and therefore they may be extremely interesting to analyse, but if we are only concerned with what is typical, we may want to impose an additional cut-off point relating to dispersion, requiring a collocate to occur in a certain number or percentage of texts.

Table 6.4 summarizes some of the different decisions that need to be made when deciding what counts as a collocate in corpus research.

With so many different decisions that need to be taken into account, it is hardly surprising that there is a lack of consistency across corpus linguistics research with regard to the 'best' or even 'usual' ways of calculating collocation. Because each piece of corpus research is different (e.g. using different-sized corpora and examining words of different frequencies), it is difficult to reach a consensus about which criteria to use. Instead, I would advise that researchers aim for transparency and consistency (at least within a particular piece of research). Be clear about the decisions that you took with regard to identifying collocates (so that your research could be replicated if someone had access to the corpus you used), and attempt to provide justifications where you can, for example, by explaining what a 'manageable' number of collocates would be for your own research, based on practical considerations. If you are following somebody else's criteria,

TABLE 6.4 *Decisions regarding identifying collocates.*

Decision	Meaning
The span	How many words either side of the node word do you consider?
Method of calculation	Do you use a strength-based measure like mutual information, a confidence-based measure like log-likelihood, a simple count of word co-occurrence or multiple measures?
Score vs ranking?	Will you use a score-based criteria (such as an MI score of 3 or more) or a ranked criteria (such as the 20 collocates that have the highest MI scores?)
Cut-off point	How high must a measure of collocation be before you consider a pair to be a collocate (e.g. if you are using MI then will you take 3 or some other number as the cut-off?)
Minimum frequency	Do you specify that a collocational pair needs to occur a certain number of times before you will consider them?
Dispersion	Do you specify that a collocational pair needs to occur in a certain number or proportion of texts in a corpus before it can be considered?

then make this clear. Additionally, once you have reached a set of decisions, stick with them for that piece of research. If you say you are using MI > 3, then do not start analysing collocates of MI < 3 or switching to LL halfway through your analysis. It is also important to know when it is appropriate to make statements like 'these two words are strong collocates'. If you are using a confidence-based measure like LL, then this wording is misleading as LL does not tell us about strength. Finally, it is always a good idea to be transparent about all of the collocates that were found, even if you do not go on to analyse them all. Putting full lists of collocates in tables or making use of Appendices will at least help to avoid the criticism that certain aspects of your analysis have been hidden away.

Studies of collocation and gender

Before discussing a case study I carried out to show how collocates can help to reveal gendered discourses (referred to in Chapter One), it is useful to survey other research in this field, which has influenced the approach I take below.

First, Pearce (2008) examined collocates of the lemmas MAN and WOMAN in the BNC, using the interface Sketch Engine (described in more detail below) which allows collocates to be analysed via the grammatical relationships that they form with words. MAN was found to be more strongly associated as the grammatical agent or 'doer' of various physical action verbs like *chase*, *climb*, *jump*, *leap*, *march*, *haul*, *race* and *stomp*. Other verbs positioning men as the subject such as *conquer*, *dominate*, *lead*, *mastermind* also indicated male dominance. However, men were both the subject and object of many physical violence verbs, and were also often positioned as criminals, being the object of verbs like *accuse*, *arrest*, *convict*, *hang* and *jail*, as well as succumbing to seduction: *bewitch*, *charm*, *enthrall*, *entice* and *flatter*. The adjectival collocates confirmed the representations of men as physically and socially dominant: males were more likely to be *able-bodied*, *big*, *broad-shouldered*, *stocky*, *tall*, *beefy* and *bull-necked* as well as *distinguished*, *grand*, *influential*, *leading* and *rich*. On the other hand, WOMAN was the subject of emotionally intemperate verbs like *berate*, *nag* and *wail*, whereas they were the object of sexual verbs like *bed*, *date*, *ravish*, *sexualize* and *shag*. Women were more likely to be the object of a set of verbs which suggested the exercise of power by others: *assist*, *compensate*, *direct*, *immunize*, *interpret*, *monitor*, *provide*, *regulate*. Also, women were more likely to be assigned adjectives which signalled their marital or reproductive status: *childless*, *fertile*, *married*, *lone*, *widowed*, *barren*, *menopausal*, *remarried*, etc. Additionally, physical attractiveness adjectives tended to collocate with women: *pretty*, *attractive*, *beautiful, pleasant-looking*, as did adjectives which suggest promiscuity: *blowsy, fallen, promiscuous, scarlet*. Overall, Pearce's research suggests that in the BNC, men and women are often stereotyped, with men more likely to be represented as powerful, large and involved in violence while women are sexualized and viewed in terms of their relationships to men or ability to have children.

A novel approach was taken by Herdağdelen and Baroni (2011), who rather than focusing on a single-gendered pair of terms, instead used a heuristic to identify all references to male or female gender in two corpora, one consisting of 34 million tweets (short messages) from the online social networking site Twitter, while the other was the 2 billion token ukWaC corpus consisting of language data from websites that end in the .uk domain, collected between 2005 and 2007. The researchers identified personal pronouns and lists of male and female names, and then identified statistically significant verb phrases which characteristically co-occurred with references to males and females in the two corpora. Therefore verb phrases rather than single words counted as the collocates. The researchers also identified a third set of verb phrases which were classed as 'neutral', not being especially associated with either males or females exclusively. The two corpora did not show a single verb phrase in common with each other for the top ten sets of most gendered actions for males and females, indicating that different reference corpora have the potential to elicit very different results. Actions more frequently linked to females in the Twitter corpus included reference to emotions or desires: *feel like, want go, feel good, make smile, make cry*, while male-linked actions on Twitter seemed to be profit-oriented: *make money, want make money, earn money*. The analysis of the ukWaC corpus did not show such distinctions, with females instead represented as having children: *give birth, become pregnant* while males were represented as taking positions of power: *take over, become king, raise up*. Neutral verb phrases included food-related actions in Twitter: *buy cheese, chew food*, and work-related actions in ukWaC: *build nuclear weapon, build product, sell magazine, teach, read, write*.

Macalister (2011) examined writing in a New Zealand publication for children that occurred across four time periods over the twentieth century, finding that *girl** was consistently more frequently pre-modified than *boy**, although he uncovered no evidence that there was an evaluative difference in these adjectives. Despite the fact that references to girls gradually became more frequent over time, and girls were more likely to be mentioned independently rather than co-occurring with boys, during all the time periods examined, boys were more likely to be represented as 'doing' things than girls. Taylor (2013) also examined collocates of *boy* and *girl*, although she used three corpora containing British broadsheet newspapers, taken from 1993, 2005 and 2010. Taylor was particularly concerned with addressing claims that corpus linguists over-focus on difference, so she tried various methods of identifying similarity. For example, she focused on c-collocates, or collocates which consistently occurred with *boy* or *girl* across all three of the corpora. She then categorized similar c-collocates into groups (such as school, violence, age, clothing, etc.) and identified c-collocates that were shared between *boy* and *girl* as well as those which were exclusive to either *boy* or *girl*. While there were numerous c-collocates which were shared between *boy* and *girl* (particularly in categories like age, violence and school), other categories suggested differences in representation: girls collocated with the verb *dance* while boys collocated with *run*, *swim* and *throw*. In a second method, Taylor used the 'theasaurus' function of the tool Sketch Engine in order to identify words which behave collocationally in similar ways to other words (see Rychly and Kilgarriff 2007). While *boy* and *girl* were found to be the most similar to each other in terms of shared collocates during all three time periods examined, Taylor noted that the word *woman* was found to behave in a similar way collocationally speaking to *girl*, although the equivalent was not true for *boy*, with *man* not appearing to be as close in meaning to *boy*, in terms of similar collocational patterns. This finding is indicative of the fact that *girl* and *woman* can often be synonymous while *boy* and *man* seem to be conceived as separate identities, although this distinction appeared to be waning in the 2010 corpus, with more examples of *boy* being used to refer to adults.

Finally, Caldas-Coulthard and Moon (2010) examined a sub-section of news articles in the Bank of English corpus, focusing on collocates of four terms: *man*, *woman*, *boy* and *girl*. They used van Leeuwen's (1996) categorization scheme as a way of classifying collocates. This scheme is based on three major categories: functionalization – defining people's identities in terms of activity or something they do, identification – defining people in terms of what they are more or less permanently or unavoidably are, and appraisment, which involves general evaluative words and affectives. In their analysis they made a distinction between a group of broadsheet newspapers and a single tabloid, *The Sun*, reflecting a hard/soft news distinction. Their results were congruent with the findings of the other researchers described above, and they conclude: 'Male categorization, especially in terms of power, "provide newspapers with the modes of discourse which already encode the attitudes of a powerful elite" (Fowler, 1991: 23). And women . . . are far from being in powerful positions, since they are constantly judged in terms of social and aesthetic esteem, especially, but not exclusively, in the tabloid press. While men are evaluated in terms of their function and status in society, a woman is evaluated additionally in terms of her appearance and sexuality – even more so in the case of a young woman, whereas young men are evaluated in terms of their behaviour' (Caldas-Coulthard and Moon (2010: 124).

Analysis of BOY and GIRL

For the remaining part of this chapter, in order to demonstrate more explicitly some of the ways that collocates can be analysed, following Macalister (2011) and Taylor (2013) I compare collocates of the lemmas BOY and GIRL using the online corpus analysis tool Sketch Engine[2] (Kilgarriff et al. 2004). Sketch Engine contains numerous large preloaded reference corpora in various languages although it allows users to upload their own corpora if they desire. Like Herdağdelen and Baroni (2011), for the purposes of this study, I am using one of Sketch Engine's preloaded corpora, the ukWaC British English web corpus (Ferraresi et al. 2008). As noted above, this is a corpus of online material taken from the web pages that end in the .uk domain in 2007. It contains more than 2 billion tokens and has been part of speech tagged and lemmatized, allowing for a more sophisticated analysis of collocates as will be shown below.

Finally, similar to Pearce (2008), I used Sketch Engine to generate Word Sketches of particular nouns, verbs and adjectives (or their lemmas). A Word Sketch is essentially a corpus-based summary of a word's grammatical and collocational behaviour. The Sketch presents all of the collocates of a word but also groups them into grammatical relationships. For example, imagine that we are interested in the collocates of the node *cat*. This word might collocate with the following words *purr, stroke, wild, flap, dog* and *bowl*. However, each of these words typically occurs in a specific relationship to *cat* indicating different grammatical relationships as shown in Table 6.5.

It is, of course, possible to work out these grammatical relationships between collocates if we examine concordance lines by hand. However,

TABLE 6.5 *Grammatical relationships between collocates.*

Collocate	Grammatical relationship to cat	Example
purr	subject of	The cat purred.
stroke	object of	Mary stroked the cat.
wild	modifier	It was a wild cat.
flap	modifies	It went through the cat flap.
dog	and/or	I like cats and dogs.
bowl	possessed	Clean the cat's bowl.

having this process automated saves time and also ensures that certain patterns are not missed by human researchers, particularly in cases where a word may have hundreds of collocates and each collocate may require the examination of hundreds of concordance lines.

Sketch Engine also allows Word Sketches of two words to be compared together, so that we can see which sorts of grammatical patterns they have in common, those which occur more often with one word and those which are completely unique to one word. This function, called SketchDiff, is what I will be using in this analysis of this chapter. I will consider a SketchDiff of the lemmas BOY and GIRL in order to obtain an impression of how these two terms are consistently positioned grammatically in a large contemporary corpus.

SketchDiff uses the logDice statistic in order to calculate collocation. This is based on research by Curran (2004) who carried out an extensive evaluation of different methods of collocation and concluded that logDice was best. I used Sketch Engine's default range for identifying collocates (5 words either side of the node). Sketch Engine grouped collocates of BOY and/or GIRL into 19 different grammatical relationships, using colour codes to show which collocates were exclusively or mostly associated with one lemma or the other. Table 6.6 shows a small part of the output from Sketch Engine, which only gives two of the grammatical relationships, those for verb collocates which position BOY/GIRL as either subject or object. The words in dark grey (towards the top of the table) have a higher logDice score for GIRL while those in light grey (towards the bottom of the table) have a higher logDice score for BOY. Additionally, words in bold print have a difference in logDice score of 2 or higher, suggesting that a particular collocational relationship is favoured by either GIRL or BOY much more than the other.

Table 6.6 indicates some of the different (and similar) ways that boys and girls are positioned by verbs in a general corpus. For example, girls appear to be more likely the subject and object of the verbs SCREAM, MARRY and DANCE. Analysis of concordances, however, shows that some of the grammatical relationships are the result of mistagging. For example, terms like *screaming girls* and *dancing girls* have generally been incorrectly categorized as cases where GIRL is the object of the verbs SCREAM and DANCE. In fact these should either be cases where girls are modified by adjectives. It is still therefore worth examining concordances of the different collocational relationships in order to check that the automated categorization is correct. Other miscategorizations are BOY as the subject of the verb SCOUT (this is actually due to the noun phrase *boy scouts*) and BOY as the object of the verb CRY (this is due to the phrase *crying boys*).

Most of the other verbs in Table 6.6 are less problematic. Girls appear more likely to be shown as expressing certain emotions, feelings or cognitive states (SMILE, WANT, SUFFER, LOVE, DECIDE) while boys are represented as being the subjects of physical actions or states (GROW, PLAY, FALL, DIE).

TABLE 6.6 *Verb (lemma) collocates which position BOY/GIRL as either subject or object.*

subject_of	F BOY	F GIRL	LogDice BOY	LogDice GIRL	object_of	F BOY	F GIRL	LogDice BOY	LogDice GIRL
outperform	9	49	2.8	5.2	scream	0	62	0.0	5.4
dance	18	87	3.2	5.4	dance	0	71	0.0	5.3
marry	12	54	2.4	4.5	marry	31	442	3.9	7.7
scream	23	82	3.8	5.6	rape	15	84	3.8	6.2
wear	168	340	5.0	6.0	meet	241	721	4.0	5.6
smile	24	43	3.8	4.6	abduct	14	40	3.8	5.2
want	260	419	4.2	4.8	impress	36	98	4.0	5.4
suffer	79	124	3.8	4.5	murder	51	135	5.3	6.6
love	185	268	5.2	5.7	kiss	49	124	5.3	6.6
decide	83	120	4.2	4.7	seduce	15	38	3.8	5.0
sit	180	249	4.9	5.4	chase	34	69	4.5	5.4
walk	133	181	4.5	4.9	kidnap	29	51	4.8	5.5
attend	160	201	4.3	4.7	call	398	622	4.5	5.2
live	245	294	4.3	4.6	dress	88	138	5.3	5.9
jump	52	61	4.6	4.8	age	587	904	7.2	7.8
sing	116	119	5.2	5.2	assault	45	69	5.3	5.8
dream	43	41	4.7	4.6	educate	95	118	5.6	5.8
tend	88	82	4.8	4.7	rescue	65	68	5.5	5.5
reply	60	53	5.0	4.8	teach	217	207	5.1	5.0
die	243	195	5.5	5.2	kill	286	239	5.9	5.6
fall	285	214	5.3	4.8	name	498	416	6.9	6.6
cry	90	60	5.5	4.9	cry	60	51	5.1	4.8
play	654	415	5.1	4.5	bear	327	201	5.9	5.2
grow	278	169	4.7	4.0	beat	111	52	5.3	4.1
scout	33	0	4.7	0.0	outperform	63	13	5.9	3.5

That is not to say that girls are never represented as carrying out physical actions – they are (slightly) more likely to SIT, WALK and JUMP.

However, girls are more often represented as being victims in a range of different ways (they are more likely than boys to be the object of the verbs RAPE, ABDUCT, MURDER, ASSAULT, SEDUCE and KIDNAP) while boys are more often described as being killed, but generally they do not seem to be as strongly associated with as many verbs which position them as victims and are not the objects of sexual or sexual violence verbs. Instead they are *named* and *taught*, yet also described as 'losing', for example they are *beaten* and *outperformed* (both cases often refer to situations where they are seen as academically inferior to girls). BEAT is a somewhat ambiguous verb because sometimes it refers to cases like 'girls beat boys at reading' but other cases refer to violence: 'The schoolmaster was beating the boys with his fists.' A closer look at the 111 concordance lines where BEAT collocates with BOY revealed that 41 cases (37%) referred to boys being physically beaten, while of the 52 cases of girls being the object of BEAT, 31 of them (60%) refer to violence. This indicates that even though BEAT is more strongly associated with boys, when we look more closely at the various meanings of the word it still indicates that girls are more likely to be associated as victims of physical violence.

As well as the verbs which position girls as objects of violence, there is also another pattern which associates them with clothing. GIRL is the subject of WEAR and the object of DRESS. This occurs in the following sorts of contexts:

Bizzy Lizzy was a little girl who wore a blue dress with a magic flower attached.

These girls are dressed in their festival finery as part of the London celebrations.

It appears then, that girls are more likely than boys to be described in terms of what they are wearing.

An optional way of taking this analysis of verbs a stage further would be to subject the verb collocational patterns to a transitivity process analysis (Halliday 1994), based on categorizing the collocates in terms of material, mental, relational, behavioural, verbal and existential processes. This might be a way of highlighting patterns more clearly – for example, girls may tend to be the subjects of mental processes (LOVE, DECIDE) and the objects of material processes (RAPE, KIDNAP).

Therefore, the analysis of collocates allows us to identify particular contexts which seem to be more applicable to one sex than the other. So far we have only considered 2 out of the 19 grammatical relationships, yet if we start to look at the others, we can see more evidence of different types of grammatical collocates which contribute to the patterns that we have already identified. For example, if we look at collocates which are used as adjectival modifiers of GIRL, we find mental state or feeling words like *jealous*, *shy*, *fond*, *anxious*, *crazy*, *unhappy*, *eager*, *desperate* and *interested*. Such words are congruent with the emotional expression verbs like SMILE. Additionally, we find more evidence of the 'victim' representation of GIRL, in patterns like 'the victim was a young girl', 'girl is the 7th victim' and 'the girl's disappearance'. Gradually, we can start to group together similar constructions as contributing towards particular representations. Tables 6.7 and 6.8 show these grouped representations for GIRL and BOY respectively.

Comparing the two tables, there appear to be fewer representations of BOY as opposed to GIRL. As others have noticed, this is likely to be due to GIRL tending to have a wider meaning in that it can often refer to adult females, whereas BOY seems to refer more often to male children. This semantic extension of GIRL is shown by some of its collocational patterns in Table 6.7. For example, a phrase like *girls and blokes* suggests equivalence between the two groups and this is borne out when concordance lines are examined, for example:

It is quite a swanky bar and restaurant, and has all individual toilets with own basins, for blokes and girls.

Additionally, the references to girls in various service occupations (*girl behind the bar*) or in the context of modelling (*girl on the cover*) also tend to refer to young adult women rather than female children. This does not tend to be the case with the jobs associated with BOY such as *errand boy* (which usually refers literally to a male child or at least a teenager). It is also worth noting how some representations can be further grouped together. For example, the category 'Girl as victim' could be linked to the category 'Girl as servile/imprisoned' as both these categories suggest representations that position girls both passively and negatively. Additionally, the category 'Girl as unstable' could be seen as (a more negative) extension of the category 'Girl as emotionally expressive'. Two other related categories that occur across the two tables are 'Girl as effeminate man' (*big girls blouse*) and 'Boy as mothered' (*mother's boy*). Both appear to occur mainly in negative contexts and tend to be used to refer to adult males who are perceived as weak or lacking in some way, as the following two examples from the corpus illustrate:

Mauro Cameronesi should win the accolade of the biggest girls blouse in the World Cup, every time he went down he looked at the ref before clutching some part of his body in apparent agony.

TABLE 6.7 *Representations of* GIRL.

	Examples of collocate in grammatical pattern
Girl as adult female	girl and blokes, girls and guys, girl in her twenties
Girl as romantic	girls love, girls marry, girl was married, girl of my dreams, girl on his arm
Girl as victim	girls suffer, vulnerable girl, girl was raped, girl was a victim of, victim was a girl, girl's disappearance
Girl as emotionally expressive	girls smile, girls scream, unhappy girl, screaming girls, girl with a passion for, girl with a smile
Girl as unstable	crazy girl, anxious girl, jealous girl
Focus on girls' clothing	girls wear, girls dress, girls handbag, girl in a t-shirt, girl in (a) costume/skirt/dress/frock/bikini/pants, girl with an earring
Focus on girls' body	overweight girl, blonde girl, girl of exquisite beauty, girl with luscious lips, girl with anorexia, girl with blond curls, girl with pigtails
Girl with a condition	girl in a wheelchair, girl with epilepsy
Girl as sexualized	naked girl, girls virginity, girl for sex, girl was raped
Girls as doing well	girls outperform boys, girl with talent, girls on top
Girl not doing well	girl in maths
Girl as entertainer	girls dance, dancing girls, girl singer, girls dancing
Girl as pregnant	pregnant girl
Girl as servile/imprisoned	servant girl, slave girl, girl in prison
Girl in education	girls schoolroom, girl boarder, girl enrolment, girls to school, girls on its roll
Girl as model	girl on the front of (a magazine), girl on the cover
Girl in service job	girl on the desk, girl on the counter, girl behind the bar, girl behind the counter
Literature for girls	girls school stories, girls comic
Active girl	girl on a mission, girl on the go
Girl as effeminate male	big girls blouse

TABLE 6.8 *Representations of* BOY.

	Examples of collocate in grammatical pattern
Boy as bad/punished	naughty boy, bad boy, bad boy antics, whipping boy
Boys as academically poor	girls outperformed boys, girls beat boys, stupid boy, boy's underachievement, raising boy's achievement, boy at the back, girls beat boys at reading
Boy as good	golden boy, boy wonder, boy genius, boys were a credit
Boy as part of an organization	boy's brigade, boy scout
Boy as entry-level job	boy wizard, shepherd boy, errand boy, boy seaman, grocer's boy, butchers boy, gardener's boy, farmer's boy, ship's boy, baker's boy
Boy as mothered	mama's boy, mummy's boy, mother's boy
Focus on boy's clothing	boy in shorts, boy in a shirt, boy in white
Boy singer	boy soprano, boy treble
Boy at play	boys at play, boys toys
Boy with a condition	boy with autism, boys are prone to testicular torsion

Moss is a borderline-autistic mother's boy who'd rather send an email to summon the fire brigade than pick up a phone to speak to another human being.

Yet there are no equivalent cases in either of the tables where females are negatively compared to males. Cases of *daddy's girl* tend not to be as negative, for example

She adored her mother but, 'I was always a daddy's girl'. He was so wonderful, supportive, patient.

At this point we may want to consider whether the collocational patterns we have identified and grouped together can be inserted into an overarching representational framework. I have already suggested that verb collocates could be subjected to a transitivity process analysis. Additionally, I described above how Caldas-Coulthard and Moon (2010) implemented van Leeuwen's (1996) 'representation of social actors' framework in their collocational analysis. Appplying van Leeuwen's framework in this study, we could consider whether any of the collocates of BOY or GIRL result in aggregation (e.g. *most girls*), functionalization (*butchers boy*), physical identification (*blonde girl*) or individuation (*a boy called Tom*) and what functions do such representations achieve?

Another way of applying an existing framework to the collocates is to take Sunderland's 'gender discourses' approach (2004), and consider whether any of the collocational patterns can be viewed as constituting 'linguistic traces' of discourses, either discourses that others have already identified, or as-yet unnamed discourses. Some of the labels in Tables 6.7 and 6.8 that I have referred to as 'representations' could be characterized as discourses in themselves, for example 'Girl as victim'. With others, we may want to reword some of the representations as discourses, based on further grouping. For example, the representations 'Girls as doing well' and 'Boys as academically poor' could both be seen as contributing towards a 'poor boys' discourse identified by Sunderland (2004: 43). Alternatively, we could view the representations from a socio-cognitive perspective, and consider how they relate to mental representations or schemas (van Dijk 2008).

On the other hand, we may feel that the collocations would not benefit from being linked to existing categorization schemes or that such schemes would not be appropriate for the words under analysis. We should not feel compelled to engage with such schemes if we feel that they do not shed new light on our data or help us to draw out patterns that otherwise would go unnoticed. In any case, having identified various representations (or discourses or schema), some people may feel that the analysis is complete. For others, particularly those engaged in more political forms of research, this point is likely to act as a precursor to more explanatory and evaluative stages of analysis, as described below.

For example, some categories appear to be oppositional to each other, such as 'Boy as Bad', 'Boy as Good', and it seems that the quality of behaviour is considered to be especially noteworthy of boys, while this is something which does not tend to get remarked upon as much for girls. As well as simply noting how boys or girls have been represented in the corpus, a further stage of analysis involves trying to explain why the categories exist, and what they tell us about how society constructs gender. So *why* are boys (and not girls) described as either naughty or good? A potential way of trying to answer this question is to look closely at concordance lines (see Table 6.9) which shows a sample of references to badly behaved boys in the ukWaC. Here lines 1–3 describe boys who engage in 'naughty' behaviour while line 4 is from a writer who claims that while the boys in question have been characterized as naughty, their behaviour can be explained because they don't understand that what they do is wrong. The final line also attempts to explain naughtiness by attributing it to an emotional problem.

Table 6.10 shows concordance lines of cases where boys are described as being *a credit*, which is used to refer to boys whose behaviour is seen as

TABLE 6.9 *Naughty boys.*

The procession marched back to the village laughing and jeering at the farmer and his wife, who had pretended to be so rich; and some of the *boys were naughty* enough to throw stones at the house from the top of the hill.
It was about a *boy who was naughty*. He was chasing all the girls and trying to pull their pigtails.
I found a nasty looking cane in the teachers desk. It was well preserved but I could still see that a lot of *boys were naughty* at school.
The local people took a long time to understand that my *boys were not naughty* but don't understand that what they do is wrong.
I reckon that most *boys who are naughty* have an emotional problem and they just cover it up with bad behaviour.

TABLE 6.10 *Boys who are a credit.*

The *boys were a credit* to them in defeat, shook hands with their opponents and saved the tears and the disappointment for the dressing room.
The *boys were a credit* to the school at all times. They played and trained with a real enthusiasm and no lack of skill.
All the *boys were a credit* to Sussex and conducted themselves superbly on and off the pitch.
The dress of the *boys was a credit* to Parents and Staff. We can be proud of our School of 760 boys and 47 Staff.
The *boys certainly were a credit* last week, making our visitors feel very welcome.

good. These tend to be cases where boys are praised for good sportsmanship (lines 1–3) or have done well in an educational setting (lines 4–5).

Do any of the concordance lines explain why the corpus data indicates that there is more focus on good or bad boys' behaviour as opposed to girls? When boys are naughty it appears that there are sometimes attempts to excuse or explain it, and when they behave well, this is commended. The fact that the good behaviour relates to sporting contexts is of interest, suggesting that boys who engage in stereotypically gendered behaviour (e.g. playing sports) will be praised.

Caldas-Coulthard and Moon (2010), in their analysis of newspaper articles, found a somewhat different picture around the word *naughty*, noting that it actually collocated with both *boy* and *girl*, although it appears to have different functions for each. When it collocates with *girl* it tended to be used to refer euphemistically to refer to sexual behaviour, thus reinforcing a 'females as sexualised' gendered discourse. Again, this indicates that different corpora may produce different results. The pairing of *naughty* and *girl* for sexual reasons also reveals something about British newspaper discourse as well as gendered discourse.

Critical discourse analysts would encourage researchers to try to consider context in as many ways as possible in attempting to explain findings. One level of context we might want to address is concerned with methods of production and reception of the texts involved. When using the ukWaC in Sketch Engine, the concordance lines also give the website addresses of each source, so it is possible to identify or view the original pages that citations from the corpus come from. A look at the sources of the concordance lines in Table 6.10 reveals that they mainly come from the websites of educational establishments. Such websites positively represent their pupils and are therefore likely to contribute towards an overall positive representation of their institutions, perhaps encouraging prospective parents to send their children there and also furthering a marketing discourse within the British educational system where schools must engage in self-promotional practices in order to compete for pupils. A further interpretation is that these websites may act as a form of social regulation for existing pupils, imparting information about preferred behaviours as well as encouraging them.

Yet the analysis of concordance lines does not fully explain why people seem to comment on boys' behaviour more, so we may need to move beyond the texts themselves and consider the social context that the texts appear in. Perhaps these texts tell a 'truth' in that boys' behaviour is more likely to be unruly than that of girls, so the corpus reflects a 'reality', for example we write about badly behaved boys more than badly behaved girls because we encounter more of those types of boys than girls in real life. This is also likely to be influenced by society's perception of what counts as bad behaviour, for example throwing stones at someone might be seen as more noteworthy and problematic than other forms of misbehaviour. Conversely, we might comment on *good* behaviour in boys because it is seen as relatively unusual, or we want to encourage boys to behave well because there is more of an expectation that they will hold positions of power later in life. People may view boys as more likely to cause greater damage and harm than girls when they become adults, if their behaviour is not checked when they are younger. Conversely, girls' behaviour may be viewed as less extreme so less worthy of discussion and explicit evaluation.

Without referring to other sorts of research, it is difficult to know if the corpus reflects reality. In order to pursue this avenue further, I carried out internet searches to find figures relating to offences committed by boys and girls. In 2006–7 (during the same period reflected in the corpus) British boys aged between 10 and 17 were recorded as committing 295,000 offences which led to police or court action, whereas girls committed only 59,000 such offences.[3] While the corpus may therefore *reflect* the 'reality' that boys are indeed 'naughtier' than girls, it could also help to *construct* such a reality. If we expect boys to engage in wrong-doing, then they are more likely to be subjected to greater regulation and observation (e.g. being stopped and searched by police), which may lead to more of that sort of behaviour being identified. Thus another potential result of categorizing boys as naughty (or not naughty) is that everyone, boys included, may come to think of them in such terms.

Additionally, we may be more inclined to think of boys in terms of being active – for someone to be naughty or good they have to be *doing* something, and therefore such constructions contribute to an overall picture of boys as active, and conversely, girls as less active, or more likely to be acted upon, a finding which echoes Macalister's (2011) work discussed above.

Referring back to Table 6.6, it is notable that girls tend to have a larger set of words which evaluate them in terms of what they are wearing or what certain parts of their body look like, and that when girls are doing things, they are likely to be expressing emotions or entertaining others by singing or dancing. Such constructions echo Berger's quote: 'according to usage and conventions which are at last being questioned but have by no means been overcome – *men act* and *women appear.* Men look at women. Women watch themselves being looked at' (Berger 1972, 45, 47). Berger did not have access to corpus data when he made these comments, although it is remarkable how even 35 years later, an analysis based on 2 billion tokens of language data indicates that his observations (still) hold true, at least for boys and girls, indicating that the process of gender differentiation starts early.

In the final stages of analysis, we may want to critique our findings in terms of whether the patterns we have found are empowering or equalizing. This would particularly be the case if we were taking a critical discourse analysis perspective, where we would want to critically engage with our research in order to instigate social change. Such a critical perspective would require us to signify commitment to a set of values which might be based on political, moral, ethical or religious ideals. The nature and focus of such values may differ from analyst to analyst and are also likely to be culturally dependent to some extent. For example, some analysts may be committed to the belief that personal choice is good and therefore everyone should be as free as possible to choose from a wide variety of possibilities with regard to say, the sort of life they lead, the job they do, the person they love and the way they dress (within limits, e.g. their choices ought not harm others). Such analysts would be interested in highlighting restrictive or exclusive representations (e.g. if girls are not described as physically active or boys are not seen as emotional). A related commitment could be to the concept of equality, although this could take different forms, for example if we are concerned that there are so many depictions of females as sexualized, should we be less concerned if there are just as many representations of males as sexualized? In some cultures, there is a move towards seeing males and females as equally able to perform the same tasks and changes in language may reflect this (e.g. the move from *fireman* to *fire fighter*). Others may have the view that men and women are fundamentally different, and therefore they should be treated or represented differently, and that such differences should be celebrated as long as everyone is treated with respect (a 'different but equal' perspective). Equal therefore does not always mean 'identical' for everyone. Another perspective could be to focus on empowering or disempowering representations, for example are girls described as decision-makers or victims?

Having attempted to explain and evaluate the findings from the analysis, a final stage may be to make suggestions to engender societal change. For example, in the concluding part of my analysis of adjectival forms of male and female nouns in the Brown family of corpora (Baker 2010: 146), I noted the existence of generic terms like *prehistoric man* in recent texts should be curbed as a practice because they erase women. Additionally, I pointed out that the lack of terms like *great woman* and *influential woman* in recent texts suggests that more efforts could be made by people to write about women in these more positive ways. However, there is a danger in suggesting that societies make changes and particularly, attempts by 'expert linguists' or academic social commentators to influence language, even if well-intentioned, can result in a backlash. Many people who belong to scientific 'communities of experts' tend to encounter criticism mainly from within that community only, because non-experts usually do not have enough experience to authoritatively comment on subjects like animal husbandry, aviation or molecular science. However, the social sciences tend to attract debate from a wider range of people. For linguistics, as everybody uses language, suggestions that certain terms should or should not be used could be seen as patronizing, overly authoritative or in conflict with other people's views. For example, in the 1980s, proposals that everyday language use should be altered to make it more inclusive were negatively characterized as 'political correctness' particularly in the conservative media (see Cameron 1995). Some researchers may therefore want to refrain from making weighty pronouncements and instead simply present their research findings and hope that others are inspired to change. Another strategy could be to lead from example, by making changes to one's own language. My article on the Brown family found some evidence that people were more likely to stop using a word or term that had been discredited but found it more difficult to start using a new term, particularly if the new term was a completely new invented word and/or was relatively difficult to say and/or write (such as *Ms* or *he/she*).

As I outlined in the first paragraphs of this book, attempts to disseminate research findings on language and gender to an audience beyond that of academics who are already interested in the topic can sometimes feel like an uphill struggle. Popular ideas about gender have tended towards the 'gender differences' paradigm (e.g. Tannen 1990) and other perspectives may be overlooked, criticized or misrepresented in the media, particularly in outlets which specifically have the aim of maintaining the status quo. However, I believe that academics have a duty to share their findings with wider audiences in a way which is accessible and devoid of jargon (which we can sometimes over-use). A good example of a piece of successful scholarly gender and language research aimed at the public is Deborah Cameron's *The Myth of Mars and Venus* (2007). However, the extent to which our research remains purely descriptive or goes a stage further to involve some form of prescriptivism is always down to individual choice.

Conclusion

In my own experience, collocational research tends to work extremely well on very large corpora consisting of millions or even billions of words. In such cases there may be thousands of citations of the words or phrases to be analysed and an examination of collocates will enable researchers to focus on the typical and salient patterns without needing to wade through seemingly endless concordance lines. With smaller corpora, unless the word or phrase is already extremely frequent, collocates may be fewer and less interesting to investigate. The appearance of tools like Sketch Engine, which are able to incorporate an analysis of grammatical relations when presenting collocates will enable more fine-grained research to be carried out in future, although it should be borne in mind that the underlying grammatical tagging may not always be accurate, so collocational relationships should always be checked via concordance line analyses. Additionally, with the availability of a wider range of reference corpora such as ukWaC and corpora consisting of newer forms of texts such as tweets, this chapter has shown that despite the fact that the way we create texts has changed, the gendered discourses that we reference through them can often be much slower to alter. An over-arching theme which emerged through engaging with the research mentioned in this chapter, and my own study, was to do with an often taken-for-granted privilege which males in society seem to enjoy.

CHAPTER SEVEN

Triangulating methods: What can personal ads on Craigslist reveal about gender?

Introduction

In this final analysis chapter I wish to bring together a number of themes taken from the earlier parts of the book in order to investigate the value of triangulation of methods in Corpus Linguistics. The term *triangulation* is originally from land surveying, meaning that a better view is obtained from looking at phenomena from two or more directions. In the social sciences it involves approaching analysis from a number of different perspectives, each which are intended to shed light on a different aspect of the data. Cohen and Manion (2000: 254) say that triangulation is an 'attempt to map out, or explain more fully, the richness and complexity of human behavior by studying it from more than one standpoint' while Altrichter et al. (2008: 147) argue that this approach 'gives a more detailed and balanced picture of the situation'. Denzin (2006) describes how triangulation can be carried out in different ways, such as using multiple analysts, data sets, theoretical standpoints or methods. For the purposes of this chapter, I will focus on multiple methods. By carrying out different types of corpus analysis on the same data, it will be easier to compare and contrast various techniques in order to obtain a better idea of the pros and cons associated with each. This chapter therefore ought to serve as an indicator of what various corpus linguistics techniques are capable of and which ones might be most appropriate for your research.

Additionally, I wish to use this chapter in order to exemplify some issues that arise when researchers want to work with their own corpus data, which can mean having to build a corpus from scratch. In previous chapters I have relied on 'ready-made' corpora like the BNC, MICASE, COHA and ukWAC, all which were integrated into online searchable interfaces, meaning that little data preparation work was required. In Chapter Five I described the compilation of a corpus of newspaper articles, although this was fairly easy to build because it involved entering a query term into a searchable database which elicited relevant newspaper articles. Not every corpus building project is as straightforward, and in the early part of this chapter I will outline a small corpus building project which involved a few more challenges before analysis could commence.

In keeping with letting this last analysis chapter revisit themes from earlier in the book, I tried to think carefully about the type of corpus that I wanted to build. Within this book I have made a key distinction between studies of language use (e.g. the language of men), and studies of language representation (e.g. language about men), so in this chapter I wish to blur this distinction, or at least indicate that it is not clear-cut. We are all simultaneously language users and involved in representation in various ways. Therefore, I have chosen to examine men's personal adverts, which reflect a form of usage (the corpus contains language produced by men – or at least by people claiming to be men), so it has the potential to tell us something about 'men's language', but the advertisers are also constructing themselves and others (the person they would like, or in some cases, would *not* like to meet), and in order to do so they may draw on gendered discourses, perhaps relating to ideas about what constitutes an ideal man or woman, or how the sexes should interact in relationships.

People place personal adverts for many reasons although a chief motive is to satisfy a desire that cannot be met in other contexts. If one is able to find (enough) partners easily through other aspects of one's life, such as via work or socializing, then there may be less need to place an advert online. Personal adverts then have the capacity to tell us something about needs that are less easy to achieve through other means, and subsequently this could be revealing about the sorts of needs that men have, and the extent to which such needs relate to societal restrictions or norms. Rather than comparing men with women, I decided to use geographic location as a main variable, in order to determine the extent to which the sorts of linguistic patterns (and related discourses) were dependent on culture or society, or whether there were indications that certain discourses appeared to be more global in nature. To quote from a well-known gendered discourse (which is also the title of a song by the group The Used released in 2009), is it true that 'men are all the same'?

Finally, to add a further dimension to this chapter, rather than compare just two corpora together, I decided to use three, as this allows us to raise questions regarding how multiple corpora should be compared, particularly when most corpus software is oriented towards two-way comparisons. My main research questions were: (1) how do males relate to gender when advertising to meet women? (2) to what extent are there differences/ similarities between advertisers from different countries?

In the following sections I first describe how I built my corpora and then outline the three methods of analysis I carried out, noting some of the more interesting findings from each. The chapter concludes with a more reflective discussion of the different methods.

Creating the corpora

In order to find websites which contained personal adverts from men, I initially carried out a search of the term *mens personals* using the search engine Google. The site craigslist.com[1] appeared on the first page of links and a further exploration of this site revealed that it was a good candidate to collect corpus data from, for a number of reasons. First, the site had a clear categorization system for adverts, based on location and type of advert, so it was straightforward to isolate just adverts categorized as 'men seeking women' from specific cities or countries. Second, as the site was free to access, it did not employ firewalls which meant that I was able to use a website copier in order to collect adverts easily. I employed the software HTTrack in order to make copies of sections of the website which contained the adverts I was interested in analysing. Third, the site had a reasonably basic and consistent style and page layout, which meant that the later stage of cleaning the data would be considerably easier to undertake.

The choice of which countries to collect adverts from was restricted by a couple of practical issues. I wanted to use countries where English was reasonably well-known and used, although I also wanted to use a combination of countries which had societies that were quite distinct from each other. I decided not to compare America and Canada, for example, as both are relatively rich, 'westernized' North American countries and I felt that it would be more interesting to see whether men's personal adverts have common or distinct features when they were posted in countries that comprised different societies and cultures. A further issue was that craigslist did not appear to be used very much in some countries, which limited the number of options further. Eventually I decided to collect data from India, Singapore and Australia, feeling that these three countries each differed significantly from each other in terms of their politics, religion, culture, amount and distribution of wealth and ethnic make-up.[2]

Collection of the adverts occurred in November 2012 and I aimed to gather 1,000 of the most recently posted adverts from each country. However, as the online archiving of adverts only went back to a certain point in time I was only able to collect 577 Australian, 604 Indian and 906 Singaporean adverts. Each advert was saved in its original html format containing boilerplate material such as a link allowing users to email the posting to a friend or to flag the advert as miscategorized. This material needed to be removed from each advert, so I used WordSmith 5.0 which contains a utility called Text Converter, enabling sections of texts to be stripped out of multiple files at the same time. With this utility I was able to remove most of the boilerplate from the adverts. There are a range of other types of file editing software available, many which are free to download, including TextWrangler, EditPad, Multilingual Corpus Toolkit and Notepad++. Text Converter did not allow me to remove all of the boilerplate, as each advert also contained a unique identifier code consisting of a string of letters and numbers, such as xgqv3–3233029440. In order to remove these codes I first used another File utility in WordSmith called Joiner, in order to join all of the adverts together so that each corpus consisted of a single file. I then opened the files in the word processing tool Microsoft Word and used the 'search and replace' function to remove the identifier codes. Within Word it is possible to specify a sequence like Any Letter, Any Letter, Any Digit, Any Digit, Any Letter etc., and then replace it with no text at all. It is, of course possible to remove boilerplate by writing a short computer program (or asking a programmer friend to help), although this is not recommended for beginners. When 'cleaning' corpora, it is a good idea to save older versions of the corpus at various stages so that portions of text are not inadvertently removed and cannot be retrieved.

Having removed the boilerplate, a further issue involved unwanted files. During the initial process of data collection I had noticed that some advertisers had posted their advert more than once, which would result in frequencies of certain words being skewed. Software such as CopyCatch (used for plagiarism detection) can compare multiple files together and identify parts of text that are similar. However, another way of identifying repeated texts is to create a cluster or n-gram list (similar to a word list but considering the frequencies of fixed sequences of words). If the number of words in a cluster is set to say 7, then an examination of such clusters that occur more than once (particularly if they contain rare lexis) could indicate repetitions. Obviously, repetitions of long clusters do not always mean a whole text is repeated, and in newspaper texts for example, the remarks of someone being interviewed or quoted may occur repeatedly across a number of different articles.

A third way to cross-check for duplicated files is to carry out concordances of reasonably frequent words, sort them alphabetically and check to see if certain concordance lines appear to be identical. This is the method I chose to incorporate, and I carried out concordances on all three corpora of the words *and*, *the*, *you* and *I* which were very frequent. This method proved to be useful for another reason. As well as revealing a number of duplicates, upon scanning concordance lines some adverts were found to have been posted in the incorrect section of craigslist. For example, a few advertised female escorts while others involved people attempting to sell services such as carpentry. Further concordance searches of words like *girls* and *escort* enabled the removal of these miscategorized adverts, reducing the total number of adverts to 554 (Australia), 511 (India) and 827 (Singapore). This unexpected source of unwanted adverts indicates one of the benefits of familiarizing oneself with the corpus prior to analysis.

The varying numbers of adverts resulted in somewhat different word counts for each corpus (Australia 52,000, India 42,000, Singapore 76,000). It is sometimes considered ideal to work with equal-sized corpora as claims about representativeness can be made with reasonably equal confidence, and I debated whether it would be preferable to attempt to equalize the word counts by removing around 24,000 words from the Singaporean corpus to bring it closer in line with the frequencies of the other two corpora. However, I decided against this as doing so would decrease the representativeness of the Singaporean corpus, and I felt that this would be less preferable than working with corpora that were all of the same size. While it is sensible to try to be consistent when conducting analyses (e.g. by keeping to the same cut-off points for statistical significance or the span for collocates), when analysis is conducted on corpora that are of different sizes, the application of the same cut-offs can result in quite large differences in the number of collocates or keywords which are elicited. One way of addressing this issue is to use a cut-off that is based on a ranked scale (such as the strongest 20 keywords) rather than an interval or ratio scale (such as all keywords that have a keyness value of over 50). The issue of differing corpus sizes impacting on results became particularly relevant when I started to create collocational networks (discussed later in this chapter).

A final issue relating to the creation of the corpora remained. Some of the adverts contained variant spellings, as the following advert demonstrates

> looking for a girl to have fun n enjoy from my place. just revert me if u like this ad. Life is too short, don't waste ur time;) (India)

Such adverts contained orthography and grammar that would be considered non-standard, compared to published academic written English, although they were appropriate for the register of computer-mediated communication as well as reflecting differences between the three geographical varieties of English being used. I considered whether it would be worth using a spelling standardizer such as VARD 2 (Variant Detector) (Baron et al. 2009) to regulate the spelling, for example, changing *u* to *you* in the advert above. Ultimately, I decided against this as the proportion of such cases was relatively small and tended to relate to grammatical words like *and*, *you* and *your* (as in the advert above). I was more interested in content words (nouns, verbs, adjectives, adverbs), so did not feel that it would be problematic to leave a few non-standard spellings in the corpus.

A more relevant issue involved the variant representation of adjectives such as *good-looking*, *fun-loving* and *open-minded* (which could be written with a hyphen, no spacing or spacing). As I was interested in the overall frequencies of these words in order to calculate their collocates, in these cases I decided to standardize them by removing hyphens and spaces so that *good-looking* became *goodlooking.*

Tagging the corpora

Before discussing how the corpora were analysed, this section describes their annotation. I decided to base part of the analysis around the semantic concepts that advertisers referenced as I hypothesized that this would help to make sense of some of the main features of each corpus. The analysis of semantic groups can be useful, especially when working with quite small corpora containing low word frequencies. For example, a group of related words (such as 'words referring to large size') may all only occur a few times each, but counted together collectively are more likely to be recognized by corpus analysis software as statistically salient.

The corpora I collected were not very large in size, each being under 100,000 words. However, as personal adverts are a somewhat restricted and repetitive language variety, I felt that the small size would still allow linguistic patterns to emerge, particularly if semantic tagging was used. As it was unfeasible to tag each corpus by hand, I used an automatic tagger which was able to carry out the task in a few minutes.

I used an online tool called Wmatrix (Rayson 2008) in order to carry out the semantic tagging of the corpora. Wmatrix allows users to load in their own corpora, which are first part-of-speech tagged, then assigned semantic tags. Frequency lists are also generated and users can use the Wmatrix interface to compare their own corpora together or against a number of preloaded reference corpora, including samples from the BNC. The semantic tagging in Wmatrix is based around a system called USAS (UCREL Semantic Analysis System) (Wilson and Thomas 1997). The semantic tagset was originally loosely based on Tom McArthur's *Longman Lexicon of Contemporary English* (McArthur 1981) and contains 21 main fields which are further subdivided into several hundred sub-fields. For example, tag E relates to emotions and is divided into E1 (general emotions), E2 (Liking), E3 (calm/violent/angry), E4 (happy/sad), E5 (fear/bravery/shock) and E6 (worry, concern, confident). These tags are also sub-divided, so E4.1 refers to the concept: happy and E4.2 refers to contentment. Additionally, certain words may be assigned multiple + or – signs to indicate both negative or positive meanings as well as strength of meaning. For example, the word *playful* is tagged E4.1+ while *thrilling* is E4.1+++.

The tagger achieves a reasonably high success rate although mistaggings do sometimes occur, particularly with unfamiliar words or words which have multiple meanings. Such mistaggings can often be spotted via concordance searches so it is important to carry out extra checks on the tagged corpora before reporting findings. One tag, Z99 is used for words that are not recognized by Wmatrix, and tends to cover mis-spellings and non-standard English. For each corpus, the percentage of words tagged Z99 were 2.31 per cent (Australia), 4.07 per cent (India) and 1.93 per cent (Singapore), indicating that generally the tagger was able to recognize (if not always accurately) the majority of the words in each corpus.[3]

Once the three sets of corpora had been tagged, I aimed to carry out an analysis which would tell me which semantic tags were characteristic of each corpus, along with the tags which were common to all three. A lot of comparative corpus research focuses on comparisons of two corpora together, and as I had three corpora, the following section discusses some of the ways that I could have approached this less usual situation.

Comparing more than two corpora

Both WordSmith and AntConc allow two corpora to be compared together in order to obtain keywords, using either LL or chi-squared tests. However, neither software (currently) allows multiple corpora to be compared in this way, and there appears to be less consensus over the best ways to conduct comparisons on more than two corpora. In deciding upon which technique to use, it is first worth considering what the comparison should focus on. For the purposes of illustration, consider the frequencies of three words in Table 7.1, which are taken from the four British sections of the Brown family (containing written published English). These corpora are all one million words in size, so it is possible to make direct comparisons of raw frequencies rather than needing to standardize via referring to percentage frequencies.

In Table 7.1, the word *around* appears to be rising in frequency over time, with quite different values at each point. The next word, *money* shows less difference, being reasonably consistent. One measure which will tell us the extent to which words differ greatly in frequency across all corpora, or

TABLE 7.1 *Frequencies in four time periods of the British sections of the Brown family.*

Time period	1931	1961	1991	2006
around	110	245	407	630
money	306	325	306	332
century	236	270	453	206

are relatively similar, is the Coefficient of Variance (CV). I have previously employed this measure in order to identify words which showed the greatest amount of variation or similarity when comparing the corpora in Table 7.1 together (Baker 2011). The CV is based on taking the standard deviation of a word's frequency and dividing it by the mean of the word (this helps to counter skewing as the most frequent words usually have the highest standard deviations). The word *around* received the highest CV score out of all the words I examined, while *money* received one of the lowest scores. The word *century* also had a high CV, due to the fact that its frequency in one time period, 1991, was much higher than the others.

Another way of identifying words which have differing frequencies across multiple corpora, is to use chi-squared tests, as Oakes and Farrow (2007) did to compare word frequencies across seven reference corpora containing different varieties of English. As this technique resulted in thousands of tests being carried out, they employed the Bonferroni correction (which raises the threshold needed for a word to be viewed as being key). Oakes and Farrow were able to identify distinctive lexis for different varieties of English, for example Australian English contained higher than normal references to *wool, unions, kilometres, library, Mr* and *unemployed* while Indian English contained the keywords *caste, village, temple, sari* and *upto*. More detailed analyses of such words may reveal information about cultural and linguistic features that are unique to that society.

Although WordSmith and AntConc do not enable users to select three or more corpora and automatically identify keywords, there are a number of workarounds which are worth considering. One is a technique which was described in Baker, Gabrielatos and McEnery (2013) where we aimed to identify keywords in 11 corpora of British newspaper articles about Muslims. For each newspaper we used the other ten newspapers added together as the reference corpus, and that way we were able to obtain 11 lists of keywords, one for each newspaper. We then used a cut-off point (the top 100 keywords in each list) and focused only on keywords that were unique to a particular list. For example, we derived keywords for *The Express* by comparing the frequency list of that newspaper against a reference corpus consisting of the other ten newspapers in our corpus. Among the 100 *Express* keywords that had the highest LL scores, we found words like *fanatics, terror* and *sharia*. However, these words were also key in some of the other top 100 keyword lists, so we decided not to focus on them. Instead, we concentrated our analysis on words like *veil* and *taxpayers* which were key in *The Express* but not in the top 100 keyword lists for any of the other newspapers. This helped us to distinguish particular words which made *The Express* salient from the rest of the British press.

We used the same method to identify the keywords for each separate year of news articles (e.g. the keywords for 1998 were found by comparing a frequency list derived from 1998 articles against a frequency list of all the articles from 1999–2009). However, we found that the unique keywords for each year were not always especially helpful to analyse as news stories do not usually fit neatly into one-year periods. Instead, the unique keywords tended to tell us about very brief stories which appeared for only a few months and then were never mentioned again. Keywords derived from stories which ran from say, October–February would tend not to be in unique keyword lists, because they would be likely to be key in two consecutive years.

So instead, we supplemented this approach by looking at how related groups of keywords appeared to go in and out of fashion over time rather than just considering keywords that were unique to a specific time period. For example, we found that words relating to gender and sexuality tended to be key in the period 1998–2000 and again from 2006–9. During the middle part of the corpus (2001–5), words relating to terrorism tended to be key. We hypothesized that the 9/11 attacks on America in 2001 had altered the discourse around Muslims to be more focused on terror for a time, although gradually issues relating to sex and gender crept back in to news discourse on Islam.

One issue with comparing parts of corpora against other parts in this way is that the technique will elicit differences but not similarities. If the aim of the study is only to identify differences, then this method is suitable, although as discussed in Chapter Two, there can be times when we want to put difference into perspective by considering how much similarity there is between two corpora (especially if we do not want to reify or over-state difference). Another option would be to compare multiple corpora against a completely different reference corpus. This was the method I used at the end of Chapter Two when I compared the male and female spoken sections of the BNC against the FLOB reference corpus of written English. The advantage of this method is that it allows both differences and similarities to be drawn out more easily (although we may still decide to focus only on differences). Obviously, the choice of the reference corpus is likely to impact on the types of keywords which emerge. For example, if I had decided to compare each of my 11 sub-corpora of news articles about Islam against the same reference corpus, I would need to employ a reference corpus that was ideally larger than the individual sub-corpora. The 100-million-word BNC would have been an option, although its data was collected in the early 1990s, while the news articles were from 1998–2009. Therefore, words referring to more recent concepts like *iphone* (which was released in 2007) might be key for some of the collections of news articles from 2007 onwards. A better matched reference corpus in terms of time period would not give *iphone* as key, unless iphones were very integral to some of the news articles about Muslims. Using the BNC as a reference corpus might also result in words which are concerned with newspaper style appearing as key (e.g. *yesterday*, *exclusive*, *reported*). An alternative would have been to use a different reference corpus, such as one containing recent news articles about a wide range of topics. Such a reference corpus, being closer in terms of the time period and the genre of the texts under examination, would be more likely to elicit keywords that tell us something relevant about the representation of Islam in the news, rather than the language of news or the language of the early twenty-first century per se.

Techniques for comparing corpora, particularly more than two corpora, are still in development, and it is hoped that software is created to allow more complex comparisons to be made automatically. With a wide range of options available, it is a good idea for researchers to explain which technique they decided upon and indicate the sorts of results that such a method is likely to produce (e.g. types of words, differences, similarities, both, etc.). For the purposes of the analysis in this chapter, I will employ a slightly different method to those described above, carrying out three sets of comparisons across three related corpora and focusing on only the results which are consistently key.

Method 1: Comparing semantic tags

First, in order to get an idea of similarity, in Wmatrix I separately compared each corpus against the same sample of almost 1 million words of text taken from the written part of the BNC (the tagged version of this reference corpus is available to all Wmatrix users). The three comparisons are shown in Figure 7.1 (each straight line indicates that a comparison was carried out).

This technique gave me the semantic tags that were key in each corpus when compared against the same reference corpus. Using LL tests and applying the default cut-off of an LL value of 6.63 (which corresponds to p < 0.01), a large number of tags (over 100) for each comparison were produced. I decided to focus on the strongest 20 tags in each comparison, and when these three sets of tags were compared, there was found to be a high amount of similarity between them – 15 of these 'top 20' tags were shared across all three corpora. An inspection of the shared tags revealed that most of them were broadly related to the genre of personal advertising discourse, referring to types of people (S2.1: Female, S2.2: Male, Z8: pronouns), desire (E2+: Like, E4.1+ Happy), relationships (S3.1: Personal

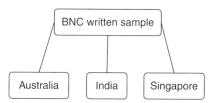

FIGURE 7.1 *Comparing three corpora to identify extent of similarity.*

Relationship: General, S3.2: Relationships, Intimacy and Sex), descriptions of people (O4.2+: Judgement of People: Beautiful, T3: Time: Old, new and young; age) and modality (Z7: If, S6–: No obligation or necessity). This is not particularly surprising – we would expect the three corpora of adverts to have some similarities as they are all from the same register (heterosexual men seeking women), which is amply demonstrated by the shared key tags.

Looking further down the lists beyond the top 20 key tags would perhaps be more revealing of differences, although I decided to take a slightly different approach in order to see which tags were most typical of a particular corpus, when it was compared against the other two corpora. In order to achieve this, I carried out three more sets of comparisons of key semantic categories using LL tests and again applying the default cut-off point at 6.63. The comparisons I made were (1) Singapore vs India, (2) Singapore vs Australia, (3) India vs Australia (see Figure 7.2).

I then compared the results of the three comparisons together, in order to see which tags appeared to be consistent. For example, when I compared Australia against Singapore, I found that one tag that was key for Singapore was F1 (Food). This tag was also key for Singapore when it was compared against India, which gives an indication that the F1 tag seems to be strongly associated with the Singaporean adverts. On the other hand, another tag which was key for Singapore when compared against Australia was L1– (Dead). However, this tag was not key when Singapore was compared with India, so I decided not to focus on this tag as the difference did not occur across the two comparisons that involved Singapore.

These consistent key tags were then examined via concordance searches and during this process some of them were found to be the result of mistagging, due to homonyms. For example, the Singapore data had K5.1 (sports) as key when compared against both Australia and India. However, when a concordance of all the 240 words tagged as K5.1 in the Singaporean corpus were examined, it was found that 62 of these K5.1 words were cases of the word *race* which always referred to ethnic background rather than sports. As a result, the category K5.1 was excluded from the list of consistent key tags. Table 7.2 lists the consistent key tags for each corpus (mistaggings are not included).

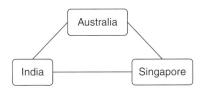

FIGURE 7.2 *Comparing three corpora to identify differences.*

TABLE 7.2 *Semantic tags that were consistently key for each corpus.*

General semantic group	Australia	India	Singapore
A (General and Abstract Terms)	A5.4+ Evaluation: Authentic	A10− Closed: Hiding/Hidden	A1.3+ Cautious
C (Arts and Crafts)	C1 Arts and crafts		
E (Emotions)	E2+ Like	E4.2− Discontent	
F (Food)			F1 Food F2 Drinks and Alcohol
H (Architecture)	H4 Residence		
I (Money)		I2.1 Business: Generally I1.3 Money: Cost and Price	
M (Moving)	M2 Putting, pulling, pushing, transporting		M6 Location and direction M7 Places
N (Numbers)		N1 Numbers N5.1+ Entire: Maximum	
O (Substances)	O4.3 Colour and colour patterns O4.2− Judgement of appearance: Ugly		
P (Education)		P1 Education in General	
Q (Linguistics)		Q2.2 Speech Acts	
S (Social Actions)	S1.2.2− Generous	S2.1 People: Female S2.2 People: Male S3.1 Personal Relationships: General S4: Kin S5− Not part of a group S8+ Helping	S7.1 Power, organizing
T (Time)		T3 Time: Old, new and young, age	T1.1.2 Time: Present simultaneous T1.2 Time: Momentary T2++ Time: Beginning
Z (Unmatched)		Z99 Unmatched	Z3 Other proper names

It is worth noting which tag groups did not emerge as key for any of the categories. These were anything tagged as B (the body), G (government and politics), K (entertainment), L (life and living things), W (the universe) and X (psychological states). As these tag groups did not occur as key, they are not included as rows in Table 7.2. Collectively, the key semantic tags (semtags) reveal a wide range of distinct aspects of the adverts, some relating to what the advertisers are looking for, others relating to how they describe themselves, and others still relating to orthographic or stylistic aspects of the adverts. Using Wmatrix it is possible to bring up a list of all of the words which contribute to a particular tag. For example, with the Australian corpus, I can click on the semtag for H4 (Residence) which produces a table showing words tagged H4 along with their frequencies and relative frequencies, ordered by frequency. Additionally, I can obtain concordances for every word tagged as H4, or individual words tagged as H4. The analysis of these word lists and their concordances helps to explain the context in which certain concepts appear in adverts, although such analyses do not, of course, explain *why* they appear.

With over 30 tags in Table 7.2 to consider, it is beyond the space limits to provide accounts of each one in detail here. Below I concentrate on the analysis of a few tags from each corpus in order to reveal some aspects of the advertisers which make them distinct to their country.

Australia

Advertisers in Australia appeared to use more tags which related to physical descriptions of themselves and the sort of partner they were looking for. The tag A5.4+ referred to Authenticity and was mainly comprised of the word *genuine* but also contained the word *sincere*, and phrases like *for real* and *be yourself*. Advertisers who used this tag refer to their advert or themselves as genuine, and/or also stated that they are looking for a genuine woman:

> Hi, this is a genuine advert [275 words deleted] Once again, this is a genuine advert so genuine replies only please.

Some advertisers expressed disappointment due to previous encounters:

> P.S. Not after any bullshit. Must be willing to meet ASAP. I do not like getting to know someone over the internet, only to have nothing come from it. It is a waste of my time. Genuine girls only.

Additionally, some advertisers ended their advert with a request for people who replied to indicate that they are genuine, by putting a code word in the subject header.

Put 'Angel' on you subject header reply so I know you are genuine and serious and not a spammer.

The word *put* occurred 50 times in the Australian advert (mainly in the construction above), and helped to contribute towards the keyness of M2 (putting, pulling, pushing, transporting). This practice of asking repliers to use a code word perhaps indicates that spammers (people who use mass mailing techniques to sell products and services) tend to frequently target Australians who use Craigslist, and/or that Australian advertisers are less likely to be tolerant of spammers, compared to advertisers in India or Singapore.

Another word in M2 was *send* (106 occurrences) which was almost always used in requests for repliers to send a picture. Related to this, the tag C1 (Arts and Crafts), occurring 273 times, was largely due to the 230 occurrences of the following words: *pic(s)*, *picture(s)* *photo(s)*:

Please reply with a pic if interested

Such requests for a picture could co-incide with the desire for authenticity – Australian advertisers seem to be particularly concerned with not having their time wasted and knowing what their respondent looks like in advance of meeting them. While both Indian and Singaporean advertisers also requested pictures, they did not do this as much as Australians.

As well as emphasizing authenticity, Australian advertisers made more reference to colours (tag O4.3), particularly *brown, blue, white, green, black* and *blond*, which were generally used in descriptions of their own hair and eyes:

I am 28 years, 5'8", light brown hair, blue/green eyes and have fit physique. I have a picture available on requset.

Perhaps this emphasis on hair and eye colour relates to these features being more variable among Europeans (Frost 2006) whom many Australians are likely to be descended from. There are only a handful of advertisers in Singapore and India who describe themselves as having blonde hair or blue eyes, and in their adverts they indicate that they are Caucasian (usually visiting an area or having relocated there for work). Another distinct aspect of description among Australian men was tag O4.2– (Judgement of Appearance: Ugly) which comprised words like *dirty, ugly, awful, junk, horrible* and *unattractive*. The most frequent word in this category (*dirty*) was often used positively, to describe sexual interests or activity:

Where are all the dirty minded girls that think like me?

However, other advertisers used such words to distance themselves from such identities.

I'm not a sleazy old man looking for a quick pick up :)

Ladies/Women/Girls dont dismiss this ad – im not ugly, im not horrible – im normal and genuine.

Another Australian semtag was S1.2.2– (Generous) which mainly comprised the word *generous* and related forms. This tag sometimes implied that the advertiser was offering payment in return for sex or companionship

Will reward generously.

Slim, generous guy with 200 to spare, seeking a slim, passionate girl to play tonight.

However, at other times an advertiser who used this term was specifically that they were *not* looking for a client–prostitute relationship (although the advert below appears somewhat ambiguous about the exact nature of the relationship and its terms):

Generous but bored visiting business professional seeks young lady to keep me company several times a month. [56 words deleted] No professional girls please but if you have an interesting personality, friendly and articulate, this could be ideal.

The final tag I want to consider from the Australian corpus is E2+ (Like). This tag was mostly due to high use of the verbs *like*, *love* and *enjoy* as well as a few less frequent adjectives which described positive traits like *loving*, *caring*, and *affectionate*. The most frequent word (*like*) was mainly used in the three word cluster *would like to*. It is difficult to generalize from the wide range of interests and desires which *like* and *love* occurred in, ranging from hobbies and interests (*skating*, *gardening*) to certain types of women (*asian girls*, *a woman with a brain on her shoulders*) or romantic or sexual activities (*rough sex*, *taking my time*, *the simple pleasure of falling asleep in someone's arms*). We should not assume that this means that Australian advertisers are more likely to be specific about what they are looking for as there may be other ways of expressing such needs (e.g. by using a word like *want*), but it is notable that Australians do appear to construct their desires and interests via *like* and *love*, and this could be an aspect of writing style.

India

While Australians seemed to be quite interested in visual aspects of identity, in the Indian corpus a number of tags indicated that social and marital status appeared to play a more important part in the personal adverts.

The tags I2.1 (Business: Generally) and P1 (Education) were often used to construct the advertiser as either a businessman or well-educated:

> I am a generous well groomed businessman in my late thirties [36 words deleted]. I have been very successful in my business. But the management of this business unfortunately takes up a significant part of my time.

> Am a 39 years young well settled male entrepreneur in Bangalore. Single and affluent.

> I am very successful,educated,professional and working in a good position in a MNC[4] here.

Additionally, the tag S4 referred to kin, and was most likely to involve reference to marital status e.g. *married*, *divorced*, *wife*. The tag S5– (Not part of a group) tended to also refer to marital status as being unmarried containing words like *independent* and *alone*. As with the words *love* and *like* in Australia, there were a wide range of ways that Indian advertisers could orient to these marital status words:

> (Not looking for marriage, i dont think this is a right place to do so)

> Looking for divorced or widowed woman for marriage, with or without children.

> No matter if you're married, divorced or single but if you hve a great desire and want to have a great time with a nice guy, pls message me.

One unexpected word which appeared in the S4 category was *aunties* which occurred 25 times with various spellings. This word referred to some advertisers who were seeking sexual encounters with married and/or older women:

> Looking for decent friendship with women of any age, particularly aunties, married women.

Aunties also occurred in adverts containing words tagged E4.2– (Discontent), relating to the word *unsatisfied* and A10– (Closed; Hiding/Hidden), relating to words like *secret*, *private* and *confidential* and these concepts sometimes appeared as part of adverts from male advertisers who were offering or selling sexual services to sexually frustrated women, promising discretion.

> Any unsatisfied aunties looking for secret sex relationship can text me back for NSA relationship.

> College students and for unsatisfied aunties. I charge one thousand for short time (Max two to three hrs) and am open to all your wishes. If i like the figure, we can spend time for free.

The tag S8+ (helping) also tended to be used by male escorts (or men who simply wanted to provide free sex), and sex was regularly euphemized as a *service*, even by those who claimed they did not require payment.

> My service is free as long as you can arrange for a place.
>
> my service is absolutely free. since iam virgin
>
> I offer all sort of personal service for women with utmost discretion
>
> i am their to help you comeout all the problem . . . need more fun and more statima guy with slim body can co-operate you in all the ways,fun is needed at the same need to think about the secret and privacy . . .

As well as offers of service, the tag I1.3 referred to money generally, comprising words like *expenses*, *cost*, *price*, *charge* and *worth*, and mostly referred to financial arrangements:

> here for a few months. looking for NSA relationship from educated women. will take care of their expenses . . .
>
> Need Independent girl for outcall. Expecting to do some shopping for you, take you to dinner, and then home for sex. Something like a 'girlfriend experience'. Please message me with contact information and your charges.

Two related tags in the Indian corpus were S2.1 (Female) and S2.2 (Male). These words referred mainly to the nouns *woman*, *girl*, *man*, *boy* (and their plurals) and as well as the adjectives *male* and *female*. Concordance analyses revealed that these terms were most likely to be used in descriptions of the self and what the advertiser was looking for.

> Looking for a homely girl from poor family – 24 (chennai)
>
> Am looking forward to spend sometime quality with a woman
>
> Hi iam seeking for women . . . for dating and sexxxx too.
>
> i am a guy looking for a female frnd i delhi and around – 26 (delhi)
>
> 26 M decent and sober guy looking for a pretty girl for intimacy – 26 (Delhi)

Considering that the adverts are all placed in the category 'men seeking women', it is notable that one set of advertisers used these terms more than the other two and it is difficult to postulate possible reasons for this, although collectively, these words appear to place a particular emphasis on gender in the Indian adverts which is not so apparent in those from Singapore or Australia.

Finally, the Indian advertisers also appear to be more specific about the type of relationship that they are looking for than the other advertisers. The tag S3.1 comprises words like *relationship*, *meet*, *friend*, *partner*, *escort* and *companion*, and as with the words relating to gender, makes the Indian adverts appear to be closely sticking to a formulaic structure more stereotypical of the personal advert genre.

Singapore

Two key semtags which appeared to be related to each other in the Singaporean corpus were F1 (Food) and F2 (Drinks and Alcohol). The reason for the presence of these tags was due to Singaporeans wanting to meet for drinks or a meal. The most popular F1 tag was *dinner*, although *lunch*, *food*, *meal* and *eat* were also popular:

> I am a mature established working mix race local guy interested to meet someone for casual dates, dinners and lunches.

F2 also occurred in similar constructions while the tag T1.2 (Momentary) mostly referred to the word *date* and was used in the sense of the above advertisement of wanting to arrange a date.

A word in F1 which did not contribute to the requests for drinks/dinner/date was *sugar* (the second most common word in this category, occurring 44 times), which was always used in constructions like *sugar mummy*, *sugar babe* or *sugar girl*. The word *sugar* implied a situation where it was understood that gifts or money would exchange hands, in return for sex and/or companionship, either with the advertiser looking for a *sugar babe* or *sugar girl* (to spend money on), or a *sugar mummy* (to pay him):

> Caucasian Sugar relationship – 32 (my place) We will meet a few times a month. Dinner, events, shopping and lots of fun at my place. Possible weekends away.

Tag A1.3+ (Cautious) largely comprised of forms of the word *discreet* and related to advertisers who wanted to keep their relationship secret.

> I am living in singapore and interested in discreet relationship.

> Im not looking to hurt anyone in my family, nor yours so if you need discretion you've got it.

> Stably married but looking for that other long term companion by the side? One who does not want to rock the boat at home yet wanting to lend each other a listening ear? And expecting discretion in return?

As noted in the last two adverts above, discretion was linked to married advertisers who wanted to arrange extra-marital affairs, which also explains the presence of key tag S7.1 (Power, organizing). This tag comprised just one word: *status*, and actually related to marital status, with advertisers almost always intimating that this was not an important issue to them:

Race, age and marital status are not important.

Not looking to change my or your status :)

I'm not intersted in your marital status so don't bother asking about mine.

Compared to the other two countries, Singapore appeared then to have a high proportion of married male advertisers seeking 'affairs', although Indian adverts seemed to feature single males offering sexual services to attached women. Neither trend was observed to be especially popular in the Australian corpus.

Discussion of Method 1

Despite the analysis identifying a number of key semantic tags associated with each country, a closer examination of such tags has sometimes revealed more similarities than differences. For example, in all three cases, a proportion of the male advertisers were using Craigslist to sell or buy sexual services. However, such advertisers were realized by their use of words in different semantic groups. Australian advertisers were more likely to describe themselves as *generous*, Indians referred more explicitly to cost and services, as well as using the term *escort* while Singaporeans used euphemisms around the word *sugar*. Individual advertisers were sometimes very clear that they wanted to pay for sex, others seemed to be offering less specific rewards in return for some sort of romantic or sexual arrangement and others were even more ambiguous, implying a financial exchange but not wanting a 'professional girl'. Only the Indian adverts appeared to involve a number of males advertising their own sexual services, although here there was also ambiguity in that some males seemed to emphasize that payment would not always be required and that they were simply happy to provide a service. To step outside the corpus for a moment and take social context into account, I note that prostitution is legal in all three countries (although with restrictions, and only in parts of Australia is it legal to manage a brothel). Continuing taboos surrounding prostitution may thus explain why advertisers resort to euphemism.

Information about divorce rates may also help to explain some of the differences found. In 2003, Australia's divorce rate was 2.67 per 1,000 people while Singapore's was 0.83 (United Nations Statistics Division).[5] India does not appear to track divorce statistics, although anecdotal reports claim it is very low, and some estimates have indicated that India has one of the lowest divorce rates in the world, although it has been rising since around 2007.[6] A combination of legal difficulties in obtaining divorce and societal taboos surrounding being divorced may help to explain the Singaporean advertisers seeking extra-marital affairs and the Indian advertisers offering sexual services for 'dissatisfied aunties'. Both India and Singaporean advertisers used categories which indicated desire for covertness in conducting a relationship although again, the semantic category that such words fell into was different – for Indian adverts the emphasis was on words relating to Closed; Hiding/Hidden (*private*, *secret*) while for Singapore the key concept was discretion. The lack of such words in the Australian adverts perhaps indicates that sexual relationships can be conducted relatively more openly in that context, which may explain why Australian advertisers were more likely to require photographs and tended to provide lists of their interests – of the three sets of advertisers, Australians seemed to be more specific about the sort of person they were and wanted to find. Indian and Singaporean advertisers may be less likely to expect or offer photographs due to a higher stigma attached around using the internet to find certain types of relationships.

In relating the results of the analysis back to the research questions, it would seem that the key semantic tags have been more revealing about how different cultural contexts filter the ways that desire is expressed, and perhaps this approach by itself is too broad to reveal much about the sorts of gendered discourses that advertisers refer to or the ways that they construct their own identities.

And ultimately, the analysis has not revealed that the male advertisers in these three countries are especially different from each other or that conceptualizations of masculinity differ very widely. I did not find key categories relating to measurement (e.g. *tall* N3.7+) or body (e.g. *muscular* B1) which would have suggested that in certain countries a particular body shape is more likely to be highly regarded and worth mentioning. Perhaps the only indication that masculinity was conceived of somewhat differently was the greater number of words in India which related to professional status and education – Indian advertisers seem to feel that mentioning such attributes will impress potential partners, and perhaps in a country which has a relatively low literacy rate (74.04% in 2011[7]), referring to education is a way of making oneself more distinct and attractive. In a similar way, I noted that in the 1980s, during a period of high unemployment, gay male British advertisers were more likely to stress that they were professional and owned their own house and car than in other time periods examined (Baker 2005: 149–50).

In summary, this approach has revealed some of the differences and similarities between the advertisers from different countries, but it has not revealed much specifically about how males relate to gender. Perhaps an approach which is more targeted would be better placed to address that issue.

Method 2: Collocational networks

In order to focus on how the advertisers related to gender, I decided to move from a corpus-driven to a more corpus-based approach by examining combinations of adjectives that the advertisers used to describe themselves. I hypothesized that choice of adjectives would potentially be revealing about the sorts of traits that male advertisers felt would be valuable and likely to elicit replies from women. Such traits had not appeared as key in the semantic analysis described above, and I wondered if this was because the semantic comparisons had perhaps been too 'broad-brush' to allow them to emerge. A different approach might help to either confirm that there was little difference in the way that male advertisers described themselves across the three corpora, or would point to the ways that multiple methods can uncover different results.

To examine self-descriptors I first obtained a frequency list for each corpus and then identified the 20 most frequent adjectives in each. A problem arose in that some of the adjectives in the lists did not appear to be used as self-descriptors but instead seemed to be describing the sort of relationship that the advertiser wanted or the sort of woman he hoped to meet. One way of resolving this issue would be to incorporate tagging into each advert in order to mark self-descriptors, other-descriptors and anything else in the advert. This was the method I applied in Baker (2005), which worked well, although the tagging of 1,350 adverts needed to be carried out by hand. For this study, I had approximately 1,900 adverts so this sort of hand tagging would have been feasible, although I wondered if it was possible to apply a quicker method this time. An alternative option could be to consider words which appeared between 1–3 words to the right of a phrase like *I am* or *I'm*. I trialled this approach on the Australian data, eliciting 868 instances of the two phrases. However, the collocates produced were mostly of low frequency: *tall* (32 cases), *single* (18), *slim* (11), *fit* (11), *clean* (8), *shy* (7), *Australian* (7), *attractive* (6), *caring* 6), *young* (6), *married* (6), *honest* (6), *Asian* (5) and I was concerned that I would miss some words altogether. Instead, I decided to return to the original top 20 list of adjectives and carry out concordances on each adjective. This allowed me to quickly determine whether the adjective was mainly used as a self-descriptor or occurred for other reasons. I decided to retain adjectives which were used as self-descriptors in at least 2/3 of the concordance lines. Those which tended to refer to the sort of woman the advertiser wished to meet (e.g. *pretty*) were removed. This method produced Table 7.3.[8]

What does the table reveal about the way that the advertisers describe themselves? If we hypothesize that the advertisers want to maximize their chances of receiving replies, then we would expect the self-descriptors to be mainly positive, which seems to be the case from Table 7.3, although there is one negative-sounding adjective (*lonely*) as well as some adjectives which describe marital status, ethnicity, location or (in the case of India) gender and may not immediately suggest clear positive or negative evaluation. Table 7.4 collapses the words in Table 7.3 into similar traits (e.g. words like

TABLE 7.3 *Top 20 self-describing adjectives in each corpus.*

	Australia	#	India	#	Singapore	#
1	nice	113	married	71	Chinese	156
2	genuine	82	educated	61	married	151
3	single	78	Indian	50	local	114
4	fit	62	handsome	45	Caucasian	107
5	tall	62	professional	43	tall	96
6	clean	61	tall	41	goodlooking	85
7	married	59	goodlooking	37	single	84
8	slim	59	young	32	Asian	74
9	young	50	clean	27	fit	73
10	attractive	48	fair	24	young	71
11	average	38	intelligent	24	slim	68
12	discreet	38	smart	24	Indian	63
13	caring	37	funloving	23	professional	60
14	professional	34	slim	23	clean	58
15	goodlooking	31	discreet	22	average	57
16	intelligent	31	fit	21	decent	57
17	honest	28	rich	19	educated	52
18	Australian	26	athletic	18	attractive	51
19	lonely	26	romantic	17	white	49
20	friendly	25	American	15	friendly	38

TABLE 7.4 *Frequency of self-descriptor traits.*

	Australia	%	India	%	Singapore	%	p<0.01
Personality	349	35.32	62	9.37	95	6.07	yes
Physical	300	30.36	209	32.81	430	27.49	no
Ethnicity/ Nationality/ Locale	26	2.63	65	10.20	563	35.99	yes
Intellect/ Profession	65	6.57	171	26.84	112	7.16	yes
Marital/ Availability	137	13.86	71	11.14	235	15.02	no
Age	50	5.06	32	5.02	71	4.35	no
Hygiene	61	6.17	27	4.23	58	3.07	no

professional, *educated* and *intelligent* were summed together to make the category Intellect/Profession).

Chi-square tests were carried out to test the null hypothesis that there was no significant difference in the frequency of each trait across the corpora, using an online chi-square calculator.[9] The final column of Table 7.4 shows whether the null hypothesis could be rejected at the p < 0.01 level for each test that was carried out. For three of the traits the null hypothesis could be rejected at p < 0.01 (Personality, Ethnicity/ Nationality/Locale and Intellect/Profession) while for the other four traits the null hypothesis could not be rejected.

Taken together, Tables 7.3 and 7.4 indicate some differences (and similarities) in the sorts of traits that advertisers of different countries appear to foreground. Almost two-thirds of the self-descriptors in the Australian adverts are concerned with physical appearance or personality. The top Australian word *nice* is notable because it did not appear frequently enough as a descriptor to be in either the Singapore or India top 20 lists. Australians tended to use *nice* as a generic personality description:

> Nice slim tall athletic man, 45, fun, intelligent, open relationship, looking for nights out with fun women 35–55.

> I'm a nice guy, probably too nice. I usually don't have a problem being friends with girls, but it's never gone beyond friendship.

As well as *nice*, Australian men described themselves as *genuine*, *caring* and *honest* – terms that did not appear in the top 20 lists for the other corpora. This construction of a 'good guy' personality is perhaps indicative of the sorts of qualities that Australian advertisers think will be attractive to women, so it is worth bearing in mind that these self-descriptors may be revealing of women's desire as well as men's (or at least men's attempts to second-guess women's desire).

While personality traits appear to show a difference that is statistically significant between the three corpora (due to Australians referring to personality more), traits relating to physical appearance descriptors did not result in a significant difference – confirming this 'non-finding' surmised from the comparison of semantic tags in the previous analysis.

However, Singaporeans were found to be more likely to highlight their ethnicity (*Chinese*, *white*, *Indian*, *Asian*, *Caucasian*) and Indian advertisers were more likely to refer to aspects of their intellect (a finding already noted with the semantic tagging analysis). It is possible that the semantic tagging would also have revealed the Singaporean focus on ethnicity but recall how the word *race* was mistagged into the sports category. It is notable that Singaporeans often refer to themselves as *local*, which is not a strategy commonly used by the other two advertisers. With regard to the other three categories, no significant differences were found for Age (which actually referred to one word – *young*), Marital Status and Hygiene (which also referred to one word – *clean*).

I was puzzled by the presence of the word *clean* appearing in all three corpora, so I carried out more detailed concordances of this word in each of the corpora. In a few cases advertisers used the word to describe themselves as either *clean shaven* or *clean cut* (10% Australia, 22% India, 7% Singapore). However, the typical usage was somewhat different, as the following advert implies:

I am slim clean 5/11 tall 80kg and clean shaven.

One common set of words which occurred near or next to *clean* were to do with sexual health: *safe sex*, *DD free* (disease and drug free), *no drug*, *STD free*, although in rarer cases other words implied personal hygiene (*smell nice*, *neat apartment*). The most common use of *clean* then, is to imply that the advertiser will not pass on any sexually transmitted infections and/or does not take drugs.

One puzzle was why Marital Status/Availability words did not yield a statistically significant result from the chi-square test, although the semantic analysis had noted that Indian advertisers often used the tag S4 (Kin) and S5– (Not part of a group), which frequently referred to marital status, while Singaporeans had S7.1 (Power, organizing) as a key tag, which comprised the word *status* and again referred to marital status. In Table 7.4, Australians seem to use more of these words than Indians, although this is due to the presence of other words like *single* (which was tagged as N5– by

Wmatrix rather than S5–). The idiosyncrasies of the automatic semantic tagger are thus easier to spot when compared against categorizations that are more accurately assigned by hand.

Moving on, I was interested in the ways in which advertisers referred to more stereotypically masculine traits via self-descriptors. For example, *tall* was a common descriptor across all three adverts while words like *short*, *small* or *little* occurred only three times collectively as self-descriptors, for example:

> i am not a model looking guy neither am i muscular or anything, m just an ordinary guy with cute looks, a little broad body and good experience in making love. (India)

> Im single, very shy. I dont go out much and am to scared to talk to girls. I have been alone for years. Dont drink or smoke or do drugs. I work, Live alone. Im short and slim body. Small everywhere. Is there an asian girl that would like to meet me. Any age or looks welcome. (Australia)

In the first advert above, the advertiser's body is described as *little* although this might be mitigated through his use of *broad*, and other positive descriptions: *cute looks*, *good experience in making love*. The advertiser describes himself as *ordinary* and appears to balance a mixture of positive and less positive traits, perhaps as a way of appearing honest. The second advertiser also uses this strategy, noting that he doesn't do drugs but is *small everywhere* (possibly implying a small penis size) and appears open to any offers (*any age or looks welcome*). Such self-effacing adverts are not typical though of the entire corpus.

While the self-descriptors were often non-specific words like *attractive* and *good-looking*, or references to healthy bodies (*athletic, fit, slim*), words which referenced more clearly masculine bodies like *muscular, rugged, well-built* and *strong* (which I found were popular among British gay male advertisers) were not especially common (e.g. *muscular* occurred as a self-descriptor only 16 times across all three corpora and did not appear in any of the top 10 lists in Table 7.3). Nor were words which emphasized masculinity (which were again popular with gay advertisers), such as *masculine* (only three occurrences across all three corpora) and *macho* (no occurrences). It seems that heterosexual male advertisers tend not to directly emphasize masculinity, perhaps because they do not feel that this would be a strategy that would attract replies from women, or possibly because they expect their masculinity to be taken for granted (perhaps similar to the way that Australian advertisers refer to being *educated* much less than Indian advertisers). Instead, certain words like *tall, handsome, athletic, fit, good-looking* and *professional* appear to reference masculine traits in a less overt way.

I was also interested in examining how the frequent self-descriptors related to each other – having noticed that self-descriptors often appeared as lists, as in the following Australian advert:

I am clean tall slim and fun to be with.

I therefore used AntConc to examine the collocates of each of the top 20 self-descriptors in Table 7.3. I initially considered a span of 5 words either side of the search term and used the mutual information statistic with a cut-off of 3 along with a minimum frequency requirement of 5. Furthermore, I only considered collocates which also appeared in the top list in Table 7.3. Noting the relationships between each set of 20 words, I built collocational networks for each corpus. Figure 7.3 shows the network for the Australian corpus. The lines between each box indicate the words which have a collocational relationship with each other, using the criteria just described.

In Figure 7.3, a few words have lots of collocates: *fit* has six, while *tall* and *slim* have five each (all three words also collocate with each other). The middle of the figure shows a set of collocates that are mainly physical descriptors and are used to construct a positive description of a physically attractive man in terms of his face and body:

Im a tall, fit well built, clean, attractive man

mature gentleman, slim, fit, attractive body

I'm a handsome mixed race guy, tall & slim . . .

Two other collocates, *married* and *lonely*, only collocate with one another, and are somewhat separated from the larger part of Figure 7.3:

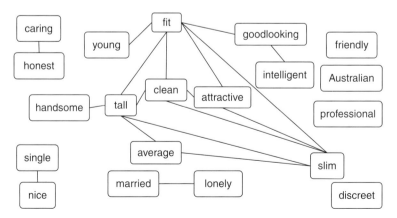

FIGURE 7.3 *Collocational network: Australian self-descriptors.*

Married but very lonely – 50 (Melbourne).

Another pair, *single* and *nice* also only collocate with one another:

Single nice guy looking for 1st girlfriend (Melbourne).

Similarly, *caring* and *honest* collocate (although *caring* also collocates with some non top-20 self-descriptors like *loving* and *kind*).

This method seemed to work well for the Australian corpus in showing relationships between descriptors, but when I tried to build similar collocational networks for the Indian and Singaporean corpora, I faced a problem. The smaller amount of text for the Indian corpus meant that a minimum frequency cut-off of 5 resulted in very few collocates – more than half of the self-descriptors did not show any relationships at all. The opposite problem was the case for the Singaporean data, however, where the larger amount of data resulted in so many relationships that it was difficult to draw a visual representation of the collocational network without the end result being too confusing to make sense of, with many overlapping lines. As noted earlier in this chapter, different corpus sizes can mean that the same cut-offs can be difficult to apply. However, altering cut-offs can make it look as if the researcher is engaging in a form of 'cherry-picking' or altering methods to get the results they want. I therefore tried to apply a different sort of criteria, which allowed methodological consistency across all three corpora but also took differing corpus size into account. This criteria set a requirement that the frequency cut-off for collocation should be (1) as high as possible; (2) need to result in at least half of the top 20 self-descriptors collocating with at least one other self-descriptor; and (3) but not to the extent that it was impossible to draw a collocational network with no overlapping lines. This required me to experiment with different minimum frequency cut-offs for collocation until one that met the criteria was found for each corpus. Using these criteria, I lowered the minimum threshold to 4 for the Indian corpus and raised it to 8 for the Singaporean corpus. Figure 7.4 thus shows the Indian collocational network.

The collocational network in Figure 7.4 comprises one group of connected adjectives with nine adjectives not connecting to any others in the network. As with the Australian network, the descriptor *tall* appears to be central, with a high number of collocates. The word *fair* stands out because it does not occur in the other two top 20 lists. A concordance analysis indicates that it is used to refer to a light-skinned complexion. There have been reports that in South Asian countries a fair skin is viewed as a marker of social prestige, and in 2010 the market in skin lightening creams in India was estimated at $432 million.[10]

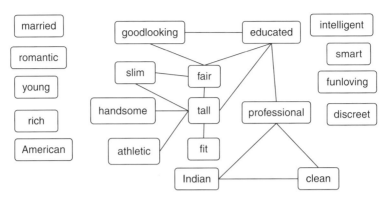

FIGURE 7.4 *Collocational network: Indian self-descriptors.*

i am 23 yr, 5'8" tall smart, fair colour, handsome . . . . .

I am 6 feet 2 inches tall, body type is athletic, fair complexion and good looking.

There are a number of trios in the Indian network (three words which all collocate with one another): *fair-goodlooking-educated*, *professional-Indian-clean*, *slim-fair-tall*. The connection of *clean* with *Indian* and *professional* is particularly interesting, contrasting with how *clean* collocates more with physical attractiveness words in the Australian network. In Australia, *clean* seems to be connected more to physical health while in India it appears to be part of a more 'socially respectable' identity. Let us move on to the Singaporean network (Figure 7.5).

In the final collocational network it was notable how the words for ethnicity or skin colour appeared to closely collocate with one another, and this seemed implausible as advertisers are unlikely to describe themselves as both *Caucasian* and *Asian* in the same way that they would list adjectives like *tall*, *attractive* and *athletic*. Concordance analysis revealed that these collocational pairs were atypical cases in that one word was a self-descriptor and another was a descriptor of the desired partner:

Caucasian guy for Asian ladies – 33 (Orchard).

Handsome white male seeks hot Asian lady for LTR.

I have indicated these exceptional connections with dotted lines as they do not function as part of lists of self-descriptors in the same way as the other collocates. The higher number of adjectives referring to ethnicity (*white*, *Indian*, *Asian*, *Chinese*, *Caucasian*), perhaps relates to Singapore's population being quite ethnically diverse. The 2010 Census indicates that 22 per cent of the population of Singapore were born outside of Singapore, and while 74 per cent of the population are classed as Chinese, there are

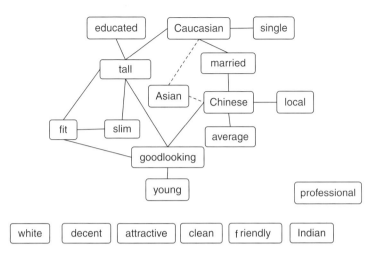

FIGURE 7.5 *Collocational network: Singaporean self-descriptors.*

also significant numbers of Indians, Malays and people classed as 'Other'.[11] Related to this, the word *local* is also worth mentioning as it was the top self-descriptor for Singaporean men in Table 7.4 but did not occur in either the Australian or Indian lists. *Local* could indicate someone who was either born in Sinagpore or has lived there a long time:

> I'm a 42 yr old Expat, Caucasian. Been here many years, so feel quite local.

> Ideally you'd be local since I don't know anyone in this island – just moved.

As with the other two networks, *tall* appears to be a central self-descriptor, collocating with five other words. The only trios in the network are *tall-fit-slim* and *tall-fit-goodlooking*, both comprising physical descriptors. Some of the connections are perhaps less expected – *educated* only collocates with *tall*, for example – although these two traits do not necessarily appear to be as semantically similar as *fit* and *slim*. However, both *tall* and *educated* are positive traits, and Judge and Cable (2004) have noted that height is more likely to be linked to career success for men than women. Thus, advertisers who use these two terms are implicitly signalling their capacity for social dominance.

The method of focusing on a smaller number of frequent words in the corpus, which directly relate to the self-description of the advertiser has not only helped to confirm some of the findings from the key semantic tag analysis (such as the Indian tendency to highlight profession and education), but has also highlighted how a user-defined categorization scheme can also be helpful (such as indicating that while references to marital status are perhaps more similar than first thought between adverts, there is more of a difference relating to ethnic status and personality). The collocational networks showed how certain adjectives appear to reinforce one another – particularly lists pertaining to an attractive body, although it is also worth noting which words were not as popular – those relating to more explicit or obvious constructions of hegemonic masculinity.

While this second method has revealed more fine-grained differences between the groups, as well as beginning to provide some clues about how the advertisers construct their own gender identities, I do not feel that the research questions have been adequately addressed yet. Perhaps a third approach will be more revealing.

Method 3: Concordancing women

The final method of analysis involves a more qualitative approach, via reading concordance lines, mirroring the technique used in Chapter Five when I examined discourses surrounding homosexuality. In order to obtain a better idea about how males relate to gender I decided to try to identify the sorts of gendered discourses (Sunderland 2004) that they articulated, by carrying out concordance searches of a small set of terms which directly related to gender.

Up until this point I had not focused on how the advertisers constructed their desired partners. The first method had given a general overview of the corpora while the second had concentrated on self-constructions which I had related to masculinity. However, I felt that a final approach which looked at how the advertisers characterized women might tell us more about gender. It is worth noting that in 2012 (the same year this study was carried out), a global poll of 370 gender experts by TrustLaw (a news service run by Reuters), found that India was the worst place to be a woman of the G20 countries (the major economies of the world), while Australia came in the top five (Singapore was not considered).[12] It would therefore be interesting to see if these differences would impact on the sorts of gendered discourses found between the three sets of adverts.

Words relating to gender were very frequent in all three corpora, and scanning the frequency lists, four terms in particular tended to be widely used: *woman*, *girl*, *lady* and *female*, along with their plurals. I therefore conducted concordance searches of these eight terms in each corpus, sorting each concordance alphabetically and reading through the 2,634 lines produced, often expanding lines and collecting cases where advertisers appeared to be articulating a gendered discourse. As described in Chapter Five, this is a somewhat subjective process as discourses are filtered through the cognitive and social biases of the analyst who may overlook particular discourses because they are taken for granted from the analyst's perspective. I tried to focus on concordance lines where advertisers made generalizing comments about women rather than specific ones, particularly when they referred to the notion of a generic woman. Additionally, I was drawn to adverts where the advertiser expressly referred to societal norms in some way. Adverts which also related women to men (e.g. by comparing them together) also proved to be a good 'site' for the identification of gendered discourses.

In order to limit the amount of data I collected to a manageable amount, I focused on cases where a particular discourse seemed to be repeated by several advertisers. In the sections below I have tried to 'name' the discourses by first grouping similar adverts together. I have not categorized the discourses into different countries, as they occurred reasonably equally across all three corpora, a finding which ran slightly counter to intuition, considering the differences in the TrustLaw poll described above.

Discourse 1: Women's sexuality suppressed

> women tend not to talk about their needs . . . Women who are very open about their needs are 'still labelled and judged' . . . (India)

This discourse could be described as a resistant discourse in that it acknowledges and refutes a mainstream discourse. First, it not only constructs women as having sexual desires but also notes that societies discourage women from expressing them. However, the discourse cited in the adverts in this subsection is resistant because the male advertisers are critical of society, instead urging women to acknowledge and follow their desires.

In India this discourse occurred in adverts for male escorts as in the one above, and in the following advert where the advertiser advocates a 'gender equality' discourse, as a way of encouraging women to use his service.

> You are very open minded and hate people who label & judge you becoz of this. You would really like to see more women act upon and make choices for themselves . . . to have the same freedom that men have. You can have your choices, be confident and you are free to do what you like. (India)

In other countries, this discourse is used to encourage women to contact advertisers who are *not* (explicitly) offering sex for money:

> So many women lock themselves away at home . . . perhaps lonely . . . frustrated . . . isolated . . . but feel that underlying urge to express themselves . . . SOMEHOW Perhaps its just to get out of the house for a while . . . or

a need to simply flirt and confirm to themselves that they are still 'sought after' . . . or perhaps even more with discretion . . . (Australia)

This is therefore an interesting use of a discourse then, because the male advertisers who are offering sex feel required to spend some time justifying why it is acceptable for a woman to reply to them. However, it could be argued that the articulation of this discourse is *strategic*, because the male advertiser (potentially) benefits from it, either from obtaining sex and/or payment.

As evidence that the adverts quoted in this section are actually referencing a *gendered* discourse, it is worth pointing out by this point in the analytical process I had read many adverts from all three corpora and had not noticed male advertisers engaging in this sort of rhetoric to validate their own sexual needs. Apart from cases where a man outlined a particular unusual desire or circumstances which meant he was transgressing another social norm (such as being married and wanting an affair), male desires were usually expressed in a more straightforward way.

Some advertisers referenced this discourse but in a more complex way which combined with traces of other discourses, as in the example below which uses a euphemistic term (*root*) for sex.

> I have heard it said that some women just want a good root. I have never been able to verify this. The only evidence I have of women wanting a good root is with conciderable payment. In other words these women want money more than they want a root. This tends to imply that all women are prostitutes and price is the determining object of whether they do or dont. Of course I am not talking about married women who are devoted to their husbands and do not stray outside of marriage vows. My question is are there any women about the place, not devoted to a relationship/commitment who just want a good root? (Australia)

This example begins with the advertiser claiming that he has heard that women want sex but this is qualified with the determiner *some* and later in the excerpt the advertiser gives two exceptions – prostitutes and married women who are devoted to their husbands. Unlike the above adverts then, the advertiser does not appear to uncritically accept the discourse, but instead hopefully postulates that it *might* be an accurate reflection of the world, although with exceptions. He then appears to reference a 'good girl-bad girl' discourse which divides women into two categories, and which he positions his own search against – a desire for a woman who does not fit into either category, but one whom he does not seem to have found before.

The following advertiser critically acknowledges that society disapproves of woman who use 'sexual power' but this discourse is combined with the 'sex differences' discourse – women's 'sexual power' is contrasted against men's 'physical strength':

> . . . a woman's sexual power is one of her greatest assets and I can't understand why society judges the use by woman of that power. If a woman disclaims a source of her own power, I think that's as foolish as a man would be if he refused to use his physical strength. (Singapore)

Some advertisers attempt to reappropriate pejorative terms for women, as in the case below, which contrasts respectable traits: *attractive*, *professional*, with another 'side' to them: *absolute whore*.

> I am looking for attractive, professional women that want to spend some time exploring that side of themselves that is just an absolute whore. (Singapore)

Like the Australian advertiser above, this advert also indicates that there is a dual nature to female sexuality, although in this case the 'good-girl-bad-girl' discourse is represented as inherently internal to individual women, rather than being a way of dividing women into two separate groups.

While the 'society wrongly suppresses female sexuality' discourse appears to be empowering to women then, the fact that it occurs in a very specific context (individual males urging women to ignore societal mores and have sex with them) for what could be interpreted as strategic purposes, lends ambivalence to its deployment. Additionally, its linking to other discourses like 'gender differences' and 'good girl-bad girl', suggests that its liberating message may not be straightforward. For some men, it seems that society is required to construct women (but not men) as 'absolute whores', in order for them to be viewed as attractive.

Discourse 2: Women, know your place

A few advertisers explicitly referenced feminism and sexual equality in their adverts, making their stance towards it clear:

> Frankly, I am looking for a woman who knows her place. The fact is, what with this feminist shit that society is putting up, the real women who know their place aren't proudly admitting it. I am looking for a female who knows she is just that, a female. And knows her place in front of a male. Write to me. (India)

> I don't mind if you complain about things. I actually think it's cute sometimes. But acting like a man is NOT CUTE. In fact it's fucking annoying which is why I hate 99% of Australian women. They try to be the boss. I'm the motherfucking boss – I'm the guy. You're the girl. If you are some raging fucking feminazi, now is the time to stop reading and live alone forever. (Australia)

While the identification of the 'women, know your place' discourse was relatively easy due to its lack of subtlety, attempting to interpret and explain its presence is more complicated. As both of the above advertisers display a clear contempt for gender equality, it could be argued that this would be interpreted as unattractive and therefore not elicit responses from women, which raises a question about why the adverts were placed. Indeed, the advertisers may not have expected replies, but instead may be using Craigslist more as a platform for their views or as a form of 'trolling', taking pleasure from posting a deliberately offensive advert that will garner angry responses.

However, these adverts might have been genuinely posted in the hope of gaining a partner, with the poster perhaps not realizing how offensive he is being and/or hoping to find a woman who is prepared to accept his terms and let him be dominant. These adverts could even be interpreted as advocating dominance towards women as a form of sexual fetishization, with hatred of sexual equality used as part of this fetish, in order to attract a woman who wants to participate in a BDSM (Bondage, Discipline and Sadomasochism) relationship.

One aspect of this discourse is that women from certain societies are viewed as unattractive, as with the above advertiser who claims to hate 99 per cent of Australian women. American women are also derided in some adverts as either promiscuous or eschewing traditional values:

Tired of USA Whores (India)

American women do not care about marriage (India)

Other advertisers find women in the workplace to be problematic:

Well I don't look forward to dating those aggressive girls at work no matter how gorgeous they look. (Singapore)

However, another advertiser refers to and subverts the 'women, know your place' discourse, implying that men are afraid of successful women. He instead presents himself as someone who finds successful women attractive:

Do you agree that guys are often afraid of successful, beautiful, independent woman? No matter if its true or not, I have to say that I am extremely attracted to women who are super educated, who know what is happening around the world, who has their own opinions, who are creative, who are actively interested in various aspects of life and arts . . . (Sinagpore)

Not everyone who claims to agree with sexual equality actually appears to be fully committed to that stance though.

I believe in sexual equality – why is that bad? Cos i like women who pay for their own shit, well if you want sexual equality, you need to act that part right? (Singapore)

The above advert appears to be another case of the strategic articulation of a discourse, in that the advertiser claims to be in favour of sexual equality because he will benefit financially from it. The dismissive way that the word *shit* is used to refer to female purchases, plus the patronizing tone taken in the direct address to women which follows 'well if you want sexual equality, you need to act that part right' suggests that the advertiser is perhaps not committed to sexual equality, or is belittling the concept by making a joke about it. Thus one interpretation of this advert is that it actually articulates a hatred of sexual equality rather than the reverse.

Discourse 3: Treat her like a queen

In contrast to the previous discourse, the final one that I identify here appears to be more positively inclined towards women. Some male advertisers seem to place women on a pedestal and the verb *treat* (or *spoil*, *worship*, *pamper* and *dote*) often signals the presence of this discourse:

I treat women with care and appreciation. (Australia)

I am a professional, who knows how to treat an women as Queen, please her and make her smile. (Singapore)

I'd love a mature gf who I could spoil and treat like a queen. (Australia)

I'm 6'4" tall medium build and treat a lady like a queen. (Australia)

The phrase *like a queen* or similar phrases also acts as a linguistic trace of this discourse, constructing women as royalty, as shown in the last three adverts. However, women are also described as princesses and goddesses:

I am a Man who treats the girl like a girl. They are to be treated like princess (Australia)

In bed – perceive women as Goddesses – Goddesses – creatures that ought to be worshipped, pampered, made to feel special and sometimes downright shagged hard. (Singapore)

Some of the adverts refer to 'treats' that are more material in nature:

I love when i take a woman out on a date. (Australia)

On the other hand, some suggest that the 'treats' are sexual, with the effect that male advertisers position themselves as knowing what women want and how to sexually pleasure them.

> All ladies truly deserved to be doted, pampered, and fulfilled through good, warm intimacy. (India)
>
> I'm skilled at making ladies squirm with pleasure. (Australia)
>
> I know its selfish of guys to always cum first so I always make sure the girls cums first. (Singapore)

While these adverts acknowledge female sexual pleasure and position women with positive and potentially empowering words like *queen* and *goddess*, it is also possible to interpret this discourse as disempowering in that women are passivized, being the recipients of verb phrases where the man is the active participant. The male advertisers also imbibe themselves with the knowledge of what women want and the ability to give it to them, positioning themselves as relatively more powerful. Additionally, some of the word choices that occur in the excerpts above raise questions. For example, the description of women as *creatures* feels dehumanizing, while the verb *spoil* is suggestive of a child (in the BNC the lemma SPOIL collocates with *child* but not *man* or *woman*, indicating that this verb is typically more used to characterize children). Disturbingly, Keeling and Fisher (2012), who interviewed women who had been subjected to domestic violence by male partners, noted that several women talked about what the analysts called 'the princess effect', whereby at the start of the relationship, prior to the man becoming violent, 'the woman was made to feel like royalty, removed from the normality of life and all its associations with feelings of being placed on a pedestal' (ibid.: 1562). Keeling and Fisher (ibid.: 1562–3) describe this as part of a grooming process, an exercise of power designed to subjugate the partner. Although it is dangerous to assume a direct link between men who use the 'treat her like a queen' discourse and subsequent domestic violence, it is interesting to note the discovery of two such discourses in such different contexts.

In any case, while the males who articulate the 'treat her like a queen' discourse appear to be positively inclined towards women, we could interpret it as contributing towards women's disempowerment. The contradictory nature of discourses has been remarked on by others. For example, talking about the workplace, Baxter (2003: 9) notes, 'individuals are rarely consistently positioned as powerful across all discourses at work within a given context – they are often located simultaneously as both powerful and powerless.'

It should be noted that in terms of the concordance lines examined, these three gendered discourses appeared in only a small number of adverts (although concordance searches of other words may have unearthed more cases). However, the fact that each discourse was identified in all three corpora indicates that they are not restricted to a single country or culture but are likely to be revealing of a more wide-ranging set of views regarding women and gender relationships. It is notable that the other two forms of analysis did not indicate the presence of any of these gendered discourses – and what the qualitative analysis has revealed are somewhat contradictory or ambivalent views about women, put forward by some male advertisers.

Conclusion

At the start of this chapter I advocated that researchers combine different methods of analysis in order to triangulate their findings. I demonstrated how triangulation might work by conducting three different types of analysis, each with different levels of focus – one based on comparisons of key semantic tags, another which used frequent self-descriptors and considered how they related to each other, while the final technique involved a qualitative examination of concordance lines in order to identify gendered discourses. I was interested in seeing what the analyses would tell us about the ways that advertisers oriented to gender, as well as uncovering the extent to which advertisers from different countries were different or similar.

The most wide-ranging analysis, involving semantic tags, initially indicated a high amount of similarity – with 15 out of 20 of the most key tags being the same when each of the three corpora were compared against the same reference corpus. However, when the corpora were compared against each other, differences emerged, which sometimes appeared to be related to aspects of a particular culture, although at other times further analysis revealed that the differences were actually hiding similarities (such as the fact that advertisers in different countries wanted to buy or sell sexual services but used different words to indicate this). The differences found did not appear to relate to the research question on gender so much, perhaps reflecting the all-encompassing approach of semantic tagging. For example, the analysis of one tag revealed that the Australian advertisers seemed to be more concerned about receiving unwanted adverts from spammers in their responses – potentially an interesting finding but not revealing a great deal about gender. However, the analysis did reveal a few relevant details – such as the fact that Indian advertisers were more likely to describe themselves with words to do with education and business, emphasizing social status and also implying their ability to be a 'provider', which indicates a preoccupation with a certain type of masculinity.

This last finding was confirmed in the second stage of analysis, when I focused only on frequent self-descriptors used by the advertisers. However, the analysis also made discoveries that had not occurred with the semantic tags – such as the propensity of Australian advertisers to describe themselves in terms of their personality more than Indian and Singaporean advertisers. As 'personality' covers a wide range of words, this was not something which could be picked up by the automatic tagging system, and a categorization scheme which was created via human engagement with the actual data, was therefore required in order to make this finding.

The analysis of top 20 self-descriptors also revealed similarities not uncovered by the semantic tagging – such as the use of the word *clean* to mean drug- or disease-free, while an examination of collocational networks revealed that certain groups of words tended to co-occur in all three adverts, particularly those relating to a positive descriptors of the body such as *tall*, *fit* and *slim*.

The final form of analysis was not quantitative, but involved reading-sorted concordance lines in order to identify and group similar patterns together. This was a more interpretive form of analysis than the other two, and it produced discoveries that were completely different to what had gone before. Across all three corpora, some advertisers acknowledged that society found female sexual desire to be problematic (and urged them to overcome this), others expressed a strong dislike of sexual equality politics while another group indicated that women should be treated like queens. All three discourses were interpreted as problematic for different reasons, although it should also be acknowledged that this may have not been the intention of individual advertisers, and that interpretations are multiple and subjective.

With just a few thousand words devoted to outlining each stage of the analysis, I cannot claim to have covered everything, and there were some aspects I had to leave out due to space (for example, I identified other gendered discourses such as 'women are emotionally unstable'). However, what I hope to have shown instead is how different techniques can help us to interrogate our corpora from different perspectives. This can sometimes help to confirm a finding – if more than one method produces a similar result, then this can be an indication that we have not over-interpreted something. However, each method also uncovered new or unique discoveries, resulting in a richer understanding of our corpora.

I carried out a related form of triangulation by asking five researchers to conduct analyses on the same corpus (containing newspaper articles about foreign doctors), and then compared their techniques and findings (Baker 2013a). Reassuringly, there was a high amount of agreement with regard to the majority patterns in the corpus – everyone noted how journalists tended to be negatively disposed towards foreign doctors. However, the five analysts uncovered different ways that such negative evaluation was expressed, depending on the type and number of techniques that they used. Two analytical strategies were found to be particularly 'productive' in that they uncovered a higher number of findings – one was to carry out a very thorough, exhaustive analysis – such as reading through hundreds of concordance lines of a high-frequency term that was central to the corpus. The second was to carry out a combination of different techniques (as also shown in this chapter).

Limitations regarding time, word count, access to resources and the abilities of individual researchers may mean that triangulation is not seen as feasible or even desirable, and additionally, the research questions being examined may be reasonably specific and answerable via a single technique. I therefore do not advocate that triangulation should always be carried out, although hopefully this chapter has shown that it is worth considering, alongside a survey of the wide range of different qualitative and quantitative techniques that are available.

CHAPTER EIGHT

Conclusion

Introduction

This final chapter provides a brief summary of the main findings of each of the analysis chapters, as well as trying to identify some emerging themes across the book. First, I sound a note of caution by discussing some of the limitations that need to be taken into consideration when carrying out corpus research on issues of gender. Following that, I reflect on the extent to which a corpus approach helps to reduce or even remove some of the biases that occur when humans try to carry out social research. And finally, I revisit the earlier chapters of the book, asking what the analyses I have carried out have been able to tell us about gender relations.

Considering limitations

For social research I would argue that at times we should be aware of a danger in exclusive reliance on both corpora and corpus techniques in order to answer research questions. A corpus in itself does not always yield explanations for language patterns and only by considering other forms of context can we fully account for our findings. This is something I have found numerous times in my own research, and it is demonstrated at various points in this book when I have drawn on statistics involving, for example, women in the workplace, divorce rates, literacy rates and crimes committed by boys and girls. At other points I have considered other types of social context, including changes in laws relating to sexual identity and guidelines for complaints about newspapers, in order to explain my findings. Sometimes, an explanation *can* be derived from the corpus itself, by expanding concordance lines or reading full texts within corpora but

I would also advocate that corpus research is improved when the analyst can rely on a healthy amount of general knowledge or at least has the skills and resources to know where to look in order to supplement deficiencies. Knowing which experts to turn to or how to conduct relevant searches on the internet (and then identify reliably accurate, well-researched information accordingly) are qualities that should not be underestimated.

Even if we remain committed to the corpus and do not feel the need to draw on other sources of information, the tools of corpus analysis, based around frequency and concordancing, are admittedly transformative for research purposes, but a good researcher needs to gain a feel for when and how they are most appropriately used, and whether a case should be made for other forms of analysis, such as reading the corpus (or a sample of it). The deployment of targeted concordance searches to identify agreements in a spoken corpus, in Chapter Three for example, was relatively successful but did not uncover all cases. Concordancing was faster than reading the corpus texts but individuals must decide on the extent to which full coverage is sacrificed for speed and convenience. For some, this may not be negotiable, verging on methodological heresy to even consider, while others may be more willing to live with a compromise. I suspect that corpus linguists, used to working with automatic taggers that proudly claim percentage accuracy in the high 90s, may be less concerned about finding all 100 per cent of all cases in their corpora, as long as the vast majority are uncovered.

Similarly, in Chapter Five, legitimation strategies were generally not forthcoming by simply looking at a list of words that collocated with *gay* or *homosexual*, nor were they especially apparent when looking at the few words of context provided by a concordance line. It was only in cases when the concordance line alone was inadequate at revealing how a collocate of *gay* or *homosexual* contributed towards a particular discourse that legitimation strategies were uncovered. In such circumstances I had to expand concordance lines to read an entire paragraph of text, or at times, a whole article. And in reading longer stretches of text I was able to point out cases that looked like legitimation, as well as recalling similar instances that I had noticed earlier. So my identification of legitimation strategies was somewhat fortuitous (and reliant on the application of knowledge regarding context) rather than being the result of carrying out targeted searches to elicit them.

Through examples, I have tried to impart information about what a corpus can do well, can do reasonably well and not do well at all in this book, although individual readers also need to supplement this information with consideration of their own abilities. Do they have the patience to apply a complicated categorization system to 5,000 concordance lines, should they just work with a sample or try something else? Can they write a perl script to remove all of the boiler-plate (and nothing else) in a corpus? Can they confidently isolate the right statistical test to perform on their table of frequencies? It is a rare researcher who can do everything corpus-related, and I increasingly see the value in assembling teams with complementary skill-sets.

Reducing researcher bias

Baxter (2003: 59–60), in her discussion of post-structuralist feminist discourse analysis advocates that researchers employ self-reflexivity in their research, which involves clarifying one's theoretical position and epistemological assumptions that are to be applied to any act of discourse analysis. Additionally, researchers should be self-aware about the fictionality and textuality of the research process, particularly the fact that any act of research comprises a series of authorial choices and strategies. While Baxter has not used techniques associated with Corpus Linguistics, I have found her suggestions to be useful when considering social and critical research that uses corpus methods, particularly because this is still an emerging field (or combination of fields), and critical engagement around what we do and why we do it is important, lest others are inadvertently misled from the outset.

Additionally, I urge self-reflexivity because corpus linguists can perhaps be more prone to make claims about objectivity due to the fact that the computer programs they use do not make errors and are not subject to the ideological and cognitive biases found in humans. However, both the *designers* and *users* of such programs are subject to such biases, and as I have tried to demonstrate, particularly in Chapter Two, an uncritical reliance on the techniques offered by corpus tools can at times help to reinforce certain ways of thinking, leading us to discount the fact that we are making choices from a finite range. For example, the keywords technique pits corpus x against corpus y, producing lists of words which show the largest relative frequency differences. Used on social groups (e.g. men vs women) this can lead to the reification of difference if we overlook all the phenomena where the difference is statistically negligible. Getting the popular corpus tools to tell us about similarity is possible but generally not as straightforward – and it is telling that we talk of keyword analysis rather than the opposite (I coined the term *lockword* to refer to words which have a similar frequency across two or more corpora, referring to how the frequencies of such words are locked into place, Baker (2011: 66)). Additionally, current corpus tools tend to be binary-oriented, allowing us to compare x against y, rather than easily enabling statistical tests across more than two corpora (x, y, and z) or to consider multiple factors.

One aspect of the 'fictionality' of research is that when we write papers, we try to present a coherent, linear narrative of the research process, which is easy for readers to follow but may not always be entirely accurate. We may simplify the order in which we took certain steps or disregard activities that resulted in dead ends. Corpus Linguistics research is sometimes imperfect and messy, and I have not tried to gloss this over in this book, instead pointing out where the automatic tagging of my corpora was incorrect, resulting in me being directed to less-than-helpful collocational pairs (e.g. *man* and *Utd* in Chapter Six), the miscategorization of *scout* as a verb rather than a noun (also Chapter Six) and the mistagging of *race* as belonging to the semantic group of sport in Chapter Seven. I have not hidden the fact that despite my best efforts I was not able to identify every incidence of disagreement in Chapter Three via concordancing or that in Chapter Seven, my initial efforts to apply the same cut-off points for collocation on three corpora of different sizes produced wildly unhelpful results. Nor have I obscured the fact that, in Chapter Five, when I revisited the same analysis of *Daily Mail* articles a few years later, I realized that I had initially missed nine cases where gay men were described somewhat positively. I would be presenting a dishonest picture of both my own abilities as an analyst and the capabilities of Corpus Linguistics if I had not been explicit about these less tidy aspects in this book, and that would risk the creation of unfair expectations for other researchers who use the techniques described herein.

However, it is important to remember that no method is immune from researcher error and procedural bias, but that should not mean the method ought to be rejected. Instead, shortcomings should be faced, errors fixed if possible and limitations acknowledged if not. The use of different forms of triangulation is one possible way of countering such limitations, subjecting the same corpus to different techniques, combining corpus techniques with those from other fields, or asking more than one researcher to work on the same corpus.

In Chapter Five I noted that 'the identification of discourse prosodies is very much a subjective matter, and that people who approach the data from a different political stance may notice or interpret different aspects of it to me.' When conducting the same analysis on the same corpus approximately six years later I elicited a slightly different set of findings, while in Chapter Seven I describe another study where I asked five researchers to carry out an independent analysis of the same corpus. Their findings overlapped but most of them pointed out phenomena in the data that the others had not noticed. This raises a question about the extent to which researchers ought to reflect on their own identities and abilities and the ways that they may have impacted on the research outcomes. For example, as a gay man who has at times experienced homophobic bullying and prejudice, am I more likely to be sensitive to homophobia (say, in terms of interpreting ambiguous or subtle cases as such) than most other people? Some researchers strongly dislike bringing their own identities into a piece of research, perhaps being uncomfortable with revealing information about themselves or concerned that such disclosures will lead others to discount their findings as resulting from their own biases. A post-structuralist perspective would eschew the idea of an objective researcher (even one who used corpus-driven techniques) and could be critical of anyone who claimed full objectivity. Instead, post-structuralism would advocate a more reflexive stance, where the researcher addresses his or her subjectivities and perhaps tries to counter them through various means (such as asking other researchers to interpret the same texts or using multiple methods of analysis on the same data). Alternatively, critical discourse analysts tend to be less concerned about presenting themselves as neutral, instead arguing that it is good to conduct analysis from a deeply-held 'position'. My personal view is that it is beneficial to be reminded that a human being has carried out a piece of social research and that a modest amount of reflection by that human being on her or his relationship to the research topic and process is welcome, although also bearing in mind that people are entitled to privacy and research ought not be needlessly confessional.

Women are from Earth, Men are from Earth

Collectively, what have the analysis chapters in this book told us about the relationship between language and gender? While the corpora I used and collected are meant to be representative samples of language, we need to be cautious in claiming that they can allow us to make generalizing statements which apply worldwide or throughout time. The corpora I used are representative not of all language but of language at various points in time and location. Findings only apply to English-speaking countries, with the United Kingdom and America being better represented than others (another reason why I chose to look at Australia, Singapore and India in Chapter Seven).

In terms of the relationship between language *usage* and gender, Chapter Two indicated that in terms of words, we could characterize males and females as having a great deal of shared language use, with a few generalizable differences. The popular metaphor of men being from Mars and women from Venus is somewhat challenged by my analysis, especially considering the fact that the gender differences found in the BNC can sometimes be attributed to context, such as the fact that women were more likely to be recorded in domestic settings when they were engaged in childcare and other home-based work. Also, some of the more spectacular differences could be attributed to variation within the sexes, or rather, small numbers of female or male speakers who used certain words repeatedly but were actually atypical of their sex. I thus argue that in order to obtain a better perspective around gender differences we need to consider extent of similarity, social context and dispersion patterns within groups, otherwise we risk making too much out of difference. I do not completely reject the idea that there are no generalizable linguistic differences between male and female speakers (and I did not examine other phenomena such as prosody, accent and grammatical choice which could have uncovered other sorts of difference) but would caution that it is very easy to overstate the case for difference.

It is pleasantly surprising when a corpus analysis elicits something that looks odd but then makes sense when examined more closely, telling me something about the world that I did not know. This was the case in Chapter Two when the word *Christmas* emerged as a good candidate word for gender differences, spoken more by women and reasonably well-dispersed among them. Concordance analyses revealed that this was another context word, demonstrating that the organization around this holiday period was likely to be the concern of women (at least in early 1990s Britain when the corpus data was recorded). Perhaps as a measure of how much (or little) society has changed since then, it is notable that in 2012, a television advert for the supermarket Asda attracted 620 complaints to the Advertising Standards Authority about sexism.[1] The advert, which showed a montage of a mother making preparations for Christmas Day, presumably over the period of several weeks, used the strapline 'Behind every great Christmas there's Mum', implying that men or fathers do not (or perhaps need not) have a role in contributing to the organization around Christmas. To an extent, the line does reflect the data shown in the BNC, and the agency who created the advert claimed that it was based on survey data from 4,000 mothers. However, the fact that the advert attracted complaints does indicate that its underlying message was interpreted negatively by some, even if it was partly based in fact.

In Chapter Three I advocated that corpus approaches can enable perspectives other than one based on gender comparison, by arguing that there is value in examining the language use of just one group of people, not necessarily comparing them against anything else. Such an approach frees us from thinking in terms of gendered 'over-use' or 'under-use', does not pit the sexes against one another or implies that certain groups are deviating from the 'norm' in some way. I chose to focus on the language of women in a particular workplace context, hoping to address some of the issues that were raised in Chapter Two which had tended to examine women who were recorded when they were not in work. I also wanted to contribute towards a growing body of literature which has looked at the 'double bind' when women are in positions of power, being expected to show authority but not in a way that makes them appear to be 'masculine'. Other researchers had shown that some women in managerial positions appear to be more linguistically adept or have to engage in more discursive work around their talk in order to achieve their goals and again, I was interested in the extent to which certain work contexts enabled women to be authoritative. Examining how women engaged in a potentially FTA (disagreeing) in the relatively liberal setting of a university, I found that a range of different strategies were employed, some which attempted to save face by mitigating the amount of disagreement or being indirect about it, but in many cases female academics were able to indicate disagreement in an on-record way. However, no single strategy was able to account for at least half of the cases of disagreements and an examination of the women who disagreed multiple times indicated that while some appeared to have a fairly narrow repertoire of strategies, others tended to vary the way that they disagreed each time. As a 'social group' then, these female academics did not appear to be especially homogeneous (or even consistent within themselves), and taken with Chapter Two, I would argue that both these chapters indicate variation *within* the sexes, which is filtered through context. What Chapters Two and Three indicate is that where gender differences emerge, it is likely that they are due to expectations about how males and females should use language, based on the contexts they are in.

Perhaps research which focuses on language usage is somewhat more problematic within the field of Gender and Language, compared to discursive analyses of gender representation. There are dangers in essentializing a group or making over-generalizations from a small amount of data, although I would advocate that studies of usage should continue to play a strong role in the field, particularly if we view gender through the lens of performativity and consider how various societies sanction or taboo certain gendered performances as appropriate or not for certain types of men or women. Studies of usage can amply allow focus on intersectional aspects of identity, the fact that gender interacts with a range of other identity characteristics that people possess, while a second focus on usage could be on the ways that different contexts are likely to alter the gender performances of individuals or groups, helping to demonstrate the fiction of a stable, unchanging gender identity for most people. Corpus approaches to gendered language usage, with their reliance on very large bodies of transcribed data, are potentially well-placed to engage with such research, although the acquisition of large amounts of spoken corpus data is a stumbling block, and my reliance on the BNC (20 years old at the time of writing) in Chapter Two, as well as MICASE (another corpus collected in the twentieth century), is indicative of another reason (apart from concerns about essentialization) why such studies are not always forthcoming.

However, with the emergence of new forms of language usage appearing in computer-mediated contexts, it could be argued that we are at the beginning of a period of unprecedented access to texts, resulting in enormous potential for large-scale linguistic research. Terms like *opinion mining* (Pang and Lee 2008), *sentiment analysis* (Tsolmon et al. 2012) and *culturomics* (Michel et al. 2010) refer to computational analysis of very large amounts of electronic information although such approaches differ somewhat from corpus linguistics in that they tend to place more reliance on automatic techniques and quantitative analysis of extremely large amounts of data (such as the entire output of Google books or seemingly endless Twitter feeds), rather than carrying out concordance analyses and considering other means of taking context into account as described in this book. However, the emergence of such fields are indicative of a growing body of work which is exploiting the vast amount of language data available online in order to tell us something about society and culture. Indeed, I would have experienced difficulties in collecting some of the corpora used in the analysis of particular chapters of this book had it not been for the existence of the internet. In Chapters Three, Four and Six I used corpora which had been created by others and made available via online interfaces while in Chapter Five I used the online database Nexis in order to build a corpus of newspaper articles around a particular topic, and in Chapter Seven I was able to collect texts that had been posted online to a personals website. While the internet offers both a range of unique text types to explore issues relating to gender usage and representation in online contexts, as well as making it much easier for researchers to share and enable analysis of their corpora, I would continue to argue that there is value in building corpora of 'old-fashioned' spoken interactions, even though there are (at present) few automated procedures associated with obtaining and transcribing such corpora, making their collection relatively slow and expensive. It would be a pity if the ease in which computer-mediated texts can be collected inadvertently results in less focus on other forms of corpus analysis though.

Male bias not yet over

Moving on to the chapters of the book which focused on gender representation, the outlook which tends to characterize this area is continuing male bias, diminishing in places. Chapter Four, which focused on a number of aspects of sexist (and non-sexist) language in a large diachronic corpus of American English, stretching back to the early 1800s, found quantifiable bias in different ways – the tendency for males to be talked about more than females, for males to be mentioned first, and for males to be referred to as generic humans, although there is evidence that at least across the twentieth century, and especially since around the 1960s, some of these practices are seeing falls. It is notable that functionalizing suffixes like -*man* and -*woman* tend to be associated with certain types of work, particularly those involving influence and leadership for men, and service-related tasks for women, and that explicit gender marking (in cases like *lady doctor*) tends to occur in contexts which indicate exceptions to the general trend. The changes in the corpus over time are encouraging, in that they suggest gains for sexual equality, at least in terms of linguistic representation, but they also indicate that there is still some way to go.

Similarly, the analysis of two sets of *Daily Mail* articles containing the words *gay* and *homosexual* indicated that this British national newspaper, which has tended to function as a bastion of traditional, conservative values, is showing signs of having to change with the times. It may have initially opposed the legal recognition of gay relationships, but a comparison of articles taken from 2001–2 and 2008–9 indicate that during this short period a noticeable shift in discourse had taken place. The more negative discourses associating gay people with shame, crime, violence, promiscuity and sleaze are being replaced with those which acknowledge the concepts of gay rights and relationships and homophobia. While the *Daily Mail* has started to use terms like *gay marriage* and *homophobia*, this does not mean that the newspaper always accepts that such concepts are right or even exist at all. But its adoption of the language of gay equality movements indicates the direction that it is increasingly being led in. And the fact that one 2009 article which made thinly veiled references to some of the more negative discourses about gay people elicited 25,000 complaints as well as criticism from other *Daily Mail* columnists also suggests that the newspaper will need to approach the subject with greater caution. As the second most popular national newspaper in the United Kingdom, the *Daily Mail* acts as a good barometer of 'popular conservatism' in that country, and continued analysis of its changing discourses will be informative about gains relating to gender and sexual equality as well as the representations of a range of other social groups.

In Chapter Six I focused on collocates as a way of examining gender representation, noting that representations of boys and girls in a large corpus of online British texts tended to reinforce stereotypes with girls being linked to emotional expression, romantic relationships, clothing choices and representation as victims, while boys were associated with physical actions, being academically poor, entry level jobs and having their behaviour judged. The analysis also uncovered cases of collocation which indicated that *girl* is often used to refer to adult women, although the equivalent is not the case for *boy*. While the findings perhaps paint opportunities for girls and their accompanying representations as somewhat more restrictive than those for boys, it is notable that some collocational patterns in the corpus like *mother's boy* and *big girls blouse* (both used pejoratively on boys) indicate a form of social control in that qualities associated with being soft are seen as inappropriately feminine. Similar mocking collocates which aim to regulate masculine behaviour in girls were not found, suggesting one way that boys may be disadvantaged (the borders of acceptability being narrower for them) but ultimately indicating a dislike of so-called feminine qualities per se, damaging girls too (just as the *Mail* shows its dislike of gay men and women by trying to degrade such men as feminine). Fine (2010: 211–12) notes how in pre-school, children learn first to be gender detectives (a term devised by Martin and Ruble 2004), then gender reinforcers, due to the fact that such a premium is placed on gender in their lives: '. . . children are born into a world in which gender is continually emphasized through conventions of dress, appearance, language, color, segregation, and symbols. Everything around the child indicates that whether one is male or female is a matter of great importance' (Fine 2010: 212–13). My analysis of *boy* and *girl* bears this out. When children hear the words that relate strongly to their own identities, they are not hearing these words in isolation, but in (often) stereotyping contexts, so it is hardly surprising that people end up reproducing such stereotypes, having first encountered them when they were least able to be critically evaluative.

Finally, in Chapter Seven I tried to bring together some of the themes already addressed in this book by combining a study that had both gendered usage and gender representation at its centre. While this chapter only looked at language in personal adverts written by heterosexual-identified men who were seeking female sexual or romantic partners, it was interesting to see how the analysis revealed the ways that different men wished to construct themselves. Australian advertisers appeared to make more of an effort to construct themselves as 'good guys', using a high number of positive personality descriptors like *nice, genuine, caring, honest* and *friendly*. This was not so for Indian advertisers who focused more on describing themselves as socially dominant through adjectives that emphasized education, earning potential or wealth (*professional, educated, intelligent, smart, rich*). On the other hand, Singaporeans tended to highlight ethnicity as being most central to descriptions of themselves. While each construction potentially tells us something about the societies that different advertisers come from, I would also argue that such popular constructions are revealing about 'what works' for women (or at least what men *think* that heterosexual women will find attractive) in different places. The analysis also revealed the presence of fairly evenly distributed gendered discourses relating to gender relations, and sexual equality. Ranging from the outright misogynistic (*women, know your place*), to the patronizing and objectifying (*treat her like a queen*) and the possibly strategic (*women's sexuality suppressed*), the overall conclusion here was a somewhat depressing one, indicating that for some men at least, even when they are trying to attract women and present their best side, it can be difficult to avoid sexist discourses which appear to have global penetration. Collectively then, the findings in this book about gender indicate that feminists still have much work to do.

Concluding remarks

In the first chapter of this book I indicated that the combination of Corpus Linguistics and Gender and Language research was still something of a rarity, with only a few published articles using corpus methods in the first few issues of the journal *Gender and Language*. I hope that this book has helped to perhaps address some misgivings that researchers might have about engaging with corpora: that it is difficult, requiring advanced knowledge of computer programming and mathematics, that the approach is stuck in the 'gender difference' years and is mere number-crunching with no consideration of context, either within the texts themselves, or of the wider social conditions that texts were produced and received in. And while there is more research on gender being carried out by corpus and computational linguists, I hope that this book will encourage them to engage with some of the debates and theoretical strides around that have occurred in the field of Gender and Language over the last couple of decades.

As a final point, I want to return to the anecdote I related at the start of this book when I failed to engage the interest of a journalist who was writing an article about gender and language. Sadly, our research is futile if we talk to each other in closed conference rooms or publish in journals that are only subscribed to by relatively rich universities. I discussed the question of whether we ought to engage in 'action research' (or more critical forms of research which are aimed at encouraging actual social change) in Chapter Six. While I suggested that it is up to individuals to decide whether they want their research to be descriptive (and possibly leading by example) or prescriptive (calling for and making suggestions for change), my personal view is that there is little point in carrying out research that is not aimed at improving people's lives or their environment in some way. As a corpus linguist who works on issues around gender, I have sometimes felt doubly crippled in that I have had to get to grips with two sets of technical terminology (*performativity, feminist post-structuralist discourse analysis*, vs *collocation, log-likelihood test*). Coupled with the fact that the stories about gender that I wish to tell journalists do not always fit well with the current 'popular wisdom' or mainstream discourses, there is a risk that the research we do will have little real impact. Social researchers need to develop better ways of engaging with non-academics and the wider media. Although it is more work for us, making our findings available and accessible via social media is increasingly important, as is developing relationships with journalists, politicians and community leaders. There is a nice view from the ivory tower, but if we stay there we risk irrelevance.

NOTES

Chapter 1

1 It is not my aim to be critical of Harrison and Shortall's study, rather I want to problematize the way that a study on reported behaviours of a small number of people in reasonably similar circumstances was held up by the journalist as an example of a generalizable difference between the sexes.

2 The concepts *sex* and *gender* are normally used within academia to refer to biological aspects of identity (e.g. number of X chromosomes and/or whether a person has a penis or vagina) and behavioural/social aspects of identity (e.g. how people act/think/speak as males or females) respectively. Sometimes people use the terms interchangeably, so *gender* can be used as a politer, euphemistic term for *sex*. Despite the existence of intersex and trans people, sex is often characterized (for most people) as a stable male/female binary. Gender on the other hand, is theorized to be more complex and subject to change, possibly involving multiple gradients (e.g. someone might be masculine in some ways and feminine in others, and this may alter as they age).

3 While the gender difference paradigm has been to be popular in the media, it has been strongly criticized within the field of Gender and Language. For example, Troemel-Plotz (1991: 490) has argued that it is a 'non-engaged and apolitical stance' which 'trivialises our experience of injustice and of conversational dominance; it conceals who has to adjust; it veils differences again and again and equalises with a levelling mania any distinction in how we experience women and men' (ibid.: 501).

4 The first wave of feminism is associated with the suffrage movement in the nineteenth and early twentieth centuries, while the second wave is linked to equality campaigns in the 1960s (Bucholtz, Liang and Sutton 1999). A third wave has been identified, starting in the 1990s which is linked to post-feminism, and associated with the idea that there is diversity among men and among women and it is reductive to view all men as wielding power over all women. Instead, the third wave is concerned with deconstructing the societal structures that are responsible for inequalities (see Brooks 1997; Tandon 2008).

5 SPSS was initially Statistical Package for the Social Sciences but then later changed to Statistical Product and Service Solutions.

6 http://ucrel.lancs.ac.uk/llwizard.html.

Chapter 2

1   Many researchers refer to the notion of differences between males and
    females as 'gender differences', although it could be argued that the term 'sex
    differences' could be applicable as it is based on a binary division of the sexes.
    However, what is also argued is that the sexes perform their gender differently
    (e.g. males are stereotypically more competitive, women more co-operative), and
    as the majority of people cited in this chapter refer to 'gender differences', this is
    the term I will use.

2   An alternative measure of lexical similarity to the Manhattan Distance is the
    Dice Coefficient, based on joint frequencies and word counts in texts. It ranges
    between 0 and 1 and can be quickly obtained using the Detailed Consistency
    function in WordSmith.

3   Rather than comparing frequencies of words, Juola compared frequencies of
    2-grams or fixed 2-word sequences like *that is*.

4   At the time of writing I was not aware of a single available corpus analysis
    tool which would provide a measure of the Manhattan Distance. Instead, I first
    obtained wordlists for two corpora using WordSmith. Then I used the Detailed
    Consistency function in WordList to bring up a table comparing the frequencies
    of both words in the two corpora. I exported this table to Excel (converting the
    raw frequencies into percentages) and then used an algorithm to subtract the
    corresponding numbers in each column from each other, convert the results to
    a positive number and then add together all of the converted subtractions. The
    resulting number was the MD.

5   I would like to express my gratitude to Andrew Hardie who provided me with
    separate files containing the speech of every individual speaker in the BNC.

6   According to Labour Force Survey figures, in 1991, 32.5 per cent of women
    and 12.3 per cent of men were classed as economically inactive (not working or
    unemployed). See www.poverty.org.uk/48/index.shtml. However, these figures
    hide the fact that many of the women who were 'economically active', worked
    part-time rather than full-time.

Chapter 3

1   The final strategy, not doing the FTA at all, is difficult to identify from a
    transcript of a conversation, particularly if it is not possible to ask the speakers
    about aspects of the interaction. Similarly, there may be cases where a pragmatic
    feature like disagreement is signalled through silence. In some cases this might
    be possible to identify, if the silence is long enough and other speakers remark
    on it, but at other times, someone's meaningful (to them) silence might be lost
    amid the contributions of the other speakers. It must be acknowledged then,
    that an analysis of a transcript is unlikely to reveal a full picture around a
    phenomenon like disagreement, but is most likely to concentrate on forms of
    expression that are more visible.

2   Table 3.1 does not show all of the search terms I carried out, I also looked at a number of other words including *inaccurate*, *improbable*, *dubious*, *doubtful*, *questionable*, *strange*, *odd*, *unusual*, *reject*, *nor* and *nah* although these terms either resulted in no hits at all, no cases of disagreements or no cases of disagreements that I had already identified.

Chapter 4

1   In fact, in the 100-million word British National Corpus, *monosexual* and related words like *monosexuality* never occur. This raises an interesting issue – if a word is frequent, it is likely to be identified via corpus processes like frequency lists. Even a less frequent word has a chance of being spotted (and noted as being rare), if it occurs in a corpus, particularly if it is related to a very frequent word in some way (e.g. as an antonym). However, if a word *never* occurs, a corpus-driven approach may not identify its absence at all – unless the word appears often in a reference corpus and we identify negative keywords (those which occur less often than expected). This can lead to a paradox whereby something which occurs, say, five times may be described as rare, while something which occurs zero times may not be described at all, even though it is more rare. Furthermore, certain concepts may be so unusual or tabooed that societies have not invented terms for them. Thus, there is value in relying on intuition at times, in order to identify what could have been written or said but is not – although this can be a difficult task as it can entail the researcher attempting to interrogate his or her own internalized discourses and putting them to one side.

2   http://corpus.byu.edu/coha/.

3   See for example http://ucrel.lancs.ac.uk/llwizard.html.

4   There was some deliberation over whether to include *gentleman* as marking gender. Its closest female equivalent *lady* is used for exception marking (e.g. *lady doctor*), but there was a concern that *gentleman* might refer to cases where a man's gentlemanly nature is being remarked upon, for example *gentleman politician*, *gentleman burglar* rather than the fact that he is male per se. In fact, only 8 cases of *gentleman* occurred before any of the roles in the table, and so these cases were included for completeness as they did not make much difference to the final ratios.

5   It is impossible to calculate ratios when one frequency is zero. A workaround for such cases is to add 1 to both frequencies, so in the case of *stripper*, the ratio would be 6:1 in favour of being preceded by a male term while *reporter* would be 60:1 in favour of being preceded by a female term.

6   For example, McEnery (2006: 35–6) notes that The British Board of Film Classification rates cunt as 'very strong' while prick is 'moderate' in terms of scale of offence.

7   Potentially, *slut* could be used in a 'reclaimed' sense, as something positive, although I did not find any examples of this meaning in the COHA, suggesting that the reclaimed usage is relatively rare in general American English.

Chapter 5

1 www.populus.co.uk/the-times-the-times-gay-britain-poll-100609.html.

2 I carry out a more detailed qualitative analysis of this single article in Baker (forthcoming).

3 This sentence is taken from an article in the *Daily Mail* about a woman who discovers that her attractive husband is gay. Ironically, even though the article is about homosexuality, the cited sentence contributes to heteronormative discourse by assuming that no woman is immune to the man's charms.

4 www.pcc.org.uk/index.html.

Chapter 6

1 The analysis of the BNC in this chapter was carried out using an online tool called BNCweb.

2 www.sketchengine.co.uk/.

3 http://news.bbc.co.uk/1/hi/7401826.stm.

Chapter 7

1 Craigslist was set up by Craig Newman in 1995 as an email distribution list of friends, focusing on local events in the San Francisco Bay area, and gradually grew into a global web-based classified advertisements service.

2 According to www.internetworldstats.com/ in 2010–12, India had 11.4 per cent internet penetration, Singapore had 77.2 per cent while Australia had 88.8 per cent. The internet users in India are therefore more likely to be the richest section of society, while social class would not be such a good correlate of internet use for Singapore and Australia.

3 Wmatrix was able to recognize some aspects of computer-mediated communication language, correctly tagging *lol* (*laugh out loud/lots of love*), although it assigned Z99 (Unknown) to *omg* (*oh my god*) and *b4* (*before*), while *ur* (*your/you are*) was tagged as (Z4: discourse bin).

4 The term MNC referred to multinational corporation, occurring 26 times in the Indian corpus. Its acronymization suggests that this would be a commonly known term for Craigslist users in India.

5 http://unstats.un.org/unsd/demographic/products/dyb/DYB2004/Table25.pdf.

6 www.bbc.co.uk/news/world-south-asia-12094360.

7 www.censusindia.gov.in/2011-prov-results/indiaatglance.html.

8 In order to further check that the adjectives in Table 7.3 actually were used as self-descriptors, I hand-tagged all of the self-descriptors for half of the Australian corpus and derived a frequency list of adjectives based only on the self-descriptors. While the ordering of the most frequent words differed slightly from those found for the Australian data in Table 7.3, the same words appeared, indicating that the method of using untagged data and scanning concordance lines to remove unwanted cases was acceptable.

9 www.quantpsy.org/chisq/chisq.htm. For each test, six numbers were entered into the calculator, the frequencies of the trait being examined in each corpus, and the total frequencies of all the traits added together for each corpus minus the frequency of the trait being examined.

10 http://news.bbc.co.uk/1/hi/8546183.stm.

11 www.singstat.gov.sg/pubn/popn/c2010acr/tA6.pdf.

12 www.trust.org/trustlaw/news/poll-canada-best-g20-country-to-be-a-woman-india-worst/.

Chapter 8

1 www.marketingmagazine.co.uk/sectors/fooddrink/article/1168853/Asda-sexist-Christmas-ad-escapes-ban-despite-hundreds-complaints/.

REFERENCES

Alsop, S., Moreton, E. and Nesi, H. (forthcoming), 'The Uses of Storytelling in University Engineering Lectures', *ESP across Cultures*, 10.

Altrichter, H., Feldman, A., Posch, P. and Somekh, B. (2008), *Teachers Investigate Their Work: An Introduction to Action Research across the Professions*. London: Routledge.

Amaechi, J. (2010), 'Homophobia Hurts Straight Men Too', *Pink News*. www.pinknews.co.uk/2010/02/12/comment-homophobia-hurts-young-straight-men-too/. 12 February 2010.

Baker, P. (2005), *Public Discourses of Gay Men*. London: Routledge.

— (2006), *Using Corpora in Discourse Analysis*. London: Continuum.

— (2010), 'Will *Ms* Ever Be as Frequent as *Mr*? A Corpus-based Comparison of Gendered Terms across Four Diachronic Corpora of British English', *Gender and Language*, 4(1): 125–9.

— (2011), 'Times May Change, but We'll Always Have Money: Diachronic Variation in Recent British English', *Journal of English Linguistics*, 39(1): 65–88.

— (2013a forthcoming), 'Does Britain Need Any More Foreign Doctors? Inter-analyst Consistency and Corpus-assisted (critical) Discourse Analysis', in M. Charles, N. Groom and S. John (eds), *Grammar, Text and Discourse: In Honour of Susan Hunston*. Amsterdam/Philadelphia: John Benjamins.

— (2013b forthcoming), 'Considering Context When Analysing Representations of Gender and Sexuality: A Case Study', in J. Flowerdew (ed.), *Discourse in Context(s)*. London: Bloomsbury.

Baker, P, Gabrielatos, G. and McEnery, T. (2013), *Discourse Analysis and Media Bias: The Representation of Islam in the British Press*. Cambridge: Cambridge University Press.

Baron, A., Rayson, P. and Archer, D. (2009), 'Word Frequency and Key Word Statistics in Historical Corpus Linguistics', in Ahrens, R. and Antor, H. (eds), *Anglistik: International Journal of English Studies*, 20(1): 41–67.

Baxter, J. (2003), *Positioning Gender in Discourse: A Feminist Methodology*. Basingstoke: Palgrave Macmillan.

— (2010), *The Language of Female Leadership*. Basingstoke: Palgrave Macmillan.

— (2011), 'Survival or Success? A Critical Exploration of the Use of "Double-voiced Discourse" by Women Business Leaders in the UK', *Discourse and Communication*, 5(3): 231–45.

Berger, J. (1972), *Ways of Seeing*. London: BBC Books/Pelican.

Biber, D., Johansson, S., Leech, G., Conrad, S. and Finegan, E. (1999), *Longman Grammar of Spoken and Written English*. London: Longman.

Bijeikienė, V. and Utka, A. (2006), 'Gender-specific Features in Lithuanian Parliamentary Discourse: An Interdisciplinary Sociolinguistic and Corpus-based Study', *SKY Journal of Linguistics*, 19: 63–99.

Brindle, A. (2010), *"Just Keep Your Pants on and in the Closet and You'll Be Fine." The Corpus Analysis of a White Supremacist Web Forum.* Unpublished PhD thesis. Lancaster University.

Brooks, A. (1997), *Postfeminisms: Feminism, Cultural Theory, and Cultural Forms.* London: Routledge.

Brown, P. and Levinson, S. C. (1987), *Politeness: Some Universals in Language Usage.* Cambridge: Cambridge University Press.

Bucholtz, M. and Hall, K. (2004), 'Theorizing Identity in Language and Sexuality Research', *Language in Society*, 33(4): 469–515.

Burr, V. (1995), *An Introduction to Social Constructionism.* London: Routledge.

Butler, J. (1990), *Gender Trouble: Feminism and the Subversion of Identity.* New York: Routledge.

Caldas-Coulthard, C. R. and Moon, R. (2010), '"Curvy, Hunky, Kinky": Using Corpora as Tools for Critical Analysis', *Discourse and Society*, 21(2): 99–133.

Cameron, D. (1995), *Verbal Hygiene.* London: Routledge.

— (1998), 'Gender, Language and Discourse: A Review Essay', *Signs: Journal of Women in Culture and Society*, 23(4): 945–73.

— (2007), *The Myth of Mars and Venus.* Oxford: Oxford University Press.

Cameron, D. and Kulick, D. (2003), *Language and Sexuality.* Cambridge: Cambridge University Press.

Charteris-Black and Seale, C. (2009), 'Men and Emotion Talk: Evidence from the Experience of Illness', *Gender and Language*, 3(1): 81–113.

Cheng, N., Chandramouli, R. and Subbalakshmi, K. P. (2011), 'Author Gender Identification from Text', *Digital Investigation*, 8: 78–88.

Clear, J. (1993), 'From Firth Principles: Computational Tools for the Study of Collocation', in M. Baker, G. Francis and E. Tognini-Bonelli (eds), *Text and Technology: In Honour of John Sinclair.* Philadephia, Amsterdam: Benjamins, 271–92.

Coates, J. (ed.) (1998), '"Thank God I Am a Woman": The Construction of Differing Femininities', in D. Cameron (ed.), *The Feminist Critique of Language: A Reader*, 2nd edn. London: Routledge, 295–320.

Coates, J. (2003), *Men Talk.* Malden, MA: Blackwell.

Cohen, L. and Manion, L. (2000), *Research Methods in Education.* London: Routledge.

Connell, R. W. (1995), *Masculinities.* Oxford: Polity Press.

Cooper, R. (1982), 'The Avoidance of Androcentric Generics', *International Journal of the Sociology of Language*, 50: 5–20.

Curran, J. R. (2004), *From Distributional to Semantic Similarity.* Unpublished PhD thesis. Edinburgh University.

Deaux, K. and LaFrance, M. (1998), 'Gender', in D. Gilbert, S. T. Fiske and G. Lindzey (eds), *Handbook of Social Psychology*, 4th edn. New York: Random House, 788–827.

Deaux, K. and Major, B. (1987), 'Putting Gender into Context: An Interactive Model of Gender-related Behavior', *Psychological Review*, 94: 369–89.

Denzin, N. (2006), *Sociological Methods: A Sourcebook.* 5th edn. Chicago: Aldine Transaction.

Dunning, T. (1993), 'Accurate Methods for the Statistics of Surprise and Coincidence', *Computational Linguistics*, 19(1): 61–74.

Durrant, P. and Doherty, A. (2010), 'Are High Frequency Collocations Psychologically Real? Investigating the Thesis of Collocational Priming', *Corpus Linguistics and Linguistic Theory*, 6(2): 125–55.

Eckert, P. and McConnell-Ginet, S. (1992), 'Think Practically and Look Locally: Language and Gender as Community-based Practice', *Annual Review of Anthropology*, 21: 461–90.

— (2003), *Language and Gender*. Cambridge: Cambridge University Press.

Edley, N. and Wetherell, M. (1999), 'Imagined Futures: Young Men's Talk about Fatherhood and Domestic Life', *British Journal of Social Psychology*, 38(2): 181–4.

Evert, S. (2009), 'Corpora and Collocations', in A. Lüdeling and M. Kytö (eds), *Corpus Linguistics: An International Handbook*. Vol. 2. Berlin: Walter de Gruyter GmbH & Co. KG, 1212–48.

Fairclough, N. (2003), *Analysing Discourse: Textual Analysis for Social Research*. London: Routledge.

Ferraresi, A., Zanchetta, E., Baroni, M. and Bernadini, S. (2008), 'Introducing and Evaluating ukWaC, a Very Large Web-derived Corpus of English', *Proceedings of the WAC4 Workshop at LREC 2008, Marrakech: ELRA*. Online document.

Fine, C. (2010), *Delusions of Gender: How Our Minds, Society, and Neurosexism Create Difference*. New York: W. W. Norton.

Fishman P. M. (1977), 'Interactional Shitwork', *Heresies*, 2: 99–101.

Flowerdew, J. (ed.) (forthcoming), *Discourse in Context*. London: Bloomsbury.

Foucault, M. (1972), *The Archaeology of Knowledge*. London: Tavistock.

Fowler, R. (1991), *Language in the News*. London: Routledge.

Freebody, P. and Baker, C. (1987), 'The Construction and Operation of Gender in Children's First School Books', in A. Pauwels (ed.), *Women, Language and Society in Australia and New Zealand*. Sydney: Australian Professional Publications, 80–107.

Frost, P. (2006), 'European Hair and Eye Color – A Case of Frequency-dependent Sexual Selection?', *Evolution and Human Behavior*, 27: 85–103.

Fuertes-Olivera, P. A. (2007), 'A Corpus-based View of Lexical Gender in Written Business English', *English for Specific Purposes*, 26: 219–34.

Gill, R. (1993), 'Justifying Justice: Broadcasters' Accounts of Inequality in Radio', in E. Burman and I. Parker (eds), *Discourse Analytic Research*. London: Routledge, 75–93.

Goldberg, P. A., Gottesdiener, M. and Aramson, P. R. (1975), 'Another Put Down of Women? Perceived Attractiveness as a Function of Support of the Feminist Movement', *Journal of Personality and Social Psychology*, 32: 113–15.

Goodwin, M. H. (1990), *He-said-she-said: Talk as Social Organization among Black Children*. Bloomington: Indiana University Press.

Gries, S. Th. (2009), *Quantitative Corpus Linguistics with R: A Practical Introduction*. New York: Routledge.

Griffin, G. (1998), 'Understanding Heterosexism: The Subtle Continuum of Homophobia', *Women and Language*, 21(1): 33–7.

Hall, S. (1997), *Representation: Cultural Representations and Signifying Practices*. London: Sage in Association with the Open University.

Halliday, M. A. K. (1994), *An Introduction to Functional Grammar.* 2nd edn. London: Edward Arnold.

Harrington, K. (2008), 'Perpetuating Difference? Corpus Linguistics and the Gendering of Reported Dialogue', in K. Harrington, L. Litosseliti, H. Sauntson and J. Sunderland (eds), *Gender and Language Research Methodologies.* Basingstoke: Palgrave MacMillan, 85–102.

Harrison, M. A. and Shortall, J. C. (2011), 'Women and Men in Love: Who Really Feels It and Says It First?', *Journal of Social Psychology,* 151(6): 727–36.

Hasund, I. K. and Stenström, A.B. (1997), 'Conflict-talk: A Comparison of the Verbal Disputes between Adolescent Females in Two Corpora', in M. Ljung (ed.), *Corpus-based Studies in English. Papers from the 17th International Conference on English Language Research on Computerized Corpora.* Amsterdam: Rodopi, 119–33.

Hellinger, M., and Bußmann, H. (2001), 'Gender across Languages. The Linguistic Representation of Women and Men', in M. Hellinger and H. Bußmann (eds), *Gender across Languages* Vol. 1. Amsterdam/Philadelphia: John Benjamins, 1–25.

Herdağdelen, A. and Baroni, M. (2011), 'Stereotypical Gender Actions Can Be Extracted from Web Text', *Journal of the American Society for Information Science and Technology,* 62(9): 1741–9.

Herek, G. M. (2004), 'Beyond "Homophobia": Thinking about Sexual Prejudice and Stigma in the Twenty-first Century', *Sexuality Research and Social Policy,* 1(2): 6–24.

Hochschild, A. and Machung, A. (1989), *The Second Shift.* New York: Viking Penguin.

Hofland, K. and Johansson, S. (1982), *Word Frequencies in British and American English.* Bergen, Norway: The Norwegian Computing Centre for the Humanities.

Holmes, J. (1995), *Women, Men and Politeness.* London: Longman.

— (2001), 'A Corpus-based View of Gender in New Zealand English', in M. Hellinger and H. Bußmann (eds), *Gender across Languages* Vol. 1. Amsterdam/Philadelphia: John Benjamins, 115–36.

Holmes, J. and Schnurr, S. (2006), 'Doing Femininity and Work: More than Just Relational Practice', *Journal of Sociolinguistics,* 10(1): 31–51.

Holmes, J. and Sigley, R. (2001), 'What's a Word Like *Girl* Doing in a Place Like This?', in A. Smith and P. Peters (eds), *New Frontiers of Corpus Linguistics.* Amsterdam: Rodopi, 247–63.

Holmes, J. and Stubbe, M. (2003), '"Feminine" Workplaces: Stereotypes and Reality', in J. Holmes and M. Meyerhoff (eds), *The Handbook of Language and Gender.* Malden, (USA, MA): Blackwell, 573–99.

Holmgreen, L.L. (2009), 'Metaphorically Speaking: Constructions of Gender and Career in the Danish Financial Sector', *Gender and Language,* 3(1): 1–32.

Hunston, S. (2002), *Corpora in Applied Linguistics.* Cambridge: Cambridge University Press.

Hyde, J. (2005), 'The Gender Similarities Hypothesis', *American Psychologist,* 60(6): 581–92.

Iyeiri, Y., Yaguchi, M. and Okabe, H. (2004), 'To Be Different from or to Be Different than in Present-day American English?', English Today, 79(20/3): 29–33.

Jackson, C. (2006), '"Wild" Girls? An Exploration of "Ladette" Cultures in Secondary Schools', Gender and Education, 18(4): 339–60.

Johnson, S. (1997), 'Theorising Language and Masculinity: A Feminist Perspective', in S. Johnson and U. H. Meinhof (eds), Language and Masculinity. Oxford: Blackwell, 47–64.

Johnson, S. and Ensslin, A. (2007), '"But Her Language Skills Shifted the Family Dynamics Dramatically" Language, Gender and the Construction of Publics in Two British Newspapers', Gender and Language, 1(2): 229–54.

Judge, T. A. and Cable, D. M. (2004), 'The Effect of Physical Height on Workplace Success and Income: Preliminary Test of a Theoretical Model', Journal of Applied Psychology, 89(3): 428–41.

Juloa, P. (2012), Using the Google Ngram Corpus to Measure Dialectical and Cultural Differences. Paper given at Chicago Colloquium on Digital Humanities and Computer Science, 17–19 November. University of Chicago.

Keeling, J. and Fisher, C. (2012), 'Women's Early Relational Experiences That Lead to Domestic Violence', Qualitative Health Research, 22(11): 1559–67.

Kilgarriff, A. (2005), 'Language Is Never Ever Ever Random', Corpus Linguistics and Linguistic Theory, 1(2): 263–76.

Kilgarriff, A., Rychly, P., Smrz, P. and Tugwell, D. (2004), 'The Sketch Engine', Proceedings of Euralex. Lorient, France, July: 105–16.

King, B. (2011), 'Language, Sexuality and Place: The View from Cyberspace', Gender and Language, 5(1): 1–30.

Kirk, J. M., Kallen, J. L., Lowry, O., Rooney, R. and Mannion, M. (2011), The SPICE-Ireland Corpus: Systems of Pragmatic Annotation for the Spoken Component of ICE-Ireland. Version 1.2.2. Belfast: Queen's University Belfast and Dublin: Trinity College Dublin.

Kitzinger, C. (2008), 'Conversation Analysis: Technical Matters for Gender Research', in K. Harrington, L. Litosseliti, H. Sauntson and J. Sunderland (eds), Gender and Language Research Methodologies. Basingstoke: Palgrave MacMillan, 119–38.

Kjellmer, G. (1986), '"The Lesser Man": Observations on the Role of Women in Modern English Writings', in J. Arts and W. Meijs (eds), Corpus Linguistics II. Amsterdam: Rodopi, 163–76.

Koller, V. (2007), '"The World's Local Bank": Glocalisation as a Strategy in Corporate Branding Discourse', Social Semiotics, 17(1): 111–30.

Koppel, M., Argamon, S. and Shimoni, A. R. (2002), 'Automatically Categorizing Written Texts by Author Gender', Literary and Linguistic Computing, 17(4): 401–12.

Lakoff, R. (1975), Language and Woman's Place. New York: Harper and Row.

Lazar, M. (ed.) (2005), Feminist Critical Discourse Analysis: Gender, Power and Ideology in Discourse. Basingstoke: Palgrave.

Leech, G. (2003), 'Modals on the Move: The English Modal Auxiliaries 1961–1992', in R. Facchinetti, F. R. Palmer and M. Krug (eds), Modality in Contemporary English. Berlin/New York: Mouton de Gruyter, 223–40.

— (2011), 'The Modals ARE Declining: Reply to Neil Millar's "Modal Verbs in TIME: Frequency Changes 1923–2006." *International Journal of Corpus Linguistics* 14:2 (2009), 191–220', *International Journal of Corpus Linguistics*, 18: 547–64.

Livia, A. and Hall, K. (eds) (1997), *Queerly Phrased: Language, Gender and Sexuality*. Oxford: Oxford University Press.

Locke, J. (2011), *Duels and Duets. Why Men and Women Talk So Differently*. Cambridge: Cambridge University Press.

Macalister, J. (2011), 'Flower-girl and Bugler-boy No More: Changing Gender Representation in Writing for Children', *Corpora*, 6(1): 25–44.

Manning, C. D. and Schütze, H. (1999), *Foundations of Statistical Natural Language Processing*. Cambridge, MA: MIT Press.

Martin, C. L. and Ruble, D. N. (2004), 'Children's Search for Gender Cues: Cognitive Perspectives on Gender Development', *Current Directions in Psychological Science*, 13(2): 67–70.

Mauranen, A. (2003), '"They're a Little Bit Different": Variation in Hedging in Academic Speech', in K. Aijmer and A.B. Stenström (eds), *Discourse Patterns in Spoken and Written Corpora*. Amsterdam: John Benjamins, 173–97.

— (2004), '"But There's a Flawed Argument": Socialization into and through Metadiscourse', in P. Leistyna and C. Meyer (eds), *Corpus Analysis: Language Structure and Use*. Amsterdam: Rodopi, 19–34.

McArthur, T. (1981), *Longman Lexicon of Contemporary English*. London: Longman.

McEnery, T. (2006), *Swearing in English: Bad language, Purity and Power from 1586 to the Present*. London: Routledge.

McEnery, T. and Hardie, A. (2012), *Corpus Linguistics: Method, Theory and Practice*. Cambridge: Cambridge University Press.

McEnery, T., Xiao, R. and Tono, Y. (2006), *Corpus-based Language Studies: An Advanced Resource Book*. London: Routledge.

McIlvenny, P. (2002), 'Critical Reflections on Performativity and the "Un/doing" of Gender and Sexuality', in P. McIlvenny (ed.), *Talking Gender and Sexuality*. Amsterdam: John Benjamins, 111–49.

Meehan, A. and Janik, L. (1990), 'Illusory Correlations and the Maintenance of Sex Role Stereotypes in Children', *Sex Roles*, 22: 83–95.

Meyerhoff, M. (1987), 'Language and Sex: Research in New Zealand', in A. Pauwels (ed.), *Women and Language in Australian and New Zealand Society*. Sydney: Australian Professional Publications, 32–44.

Michel, J. B., Shen, Y. K., Aiden, A. P., Veres, A., Gray, M. K., Google Books Team, Pickett, J. P., Hoiberg, D., Clancy, D., Norvig, P., Orwant, J., Pinker, S., Nowak M. A. and Aiden, E. L. (2010), 'Quantitative Analysis of Culture Using Millions of Digitized Books', *Science*, 331(6014): 176–82.

Millar, N. (2009), 'Modal Verbs in TIME: Frequency Changes 1923–2006', *International Journal of Corpus Linguistics*, 14(2): 191–220.

Mills, S. (1998), 'Post-feminist Text Analysis', *Language and Literature*, 7(3): 235–53.

Motschenbacher, H. (2012), *Language, Gender and Sexuality: Poststructuralist Perspectives*. Amsterdam: John Benjamins.

— (forthcoming), 'Gentlemen Before Ladies? A Corpus-Based Study of Conjunct Order in Personal Binomials', *Journal of English Linguistics*.

Mullany, L. (2007), *Gendered Discourse in Professional Communication.* Basingstoke: Palgrave.

Murphy, B. (2009), '"She's a *Fucking* Ticket": The Pragmatics of FUCK in Irish English – an Age and Gender Perspective', *Corpora*, 4(1): 85–106.

Nevalainen, T. (2000), 'Gender Differences in the Evolution of Standard English: Evidence from the Corpus of Early English Correspondence', *Journal of English Linguistics*, 28(1): 38–59.

Newman, M. L., Groom, C. J., Handleman, L. D. and Pennebaker, J. W. (2008), 'Gender Differences in Language Use: An Analysis of 14,000 Text Samples', *Discourse Processes*, 45: 211–36.

Nickerson, R. S. (1998), 'Confirmation Bias; A Ubiquitous Phenomenon in Many Guises', *Review of General Psychology*, 2(2): 175–220.

Oakes, M. P. (1998), *Statistics for Corpus Linguistics.* Edinburgh University Press, Edinburgh.

Oakes, M. and Farrow, M. (2007), 'Use of the Chi-square Test to Examine Vocabulary Differences in English-language Corpora Representing Seven Different Countries', *Literary and Linguistic Computing*, 22(1): 85–100.

Olatunji, B. O. and Sawchuk, C. N. (2005), 'Disgust: Characteristic Features, Social Manifestations and Clinical Implications', *Journal of Social and Clinical Psychology*, 24(7): 932–62.

Olsen, M. (2005), 'Écriture Féminine: Searching for an Indefinable Practice?', *Literary and Linguistic Computing*, 20: 147–64.

Pang, B. and Lee, L. (2008), 'Opinion Mining and Sentiment Analysis', Foundations and Trends in Information Retrieval, 2(1–2): 1–135.

Pearce, M. (2008), 'Investigating the Collocational Behaviour of MAN and WOMAN in the BNC Using Sketch Engine', *Corpora*, 3(1): 1–29.

Petley, J. (2006), 'Still No Redress from the PCC', in E. Poole and J. E. Richardson (eds), *Muslims and the News Media.* London: I.B. Taurus, 53–62.

Pilkington, J. (1998), '"Don't Try and Make out That I'm Nice!!" The Different Strategies Women and Men Use When Gossiping', in J. Coates (ed.), *Language and Gender: A Reader.* Oxford: Blackwell, 254–69.

Preacher, K. J. (2001), *Calculation for the Chi-square Test: An Interactive Calculation Tool for Chi-square Tests of Goodness of Fit and Independence* [Computer software]. Available from http://quantpsy.org.

Rayson, P. (2008), 'From Key Words to Key Semantic Domains', *International Journal of Corpus Linguistics*, 13(4): 519–49.

Rayson, P., Leech, G. and Hodges, M. (1997), 'Social Differentiation in the Use of English Vocabulary: Some Analyses of the Conversational Component of the British National Corpus', *International Journal of Corpus Linguistics*, 2(1): 133–52.

Remlinger, K. A. (2005), 'Negotiating the Classroom Floor: Negotiating Ideologies of Gender and Sexuality', in M. Lazar (ed.), *Feminist Critical Discourse Analysis: Gender, Power and Ideology in Discourse.* London: Palgrave Macmillan, 114–38.

Rich, A. C. (1980), 'Compulsory Heterosexuality and Lesbian Existence', *Signs*, 5(4): 631–60.

Richardson, R. (ed.) (2004), *Islamophobia: Issues, Challenges and Action.* United Kingdom, Trentham Books.

Romaine, S. (2001), 'A Corpus-based View of Gender in British and American English', in M. Hellinger and H. Bußmann (eds), *Gender across Languages* Vol. 1. Amsterdam/Philadelphia: John Benjamins, 153–75.

Runnymede Trust (1997), *Islamophobia: A Challenge for Us All*. London: Runnymede Trust.

Rychly, P. and Kilgarriff, A. (2007), 'An Efficient Algorithm for Building a Distributional Thesaurus', *Proceedings of the Association for Computational Linguistics*. Prague, Czech Republic. Retrieved from www.kilgarriff.co.uk/Publications/2007-RychlyKilg-ACL-thesauruses.pdf.

Salama, A. (2011), 'Ideological Collocation and the Recontexualization of Wahhabi-Saudi Islam Post-9/11: A Synergy of Corpus Linguistics and Critical Discourse Analysis', *Discourse and Society*, 22(3): 315–42.

Schmid, H.J. (2003), 'Do Men and Women Really Live in Different Cultures? Evidence from the BNC', in A. Wilson, R. Rayson and T. McEnery (eds), *Corpus Linguistics by the Lune. Lódź Studies in Language 8*. Frankfurt: Peter Lang, 185–221.

Sigley, R. and Holmes, J. (2002), 'Looking at *Girls* in Corpora of English', *Journal of English Linguistics*, 30(2): 138–57.

Simpson, R. C., Briggs, S. L., Ovens, J. and Swales, J. M. (2002), *The Michigan Corpus of Academic Spoken English*. Ann Arbor, MI: The Regents of the University of Michigan.

Stubbs, M. (1995), 'Collocations and Semantic Profiles: On the Cause of the Trouble with Quantitative Methods', *Functions of Language*, 2(1): 1–33.

— (2001), *Words and Phrases: Corpus Studies of Lexical Semantics*. London: Blackwell.

Sunderland, J. (2004), *Gendered Discourses*. London: Palgrave.

Swales, J. (2005), *Doing MICASE-based Investigations (II): Starting with a Category or Grammar Point*. Document at http://micase.elicorpora.info/using-micase-tips-tutorials Accessed 11 November 2012.

Tandon, N. (2008), *Feminism: A Paradigm Shift*. New Delhi: Atlantic.

Tannen, D. (1990), *You Just Don't understand: Women and Men in Conversation*. London: Virago.

Taylor, C. (2013), 'Searching for Similarity Using Corpus-assisted Discourse Studies', *Corpora*, 8(1): 81–114.

Thelwall, M. (2008), 'Fk Yea I Swear: Cursing and Gender in MySpace', *Corpora*, 3(1): 83–107.

Thimm, C., Koch, S. C. and Schey, S. (2003), 'Communicating Gendered Professional Identity: Competence, Cooperation, and Conflict in the Workplace', in J. Holmes and M. Meyerhoff (eds), *The Handbook of Language and Gender*. Malden, (USA, MA): Blackwell Publishing, 528–49.

Toginini-Bonelli, E. (2001), *Corpus Linguistics at Work*. Amsterdam: John Benjamins.

Troemel-Plotz, S. (1991), 'Review Essay: Selling the Apolitical', *Discourse and Society*, 2(4): 489–502.

Tsolmon, B., Kwon, A.-R. and Lee, K.-S. (2012), 'Extracting Social Events Based on Timeline and Sentiment Analysis in Twitter Corpus', in G. Bouma, A. Ittoo, E. Métais and H. Wortmann (eds), *Natural Language Processing and Information Systems. Proceedings of 17th International Conference on*

Applications of Natural Language to Information Systems. Groningen, The Netherlands. *Lecture Notes in Computer Science,* 7337: 265–70.

Van Alphen, I. (1987), 'Learning from Your Peers: The Acquisition of Gender-specific Speech Styles', in D. Brower and D. De Haan (eds), *Women's Language, Socialisation and Self-Image.* Dordrecht: Foris, 58–75.

Van Dijk, T. (2008), *Discourse and Context: A Socio-cognitive Approach.* Cambridge: Cambridge University Press.

Van Leeuwen, T. (1996), 'The Representation of Social Actors', in C. Caldas-Coulthard and M. Coulthard (eds), *Texts and Practices: Readings in Critical Discourse Analysis.* London: Routledge, 32–70.

— (2007), 'Legitimation in Discourse and Communications', *Discourse and Communication,* 1(1): 91–112.

Warner, M. (ed.) (1993), *Fear of a Queer Planet.* Minneapolis, MN: University of Minnesota Press.

Weinberg, G. (1973), *Society and the Healthy Homosexual.* Garden City: New York Anchor Press Doubleday & Co.

Williams, R. and Wittig, M. A. (1997), '"I'm Not a Feminist but. . ." Factors Contributing to the Discrepancy between Pro-feminist Orientation and Feminist Social Identity', *Sex Roles,* 37(11/12): 885–904.

Wilson, A. and Thomas, J. (1997), 'Semantic Annotation', in R. Garside, G. Leech and A. McEnery (eds), *Corpus Annotation: Linguistic Information from Computer Texts.* London: Longman, 55–65.

Woods, A., Fletcher, P. and Hughes, A. (1986), *Statistics in Language Studies.* Cambridge: Cambridge University Press.

INDEX